HAUNTED HIGHWAYS

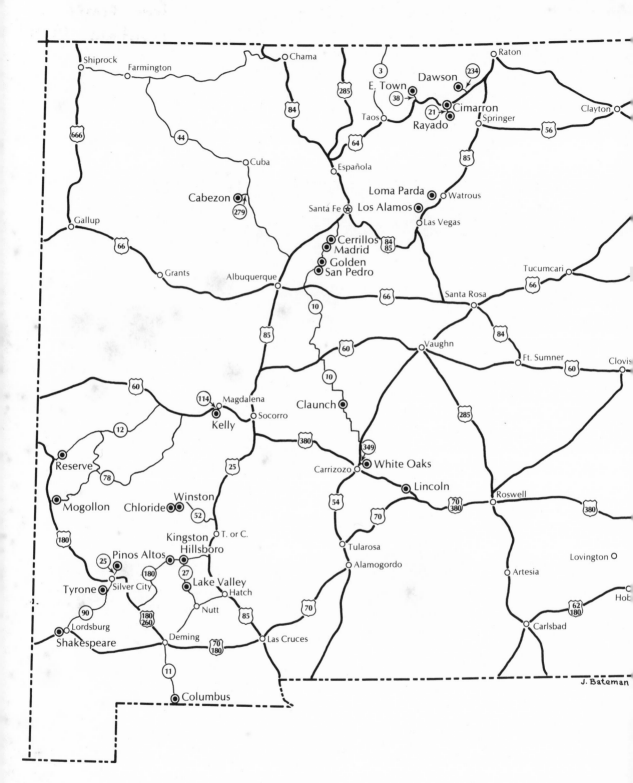

Shiprock
Farmington
Chama
Raton
666
3
234
E. Town
Dawson
285
38
Cimarron
84
21
Clayton
44
Taos
Rayado
Springer
56
64
85
Cuba
Española
Gallup
Cabezon
4
Loma Parda
Watrous
279
Santa Fe
Los Alamos
66
Cerrillos
Las Vegas
Grants
Madrid
84
Golden
85
Albuquerque
San Pedro
Tucumcari
10
66
66
Santa Rosa
85
84
60
Vaughn
Ft. Sumner
60
Clovis
60
10
114
Magdalena
Claunch
285
Kelly
Socorro
12
380
349
Reserve
White Oaks
25
Carrizozo
78
Winston
Lincoln
Roswell
Mogollon
Chloride
54
52
380
70
Kingston
T. or C.
380
180
Hillsboro
Tularosa
25
Pinos Altos
70
Lovington
Tyrone
180
27
Alamogordo
Silver City
Lake Valley
Artesia
90
Hatch
62
Lordsburg
180
260
Nutt
85
180
Hob
Shakespeare
Deming
70
Carlsbad
Las Cruces
180
11

Columbus

J. Bateman

HAUNTED HIGHWAYS

The Ghost Towns of New Mexico

Ralph Looney

UNIVERSITY OF NEW MEXICO PRESS

Albuquerque

Second paperback printing, University of New Mexico Press, 1983

Bell hanging from its log supports on Kingston's main street, used for years as a fire alarm

Contents

The falsefront that the Ladies of the Christian Endeavor Society fixed up is on the verge of collapse (Lake Valley)

Introduction

On Memorial Day in 1885 the then governor of New Mexico, Lionel A. Sheldon, dedicated a monument in Santa Fe to the famous scout and trail blazer, Kit Carson. Governor Sheldon told the crowd gathered in front of the monument that "wherever railroads run and trails are followed, Kit Carson led the way."

There are many such magic names in early New Mexico history, and they blazed many trails that today are the routes of transcontinental highways or back-country roads into hidden valleys or canyons that once bustled with activity.

Wherever people ride or walk today, they are following the ruts and footprints of history. Many men have traveled these trails in the past to leave their impress on New Mexico for all time to come — miners, cowboys, soldiers, priests — men whose names loom large on the scroll of history, and many whose names are all but forgotten.

Ralph Looney has followed the old trails — the haunted highways of history — to rescue some of the tales of men and women who were a vital part of the frontier seventy-five or a hundred years ago.

It was an era of rugged individualism and fortune-seeking adventure. At times, law and order was more a phrase than a fact. When the cowboys at Cimarron noted that "Henry Lambert had a man for breakfast," the town's gravediggers prepared for another burial in boothill cemetery.

There were long periods when it seemed as if the six-shooter was the only law. Peace officers tried to do their job — often against overwhelming odds — and gradually the roughnecks were run out of the country. The lawless breed was either killed off or finally settled down and died natural deaths.

There were many legal executions and many others not sanctioned by law. A man named William Wilson was among those who was legally hanged in Lincoln. In fact, he was hanged twice. After nine and one-half minutes he was cut down and placed in a coffin. Then it was discovered he was still alive. The rope was again placed about his neck and he was hoisted on high for another twenty minutes. "Slip-ups like these do not occur often and are to be regretted," the Lincoln correspondent of the *Las Vegas Gazette* observed.

But the frontier period was not all violence and gunfights and hangings, the men were not all "bad guys." Substantial citizens were in the majority and eventually they brought law and order and peace and quiet to their communities.

Ralph Looney has toured the highways, talked to old settlers or descendants of those who knew the mining camps and the boom towns in their heyday. He has collected facts and legends and remembrances of other days in these chapters.

For many who still live in New Mexico, it will be a nostalgic look into the past. For visitors to the state here is both a guidebook and a journey of discovery. How I envy those who will be seeing some of these places for the first time!

George Fitzpatrick, Editor
New Mexico Magazine

Santa Fe, New Mexico

The panes are gone from the window (Lake Valley)

Foreword

There is a fascination about ghost towns and the reason for it is as elusive as the wraith of Sleepy Hollow. Sometimes I think it's a kind of disease prompted by some playful spook. Or perhaps it's the unearthly aspect of such places — the vacant houses, their doors and windows gaping forlornly, their roofs swaybacked and crumbling.

Maybe it's the eerie silence, or the soft rustle of wind through weathered boards, or grass grown tall and unkempt on doorsteps, or tumbleweeds piled high against the porch. Or perhaps it's simply the mellow patina of the past and nostalgic recollection of times long gone that clings to these places. Often there is Victorian gingerbread decorating the houses, relic of a bygone day; the deep shades of brown and gray and black in wood painted only by wind and sun and sand and rain.

All the towns are alike in some respects, yet each has its individual characteristics. Some, in fact, are not yet complete corpses even though they may be suffering a terminal illness. A few still show surprising vitality. But all have one thing in common: They are haunted, if not by ghosts, at least by memory. Therein lies the fascination.

Each, of course, has a story. Perhaps a hundred or a thousand stories. Each creaking relic of a town or a city is a place rich in the dust of drifted dreams, a place where specters stalk the lonely streets.

Western America is country richly haunted by phantoms of the past. Throughout its wide and lonely reaches linger the skeletal remnants of cities. But New Mexico is singularly blessed: our enchanted world of broken butte, lofty mountain, desert and big sky contains the widest variety of such places found anywhere in the West.

Part of this is caused by the blending of three cultures. The white culture reaches back to 1540, eighty years before the Pilgrims set foot on Plymouth Rock. The Indian culture goes back to the dimmest recesses of prehistoric time. The white is divided into two: Spanish and Anglo, the latter term loosely identifying any white man not Spanish. Both have left their mark on our colorful landscape.

Partly as a result of this, New Mexico's haunted places provide a cross section of frontier history. Such towns in other Western states are usually mining camps. New Mexico has its share of these, but there are others.

Loma Parda, the wickedest "little Sodom" in the West, never knew the scrape of a miner's pick. Nor did Lincoln, haunted by the restless wraith of Billy the Kid and the unhappy spirits of gunslingers who fell in the Lincoln County War.

Add to the list towns like Reserve, where Elfego Baca held off eighty Texas cowboys; Rayado, from where Lucien B. Maxwell carved out America's greatest land empire; and Columbus, target of the only invasion of American soil since the War of 1812.

The mining towns have their stories: some of it boom and bust, some of it terror from the savage Apaches, all intriguing.

Many are far from dead, but haunted nevertheless. And their inhabitants are as vital and interesting as the towns' past.

At first glance it appears that the town is still inhabited (Cabezon)

Acknowledgments

Many people helped make *Haunted Highways* possible.

My wife and I traveled many miles through back country New Mexico to gather material and photographs. We met many wonderful people who always made us welcome and offered all the help they could.

People like Raymond Schmidt of Chloride, who told us so much about the Black Range and let me have the run of his fine collection of old photographs. And friendly Lydia Key of Hillsboro, who although she hardly knew me from Billy the Kid lent me a literally priceless trove of old glass photographic plates of boom days.

Blanche Nowlin, of Lake Valley, was tremendously helpful. So were Mr. and Mrs. Johnnie Artcher of Mogollon, who provided many old pictures.

The Hills of Shakespeare — Frank, Rita and Janaloo — have given us much information, together with a number of fine old photos.

Fred Lambert and Mary Lail of Cimarron showed us real Western hospitality. I am indebted to them for all their assistance.

Harvey Austin and Barney Cook helped me find much information on the Torrance County Singing Convention and on singing conventions in general.

Ray Bryan, the director of Philmont Scout Ranch, gave us much information on the ranch and its history.

The idea for the book glimmered from some articles I did for George Fitzpatrick, Editor of *New Mexico Magazine*. George later lent me several old photos from his own extensive collection.

Katherine McMahon, Southwest Room Librarian at the Albuquerque Public Library, encouraged me to write the book, then provided enormous help in finding sources.

Georgia O'Keeffe, of Abiquiu, America's greatest woman artist, was a source of much encouragement. Her suggestions about my photographs are always helpful.

Author A. B. Guthrie, Jr., an old friend, took time to read several chapters and make some suggestions.

Helpful in the search for old photographs were people at the University of New Mexico Library and Director Bruce Ellis of the Museum of New Mexico in Santa Fe and his aides.

J. Winston Coleman of Lexington, Ky., and Dr. Thomas D. Clark, a distinguished historian, offered much encouragement.

Gene McGehee of Albuquerque prepared the endpapers map. My father, A. Z. Looney, was always encouraging.

And my wife was the greatest help of all.

I owe them all my gratitude.

PICTURE CREDITS

Ralph Looney: 2, 5, 7, 9, 11, 13, 17, 19, 21, 22, 23, 25, 27, 29, 30, 31, 35, 38, 39, 43, 44, 45, 57, 61, 63, 64, 66, 72, 73, 75, 79, 80, 81, 85, 86, 87, 89, 90, 99, 100-1, 102, 107, 108, 109, 110, 112, 115, 117, 122, 124, 125, 131R, 133, 143, 144, 153, 154, 155, 158, 159, 161R, 166, 167, 168, 174, 175, 176, 181, 182, 183, 184, 186, 187, 188, 189, 199, 201, 202, 204, 209, 211, 212

Albuquerque Tribune: 93, 94, 97, 126, 131L
Mr. and Mrs. Johnny Artcher Collection: 134, 136, 137, 139, 140

Lorin Brown: 92
George Fitzpatrick Collection: 119, 179
Frank and Rita Hill Collection: 206, 207, 208
Lydia Key Collection: 156, 157, 160, 161L, 162, 163, 164, 165
Mrs. Mary Lail: 83
Museum of New Mexico: 14, 28, 191, 192, 195, 196, 197
Raymond Schmidt Collection: 15, 116, 146, 147, 148, 149, 150, 152, 169, 172
University of New Mexico Library: 47, 48, 53, 54, 59

A tumble-down relic of the early days in Golden

1 | The Ghosts of Highway 10

If ever there was a time-traveling highway it is North New Mexico 10.

Wandering through the rolling piñon-and-juniper-dotted hills of central New Mexico, the road is haunted by some of America's oldest ghosts. It crosses the area where America's very first gold rush took place and taps the continent's first mining region.

In a single eighteen-mile stretch is compressed 1400 years of mining history. It links the desolate ghosts of four old boom camps, three of them once pulsing with gold fever.

Seldom are ghost towns so accessible. The highway, paved throughout its length, provides a pleasant alternate route for U.S. 85 (I-25) between Albuquerque and Santa Fe, although a much slower one. It connects U.S. 66 (I-40) just east of booming Albuquerque, with U.S. 85 nine miles south of Santa Fe.

The road turns north from U.S. 66 just east of the 10,678-foot high Sandia Mountains in rocky Tijeras (Scissors) Canyon, the defile U.S. 66 follows to reach Albuquerque.

From the eastern side, you get no idea

at all why the Spaniards named this gigantic limestone upthrust "Sandia" or "Watermelon" Mountains. Only from the west does the name take on meaning. Then one can appreciate the Spaniard's passion for romantic description.

At sunset the precipitous western face of the mountains turns a vivid, almost unbelievable crimson, a phenomenon especially noticeable in winter. Because of this same effect the Spaniards named the mountain range to the south *"Manzano,"* or "Apple," and that to the north of Santa Fe the *"Sangre de Cristo"* "Blood of Christ" range.

The eastern side of the mountains, heavily timbered with tall ponderosa pine and fir and aspen, is part of the Cibola National Forest. Highway 10 skirts the edge of the tall timber.

At San Antonito, a tiny Spanish-American settlement, a paved road wanders off northwestward to ascend to the heights. It passes Sandia Peak Ski Area and its chair lift to the crest. Eventually it climbs to the very top of the mountain and a spectacular view. From the top of the ski run an aerial passenger tramway plunges dizzily toward the mesa below.

But Highway 10 continues its lazy journey northward into history, through gently rolling country looking almost parklike because of the thousands of little scrub evergreens.

Twelve miles above San Antonito, a sign pointing eastward reads:

SAN PEDRO

It is only a mile down the road to what is left of one of the earliest boom towns in North America but you must be watchful. The years have been unkind to this relic of man's greed for gold. Little remains.

Marking the site is a great glassy black pile of slag at the foot of the scrub-covered San Pedro Mountains; the crumbling adobe wall of the old church and the ruins of two charcoal ovens. Halfway up the hill the black maw of an old copper mine gapes. If you walk to the top of the hill west of the townsite you can see the faint outlines of a few house foundations. Nothing more.

This is a lonesome spot, visited by few people. It is silent, too, except for the faint whisper of the breeze in the branches of the piñons.

The picture was far different back in 1832 when the Spanish discovered gold and copper here. Hundreds descended on the pastel-colored hills to seek riches from placer gold, the kind found as nuggets and dust in sand and streambeds. It was a similar discovery that started the fabulous California gold rush a few years later, in 1849.

San Pedro thrived. By 1846, the area was abuzz with activity. Lt. J. W. Abert of the U.S. Army visited the place on a tour of New Mexico Territory and reported to Congress:

In the evening we visited a town at the base of the principal mountain; here, mingled with houses, were huge mounds of earth, thrown out of the wells so that the village looked like a village of gigantic prairie dogs. Nearly all the people there were at their wells, and were drawing up bags of loose sand by means of windlasses. Around little pools, men, women and children were grouped, intently poring over these bags of loose sand, washing the earth in wooden platters or goat horns.

Water, or the lack of it, was always San Pedro's biggest problem. The fluid is an absolute necessity to extract placer gold from gravel and sand. This part of semi-arid New Mexico is no more rich in this resource than most of the state. The desperate goldseekers tried everything, from hauling to capturing snow in pockets in wintertime, to provide water to wash out the precious metal.

Josiah Gregg, the intrepid trader who traveled the Santa Fe Trail in the early 1840's reported in *Commerce of the Prairies* that the miners preferred to work in the winter season.

Water in winter is obtained by melting a quantity of snow thrown into a sink, with heated stones. Those employed as washers are very frequently the wives and children of the miners. A round wooden bowl called *batea* about eighteen inches in diameter, is the washing vessel, which they fill with the earth, and then immerse it in the pool, and stir with their hands; by which operation the loose dirt floats off, and the gold settles to the bottom. In this manner they continue till nothing remains in the bottom of the *batea* but a little heavy black sand mixed with a few grains of gold, the value of which (to the trayful) varies from one to twelve cents, and sometimes in very rich soils, to twenty-five or more.

Obviously, miners worked mighty hard to get very little. Activity necessarily was limited.

However, the copper mine still visible on the mountain was operated more or less regularly for many years. In 1880 the San Pedro and Cañon del Agua Company tried big-scale development. A formal townsite was laid out and the company spent $500,-000 piping water from the distant Sandias for hydraulic mining. But litigation involving an old Spanish land grant put a halt to that. A lull ensued.

Then in 1887 San Pedro bloomed with renewed vigor. Activity resumed on a large

Santa Fe Gold & Copper Mining Company smelter in operation at San Pedro, 1902

scale at the copper mine and placer gold mining resumed. San Pedro even got herself a newspaper, called *The Golden Nine*. For awhile, things looked very bright indeed. "Everybody is coming to San Pedro and the rest of the world will be used as pasturage," reported the paper.

Visitors were advised to bring a tent, since there were no vacant houses in town. "Families," said the paper, "are living in coke ovens." An idea of what the place looked like is gained from this article in *The Golden Nine:*

Possibly a more varied assortment of residence buildings have never before been seen as are now going up in San Pedro. Unprecedented demand has exhausted the supply of building material. Log houses, frame houses, adobe houses, sod houses, mixed houses, and dugouts are going up by hundreds.

Between the boom in the late 'eighties and 1892 the San Pedro Copper Mine produced several million pounds of metal. But the richness of the lode diminished. The boom sputtered, then died.

There was some sporadic activity in the town during the early 1900s. During the copper shortage in World War I the big copper mine was even reopened for a time. In 1967 the Goldfield Corporation leased the old mine and began large-scale copper exploration. What will develop remains to be seen. There are other mining claims around the townsite and a few city folks do a bit of weekend prospecting. Not a one, however, is driving a Cadillac. Their main product seems to be exercise.

A quick glance at San Pedro's remains tells you that what's left won't last long. The two old coke ovens are still in a fair state of preservation. They were put to-gether without mortar and have stood up remarkably well. Their entrances are beautifully constructed arches.

Standing by the ovens, you can look southwestward toward the distant blue hump of the Sandias. To your right lies the old slag heap, black and glistening beneath the sun. The first time I ever saw the place there were literally hundreds of strange three-foot thick cones of shiny slag lying about, enormously heavy.

That was twelve years ago. Today, most of the big cones have disappeared, hauled away by visiting scavengers.

Down below, the sanctuary wall is all that remains of the church, and it is going fast. The adobe is crumbling. Yes, time is rapidly running out on San Pedro. The spindly *cholla* cactus and the tumbleweed and the evergreen scrub are reclaiming the scene. One gets the feeling that most of the spirits have fled this lonely, desolate graveyard of a town. Perhaps some have drifted across the hill on the breeze riffling the piñon, where, a mile or so away, lies

GOLDEN

To reach this gold-rush relic you must retrace your way to Highway 10. Golden lies about a mile north of the San Pedro turnoff. The highway forms the main street of this busted boom camp.

Houses and buildings built variously of rock, adobe, frame and galvanized iron straggle along both sides of the road. Several line the deep *Arroyo Valverde* that meanders along the west side of the highway. The only business in town is a large well-kept store on which is emblazoned a big sign, reading:

ERNEST RICCON, GENERAL MERCHANDISE.

Inside, amid a welter of groceries, as-

The mission church at Golden provides a backdrop for Boot Hill

sorted hardware and Navajo rugs, you're likely to find Mrs. William D. Henderson, an attractive, friendly woman. She has run the store since her father, Mr. Riccon, retired. To her, Golden is anything but a ghost town. She hotly disputes those who so refer to it.

"Why," she says, "There are fourteen families living here!"

Her concern is vandalism. Roving scavengers often wander right into the homes of residents, thinking them uninhabited. Actually, most of the houses are occupied.

Of Golden's surviving buildings the most imposing is the little mission church atop the hill at the north edge of town. The newest-looking structure here, the church is actually the oldest.

It was built in the late 1830s, soon after the gold rush began. Built to honor St. Francis of Assisi, the church has served the area ever since. In 1918, practical-minded but unromantic parishioners put a corrugated tin roof on the church. In 1958, providence in the form of a windstorm removed it.

This was when Fray Angelico Chavez, noted Franciscan author, historian and cleric, stepped in. The friar, who at the time served the parish from nearby Cerrillos, restored the building to its original character.

The slender, esthetic-looking priest did much of the work himself and supervised the remainder. He added the bell tower. The result is a handsome little church, faithful to the original adobe missions.

Inside is a marvelous old hand-carved figure of the church's patron saint. The figure was brought to New Mexico by creaking ox cart in the early 1700s to stand in the original adobe cathedral in the capital city of Santa Fe. When the present cathedral replaced the old church the figure was moved to Golden. When Fray Angelico restored the little mission State Museum experts spent a year cleaning the figure. The facial detail is amazing.

Another statue adorning the church is one of St. Peter, a primitive cement carving that came from San Pedro. It is believed to be the work of one of the many Italian miners there.

More typical of Golden's ghostly aspect is the cemetery, directly in front of the little church. Here, weathered handcarved wooden gravemarkers, many fenced by worn pickets, testify to Golden's history.

That colorful past reaches back to the early 1830s. It was then that glittering placer gold, like that found across the hill at San Pedro, was discovered in Tuerto Creek near the present townsite. The strike here preceded that at San Pedro.

Goldseekers rushed to the area, which was immediately dubbed "New Placers." The Dolores area, across the Ortiz Mountains to the north, was the first gold strike in North America, in 1828. When gold was found on Tuerto Creek, the Dolores area became known as "Old Placers."

A town blossomed, just north of Golden's present ghost. It became known as Placer del Tuerto. By 1845 the town contained twenty-two stores. It was said that the town, with 100 houses, was busier than Santa Fe.

Population fluctuated, however. As at San Pedro, most activity was in the winter, when snow could be melted to provide water to wash the gold dust from the sand.

Apparently, the little mission church so painstakingly restored by Fray Angelico is the only relic of Tuerto. The rest has vanished. The population, over the years, shifted to the community now known as Golden, then called Real de San Francisco.

Apparently nobody got rich washing gold dust. But in the 1840s the picture brightened. Veins of gold were discovered in the San Pedro Mountains.

Two Mexican prospectors from Chihuahua, Mariano Baca and Antonio Aguilar, made the strike. They called their mine the *Nuestra de los Dolores*. It produced ore which was crushed in *Cañon del Agua* (Water Canyon) nearby, then carried over the long, rough trail to Chihuahua by burro for smelting.

Once again the lack of water caused trouble, this time slowing the crushing operations. The Mexicans moved their stamp mill southward, to the town of San Antonito. After the United States annexed New Mexico in 1846, Baca and Aguilar sold the mine to the Otero brothers. Little was done with it until the early 'eighties, when a Boston syndicate bought the claim. This was when the San Pedro and Cañon del Agua Company launched its project to bring water from the Sandias to the area.

Two dams were built, in Los Tuertos and Madera canyons in the Sandias, about fifteen miles away. Twenty-two miles of fourteen-inch pipeline were laid to San Pedro.

Mellow patina of the past — a Boothill fence in Golden

Engineers figured the outlet of the line at the placers to be 700 feet lower in elevation than the reservoirs.

However, the reservoirs produced less water than anticipated and the pipeline, with its many curves, couldn't take the water pressure. Then litigation was started over the company's title to the Cañon del Agua Grant. The company had claimed *all* of the New Placers Mining District.

At one point, Ulysses S. Grant visited Golden. He was much impressed — so much, in fact, that he allowed himself to be elected president of the company, a device the company promoters used to skyrocket the stock. When Grant discovered what was happening, he quit. The stock nosedived.

Eventually, the United States Supreme Court ruled against the company. The pipeline was removed and some of it wound up in the Santa Fe water system.

Later, new strikes brought another rush to the area. Golden flourished once again. The town got a bank and even a stock exchange but by 1910 the boom had fizzled and Golden's population declined.

Today one can explore the side roads leading into the San Pedro Mountains and find old mine workings and dumps but no activity. The town itself has a lonely aspect, a crumbling village almost lost in the overwhelming vastness of the New Mexico landscape. This is *big* country. Far off to the northwest broods the long blue ridge of the Jemez Mountains. Almost lost in the haze in the distant west is the sombrero-shaped dome of Cabezon Peak. Closer at hand looms the towering bulk of the Sandia Mountains.

Golden residents tell you that the placers are still rich in gold. Only water is needed to produce the precious mineral. After a rain, they say, free gold can be found in the beds of the many arroyos hereabouts.

You wonder if deep within them the Golden folks harbor a secret belief that once again Golden will glow with life. Such a belief, born of wistful hope, is common to broken mining towns everywhere.

At Golden the hope is only that. Only water in enormous quantities could restore the town's prosperity. Various other means have been tried. Even famed inventor Thomas A. Edison tried his hand and failed.

Meanwhile, no plentiful supply of water seems anywhere in sight. But who can blame the fourteen families of Golden for indulging their hopes? Perhaps they remember that some of the largest gold nuggets ever discovered in North America were found nearby.

One, it is said, weighed almost twelve pounds. Picked up by an Indian, the precious rock was traded off for some whisky, a blind pony and a hat without a crown. Other nuggets worth $1700 and $1600 each were reported.

If anyone has found any of those king-sized nuggets lately, he isn't talking about them. At the moment, most of the gold glitters in the breathtaking New Mexico sunsets. The only riches lie in the esthetic appreciation of the vastness of the New Mexico landscape.

Moving northward on Highway 10 one can appreciate that landscape. For this is big and lonely country. A land of space . . . of time. Each mile takes you a little farther back through the pages of the past.

A big two-story building fronted by a huge porch — a rooming house in Madrid

2 | More Ghosts of Highway 10

Follow Highway 10 northward through the rolling hills, climbing easily all the way. Ten miles from Golden you'll top out at the head of a long draw. Directly ahead, far away, lie the majestic Sangre de Cristos. In between you and the mountains is an overwhelming pastel canvas of wrinkled gray and tan and green.

Now, if you are watchful, you can see evidence of old mining along the way. Tunnel mouths are visible among the scrub to the east. A level road that once bore rails connects them.

You descend the draw and finally a crumbling black tipple thrusts itself into your vision against the ridge to the east. Close to the highway, little wooden coal cars are scattered helter-skelter among the scrub. You are in

MADRID

A classic ghost town, big and empty, it is a place from which practically all life has fled.

Your first impression is the houses. Dozens of them, they march straight ahead along the highway and up the hill. To your right, just below the road, a row stands forlornly waiting. The paint is peeling from the weather-boarding. Roofs sag. Windows and

In Madrid the houses march straight ahead along the highway and up the hill

doors gape bleakly. The porches stagger like a miner on Saturday night.

Across the street, more houses stumble across the hills among the piñons and the tumbleweeds. They have the monotonous sameness of houses in company towns throughout the world, except for those tilted off center, as if ready to fall. The bunchgrass and Russian thistle and *chamiso* grow luxuriantly.

Not long after Highway 10 enters Madrid, the road turns sharply to the right. On the left are an old service station and a garage converted now to a restaurant. The gas pump is still operating in spite of the rust. Directly across from the station is a long rectangular building with a high front porch. A big sign reads: TAVERN.

This was once practically town hall for the coal miners of Madrid. Like everything else in the place it was operated by the Madrid and Cerrillos Coal Company.

Today, reopened, it is called the Mine Shaft Tavern. Bud Hughes is responsible. He deserted another ghost town, Cerrillos, to move into Madrid and open up the Mine Shaft. He refurbished the bar and redecorated a long, narrow room behind it to look like the interior of a coal-mine tunnel. An excellent buffet dinner is available at the Mine Shaft every night but Sunday and Monday.

A visit to the Mine Shaft at night is unforgettable. Places like Madrid are eerie enough by daylight. After sundown the darkness is overpowering. But the Mine Shaft creates a blazing island of light in the blackness. Honkytonk music from the jukebox inside the tavern blares across the ghost town from loudspeakers hooked up out front. The effect is unsettling, completely out of tune with the surroundings.

Except for the Mine Shaft, the only other businesses in town are the service station and a general store. Joe Huber, son of the late owner of Madrid, Oscar Huber, recently opened a museum. At last count, four families called Madrid home. There is room for several thousand.

Just behind the tavern an old steam locomotive, Santa Fe No. 874, rusts away on its tracks. Maybe the Santa Fe forgot it when it pulled up the spur leading from the main line at Waldo. Or perhaps the company figured Madrid was a fitting graveyard.

Northward along Main Street (Highway 10) looms a big two-story frame building fronted by a huge porch. A rooming house in mining days, it is decaying rapidly. The glass has long since disappeared from windows. Boards are missing from the steps.

Nearby are the empty elementary school (eight grades) and the high school. Close by

Santa Fe No. 874 rusts away on its track in Madrid

is a baseball field, with a crumbling grandstand. For many years the Madrid baseball team was a power in New Mexico.

Coal was Madrid's bonanza. This is one of the few places in the world where both bituminous (soft) and anthracite (hard) coal are found. This is one of only three locations in America where anthracite coal is found at all. In some mines here soft coal was mined on one side of the tunnel and hard coal on the other.

The earliest recorded use of Madrid coal came in 1835 when it was mined to operate a gold mill at Dolores, three miles away. Tradition has it that General Stephen Watts Kearny, conqueror of New Mexico, supplied his army from coal seams here. At one time, it is said, ox teams hauled hard coal from Madrid all the way to St. Louis.

Until the 1880s mining at Madrid was strictly small scale, with individuals working a number of small mines. Most of the coal was sold to smelters and mills in the Golden-Dolores-San Pedro area and at Cerrillos. Some supplied Army posts at Santa Fe and Las Vegas.

But in 1882 the Atchison, Topeka & Santa Fe Railway pushed its main-line tracks to the town of Cerrillos, just three miles north. It wasn't long until the railroad laid a spur to the town of Waldo and began mining soft coal in Waldo Gulch. By 1889, with the demand for hard coal increasing, the Santa Fe thrust its spur to Madrid.

By this time the railroad had acquired the coal claims. In 1893 the firm built an anthracite breaker at Madrid and transferred its coaling operations there. Three years later, the Santa Fe leased its holdings to the Colorado Fuel and Iron Company of Pueblo, Colorado. By 1899, 3000 people lived in the town. The mines supplied coking coal for the

July 4th parade in Madrid during the 1920s

The ghost town of Madrid, with the snow-capped Sangre de Cristos in the far-off background

C. F. and I., as well as coal to power Santa Fe locomotives and heat for towns all over the Southwest.

In 1906 a fire in a soft-coal mine caused the C. F. and I. to close its Madrid operations. George Kaseman of Albuquerque leased the property and resumed mining under the Albuquerque and Cerrillos Coal Company flag. The late Oscar Huber, who went to work for the firm in 1910, got control of Madrid in 1938. His family stills owns the town.

Coal production reached a peak in 1928, when production totaled 87,148 tons of an-thracite and 97,562 tons of bituminous. But production slackened as demand diminished. Natural gas was slowly cutting the need for coal. By 1934, Madrid's population dipped to 1300.

World War II brought a temporary end to the decline. The new and secret city of Los Alamos, high on a lonely mesa northwest of Santa Fe, needed coal — lots of it. The Ma-drid mines shipped 20,000 tons of coal to Los Alamos, thus helping to build the first atomic bombs.

With the end of the war, natural gas was piped into Los Alamos. With steel once again available, pipelines were being built. It wasn't long until the railroads converted from steam power to diesel. Madrid's doom was quick.

Production steadily dwindled. Then, a few years back, fire destroyed the town's power plant and even that small production halted.

Gone like the rest of Madrid's glory are its Christmas decorations, once famed throughout the Southwest. The lighted displays festooned the surrounding hills and drew nationwide notice. TWA airliners altered their flight patterns so their passengers could see the bright glow of Madrid. Turned on for the last time in 1941, the decorations were bought by the town of Gallup, to be erected there for the first time in December, 1964.

As in the New Placers district, water was the big problem at Madrid. Every drop used in the community had to be hauled from the mainline of the railroad. Joe Huber recalls that the coal company kept four 10,000-gallon tank cars running back and forth to Waldo hauling 120,000 to 160,000 gallons of water daily.

Mr. Huber still hopes to see Madrid, like Lazarus, rise from the dead. He still sees possible demand for the hard coal, although he hasn't yet found a market. And such a well preserved and authentic ghost town might have commercial possibilities as a tourist attraction.

Billie Sol Estes, bankrupt fertilizer tycoon, apparently thought so. In late 1964 Estes became interested in the town. Free on appeal bond on a fraud sentence, Estes and his associates made several trips to Madrid, announcing they wanted to lease the picturesque community, but Estes and Huber never got together. Estes went to prison when his appeal was denied and Madrid resumed its slumber.

The town is at its eerie best in the fading rays of the setting sun. The shadows are longest then, and the shades of the past the most playful. It is then, when dusk gathers somberly among the rows of gaunt, lonely houses, that Madrid is truly a *ghost* town. There is a touch of sadness about it.

Close by Madrid are two other townsites. Five miles distant, by driving through Cerrillos and heading west, is the wreckage of Waldo, where a few adobe buildings and a long concrete structure crumble in the sun. Waldo was the junction point of the rail spur to Madrid. There was little else to distinguish it.

DOLORES

Three miles away, over the Ortiz Mountains to the east, is Dolores, or Old Placers, site of America's first epidemic of gold fever. It is probably also the site of the first gold rush ever started by an ox.

Legend has it that some Mexican freighters were searching the area for some lost oxen. Finally, in a lonely canyon, they found the draft animals. But within an hour or two one of the oxen died. Curious about it, the Mexicans performed a crude autopsy with a knife — and in the stomach they found a large gold nugget.

If nothing else, it proved that gold is where you find it. But the freighters weren't satisfied. They figured that the ox swallowed the nugget while drinking at a spring or shallow stream. Promptly they made tracks for the canyon where they had found the animals. There they discovered the placers.

Within three months word of the gold strike reached Missouri. It is said that many farmers deserted their spring plowing to hie themselves down the Santa Fe Trail to romance and the gold fields. There is no evidence that any of them became rich as a result.

As in the New Placers, water stalled development. There seems to be no doubt that gold deposits in the area are enormous. In 1901 geologists estimated the sixteen-square-mile area of the Old Placers district contained $800,000,000 worth of gold. The gold-bearing gravel ranged up to sixty-five feet thick but there wasn't enough water available to get it out.

In 1832 Jose Francisco Ortiz located the source or mother lode of the placer deposits. The discovery became known as the Ortiz Mine. Ortiz hired Damasio Lopez to help him with development and soon the two were taking large amounts of gold ore from the mountain.

A town was laid out on the canyon floor near the entrance of the mine. It was called *El Real de Dolores*. Within a few months it had a population of 3000. During the first years gold yield in the area was estimated at from $60,000 to $80,000 yearly.

As it always does, the lode played out. By 1893, only about 100 persons remained in Dolores. Miss Belle Sweet, a retired schoolteacher, lived in Dolores at the time. She remembers that free gold could be picked up in the village streets after a heavy rain.

Thomas A. Edison came to Dolores in 1900 and set up a small plant where he tried to extract gold from the placer gravel using static electricity. He was not successful. Some say the experiment cost a million dollars.

Today, to reach Dolores, one must drive north on Highway 10 to a point just south of Cerrillos. An unpaved road winds southward

A memento of the past — Boot Hill, Cerrillos

eight or ten miles to a high mountain valley. There is little left of the town. The old general store and saloon has been remodeled into a modern house that serves as headquarters for a ranch. Little else remains.

There is much more to see at the town of

CERRILLOS

This relic is easy to miss as you travel north up Highway 10 from Madrid. The town seems to hide shyly beneath a cluster of giant cottonwoods a half mile off the highway, close by the wide and usually dry Galisteo River.

This adobe bakery was carefully plastered and whitewashed in front (picture taken during the Cerrillos boom)

The name Cerrillos means "Little Hills" and it is the kind of place well calculated to conjure up visions of cowboys and smoking sixguns and the Old West. Perhaps a hundred people still live here, but you'd never know it.

The business district, containing perhaps four or five stores, looks like a set for a television Western. Walt Disney saw the resemblance, and used the town in 1958 as the background for part of his TV series on New Mexico gunman Elfego Baca. Some of the Disney signs that converted Cerrillos to Frisco, N.M., still linger.

There is a board sidewalk in front of the Tiffany Saloon, a restored restaurant that serves excellent food in the atmosphere of an Old West barroom. The decaying but still occupied building that once was the Palace Hotel is impressive.

When you reach Cerrillos you are within spitting distance of perhaps the first mining in the entire Western Hemisphere. A few miles to the northwest lies Mount Chalchihuitl, where Indians of the Basket Maker culture mined turquoise perhaps as early as 500 A.D. Using primitive tools, fire and water, the Indians excavated a gigantic pit from solid rock. Lacking blasting powder, the Indians heated the rock by fires, then used cold water to shatter it.

The pit is enormous, ranging in depth from 130 to thirty-five feet. Its rim is about 250 feet across, the bottom nearly 100 feet.

A geologist (Ball) in 1941 calculated from the waste dump that the Indians had removed some 100,000 tons of rock. This old mine is on private property and is not often open to visitors.

Also near Cerrillos, across Galisteo River and up a sinuous arroyo, is the famed *Mina del Tiro* mine, or "Mine of the Shaft." Some historians say this is the mine that produced the gold, silver and lead assayed by the Spaniard Espejo in 1582. There is evidence of activity but whatever mining was done here ceased in the Pueblo Revolt of 1680. The location of the mines was lost.

Americans rediscovered silver in the Cer-rillos hills in the late 1870s. By the summer of 1879 the rush was on. More than 300 miners were exploring for precious metals among the "little hills." When the Santa Fe arrived, Cerrillos boom was on.

Two other camps erupted nearby — Bonanza and Carbonateville. Soon, Eastern capitalists reopened the turquoise mines. Among them were the noted Tiffany and Castilian mines. Turquoise was important to the area. A report in 1899 listed state turquoise production at $1,600,000. Most of it is believed to have come from the Cerrillos area. It was mined here until the late 'twenties.

"Hotel Frisco" sign was painted on for Disney movie

In its heyday Cerrillos was as wild and woolly as any other frontier mining camp. Susan E. Wallace, wife of Lew Wallace, governor of the territory 1878-81, wrote that the Cerrillos district was infested with outlaws. On a trip to the area from Santa Fe she encountered a desperado called "Texas Jack." Her description is vivid:

A powerful fellow, of giant frame and dangerous muscle, and, though unarmed, a foe to dread in any fight. He wore a shoddy coat . . . buckskin pants, with fringed sidestripes of Indian work, tucked inside of heavy cavalry boots, ponderous brass spurs jingling as he walked; a red cotton handkerchief knotted around his throat.

Among Mrs. Wallace's other observations of Texas Jack:

An immense slouched sombrero . . . shaded eyes that were restless and penetrating like a blackbird's. A shaggy, unshorn mane, reddened with dust and sunburn . . . matted beard, a very jungle, reached almost to the cartridge belt, and, blown aside by the wind, revealed the outline of revolvers in the breast pockets.

While not exactly the television version of the Western badman, Texas Jack certainly sounds like a colorful figure. Such characters vanished from the Cerrillos scene along with the mining prosperity. The town settled down to being a trading and rail center for adjacent areas.

In 1960, exploration by Kennecott Copper Corporation raised Cerrillos' hopes — if briefly. What the drillers found, if anything, was never disclosed. Perhaps it is just as well no boom developed. Cerrillos, as it stands, is a memento of the past, drowsing with its memories beneath those big cottonwoods. Like the other ghosts of Highway 10 the town had its fleeting hour of glory. Anything now would be anticlimax.

In strange contrast to so many Western towns the history of the Highway 10 ghosts was not written in bloody violence. At least, whatever violence existed apparently made little impression in the town annals.

It was a different story in a pastoral village near Fort Union in the Mora River Valley not far off the Santa Fe Trail.

Primitive concrete sculpture serves as grave marker in Cerrillos Boot Hill

They called Loma Parda "Little Sodom," a village of sin on the banks of the Mora

3 | "Sodom" on the Mora

They called it "Little Sodom," a village of sin on the banks of the Mora River in the far backwoods of New Mexico territory. In size it couldn't compare with notorious wide-open frontier towns like Las Vegas, only twenty-six miles away; or Tombstone, Arizona, or Dodge City, Kansas. At its very best the town population totaled no more than 500.

But the hamlet of Loma Parda more than made up for its lack of size with a super-abundance of sin. The place rocked nightly with revelry as it catered to all the vices of lonely men. Two string bands played con-tinuously, rotating shifts, at Julian Baca's dance hall. There was gambling. There was liquor. And there were girls.

The gambling was mostly the deadly three-card monte, a favorite in the territory. It is a game in which the odds are heavily stacked in the house's favor.

The liquor was the raw and treacherous rotgut distilled at Taos and known through-out the West as "Taos Lightning." At Loma Parda they called it "Loma Lightning." Whatever the name, the effect was the same.

About the most that can be said about the girls is that they were obliging – and there were plenty of them. To the lonely soldiers of Fort Union they were probably enchanting.

Mixing three such ingredients as gambling, liquor and women in the copious quantities dispensed in Loma Parda resulted in bloody and repeated violence. Eye-gouging fights were common. Shootings and knifings and murders were routine.

Pure chance turned Loma Parda into a sanctuary for sin. It was the decision of Lieutenant Colonel Edwin V. Sumner to build the famed Santa Fe Trail outpost of Fort Union just five miles away. Ironically, the decision to put the fort there was to protect the soldiers from vice.

C. M. Conrad, Secretary of War, thought the government should remove the soldiers from the territorial towns to cut expenses and increase their efficiency. He so instructed Colonel Sumner when he gave him command of territorial troops in 1851.

Colonel Sumner surveyed the situation and found he had 1300 troops scattered among eleven tiny outposts. Headquarters was at Fort Marcy in Santa Fe. The soldiers were supposed to protect the territory from the menacing and marauding Indians who had terrorized the area for two centuries and a half.

Sumner found his troops demoralized because of their associations in the New Mexico towns. The first thing he did was "break up the post at Santa Fe, that sink of vice and extravagance."

Looking around, Sumner found a spot on the Santa Fe Trail near the juncture of the Sapello and Mora rivers that seemed to fit his specifications. It was a strategic spot, near the junction of the Mountain and Cimarron branches of the Santa Fe Trail. It had ample supplies of grass, wood and water.

Most important of all, it was a hundred miles from the fleshpots of Santa Fe. Here Colonel Sumner built Fort Union.

Other units in the frontier army were moved to smaller posts, far from the towns and closer to Indian territory. The "vicious associations" in those towns were what worried the colonel.

He completely ignored the sleepy hamlet of Loma Parda, dozing in the shade on the north bank of the Mora. Probably settled in the 1830s or 1840s, it was a farming center. The musical Spanish name means "small gray hill." It certainly looked innocent enough. Presumably the colonel thought it so pastoral as never to be a threat to the morale or morals of his boys in blue.

Construction of the fort proceeded. And very soon after the bastion was completed it became apparent to all and sundry that it would take more than isolation to protect the troops. Certainly they showed no inclination to be protected.

A covey of prostitutes almost immediately set up shop in some caves only a few miles from the fort. In this strangely suitable environment for the oldest profession they did a thriving business — until a Captain Sykes had two of them arrested, publicly whipped and shorn of their tresses. For his trouble Captain Sykes was court-martialed but freed when the two aggrieved women failed to appear to testify against him. It seemed, however, that Captain Sykes' prudery had cleaned the camp followers out of the caves.

Meanwhile, the residents of Loma Parda began to realize what a bonanza Uncle Sam had deposited right next door. No doubt some frontier floaters also saw the possibilities.

Monotony was the chief fact of existence at frontier outposts like Fort Union. Daily life was deadly dull. Only occasional scouting, patrols and campaigns interrupted the routine. It was hardest of all on the enlisted men. Their day was long and tiring, their officers usually severe taskmasters. Punishments were tough. The pay was a pittance.

Adding to the rigors of Fort Union were leaky and bedbug-infested quarters. The Fort Union bedbugs were notorious throughout the frontier West. It was small wonder that many troopers deserted, and hardly surprising that when *cantinas* and dance halls were established in a town only five miles distant that they flocked to the place.

By the time the Civil War started, "La Loma," as it was called, was booming. Ovando J. Hollister, of the First Colorado Regiment of Volunteers, wrote how his regiment spent much of its time at the fort . . . "drinking, fighting and carousing with . . . women at the *Lome* [Loma Parda], a small 'sodom' five or six miles from Union."

After the fighting with the Confederates ended Hollister's unit went on garrison duty at the fort. Little Sodom became more and more popular. "Fandages [fandangoes]," he wrote, "*Lome* lightning and *pecadoras* [female sinners] were the attractions and rows of considerable magnitude were of nightly occurrence. The guard house was filled with *Lome* cadets, and the hospital with *Lome* patients. The hole is an unmitigated curse to the soldiers but was most generously patronized nevertheless."

Frank Olsmith, another soldier, reported Loma Parda's citizens "derived their subsistence largely from catering to the desires of the troops for social entertainment, amusement, wine rooms and restaurants. . . . Dancing pavilions, most . . . with gambling places in connection, were plentiful and were for the most part well patronized from early eve to dewy morn."

If things were wild during the Civil War, they grew even wilder when it ended. For after Appomattox, Fort Union became the nerve center for the Indian campaigns. Often there were as many as 3000 persons, military and civilian, crowding the post.

Little Sodom proved a crown of thorns for the post commanders at the fort. Among other things, the town proved to be a convenient cache for loot stolen from the fort. General James H. Carleton at one point sought to have his quartermaster lease the town, after which he planned on its "legal" destruction.

Things got so rowdy in the town in 1866 that the new commanding officer, Major John Thompson, declared Loma Parda off limits. This followed a ruckus in town on May 10 when two soldiers were badly wounded. Major Thompson's investigation showed that the residents had attacked the soldiers "without any provocation." He asked the *alcalde* (mayor) to have those responsible arrested.

The response was rapid. The *alcalde* asked the major to turn over to *him* a number of soldiers he accused of breach of the peace.

Major Thompson saw that the mayor was moving to shield the guilty parties but he feared a clash with civilian authorities and sent along the *alcalde's* request to headquarters in Santa Fe. He explained that if it was granted "then this post will be largely represented at that place, and the soldiers will be detained so long as a dollar, or a dollar's worth of property can be gleaned from them."

Meanwhile Little Sodom's mayor acted. He arrested and disarmed the very unit of soldiers sent by the major to arrest and return soldiers found in the town. The *alcalde*, proceeding to hold them hostage for awhile before releasing them at his leisure, told Lieutenant Thomas Clancy exactly how he felt about the Army:

"I do not care a damn for you, the commanding officer or any other military authority, and I will turn them [the hostages] loose when I get through with them and after that they can go where they damn please."

His words seem a pretty accurate summation of the feelings the Loma Pardans had for the U.S. Army.

In 1870, the census recorded that Precinct 13 of Mora County (Loma Parda) had 412 residents living in eighty-nine houses. By occupation they included farmers, freighters, servants, laborers, a tinsmith, herders, a stone mason, a blacksmith and merchants. Only about a fourth of the residents could read or write, nothing unusual for frontier villages.

A Bavarian, Charles Deutschman, ran a mill in the town. Leading residents were Samuel and Martin McMartin, natives of Canada. They ran a store, surely the most imposing building in town, solidly built of cut stone. Former Loma residents say the two did a good business selling goods to the soldiers. Samuel McMartin listed holdings of $4000 in real estate in the 1870 census, no insignificant sum for the time and place.

The McMartins ran a wagon taxi from and to Fort Union, charging the soldiers one dollar per round trip. Another taxi service was run by Toribio C. DeBaca. Because of the price, many soldiers walked.

While the demand for goods of one sort or another drew some soldiers to Little Sodom, the biggest magnet was women, liquor and gambling. A large and diverting selection of señoritas was always available in a big house located near the McMartins' store. There were others in the dance halls and saloons.

Julian Baca probably was the most successful man in town when it came to providing what the soldiers wanted. A surviving Loma Pardan remembers that Baca was so wealthy he was supposed to use dollar bills to light his cigarettes. Baca's dance hall had many pretty *bailarinas* to help the soldiers while away their time and spend their money. Bands played in shifts as the place operated twenty-four hours a day. The proprietor dealt a mean game of monte. Baca usually managed to avoid trouble with his patrons but once he almost had a fatal adventure with some Texas cowboys.

On a warm September day in 1872 a band of Texas cowpunchers, led by prominent cattleman John Hittson, rode into Loma Parda looking for stolen cattle. The Texans believed their cattle had been taken by *comancheros*, the pirates of the plains. These *comancheros* were traders who roamed the prairie, often staging raids on settlers and wagon trains in the guise of Indians. Little Sodom's reputation was well known on the plains. Many believed the place was a hangout for the *comancheros*, a place where they could dispose of their loot.

The Texans promptly rounded up seven steers. They were about to leave when some Loma Pardans pointed guns at them and took back the cattle. However, the Texans weren't about to let the Loma "Mexes" get the better of them.

About twenty of them returned the next day. Again, the natives barred their way with guns. Again the Texans retreated. On September 10 the Texans returned once more to Loma Parda. This time there were sixty of them. Swarming across the Mora and up Little Sodom's Main Street, they rode straight to the home of Julian Baca. They demanded to see his corral.

In the corral they spotted two horses they said were stolen. They demanded that Baca surrender them. He refused, saying he had bills of sale. The cowboys beat him black and blue.

The Loma Parda version has it that Baca's wife ran screaming into the street. Help came quickly, in the form of Toribio Garcia, who lived across the street. He grabbed a six-shooter and ran to the Baca house. Threatened by the Texans, however, he dropped the pistol and fled. A cowboy's bullet dropped him dead in the dusty street.

Samuel J. Seaman, postmaster and police chief, arrived about the same time. Loma Pardans claimed the gun-toting Seaman was knocked down with a rifle butt the moment he entered the Baca home, then dragged into the corral and shot to death. According to the Loma Parda side, as reported later by the Santa Fe *New Mexican*:

The murderers with their party now moved off down the street, yelling like Indians and shooting up the street and into the houses. The *alcalde* came on to the street with his gun in his hand and was shot at 150 yards by one of the gang, the ball passing through the fleshy part of both thighs.

The Texans also wrote to the *New Mexican*, claiming everyone in town was cooperative except Julian Baca. Seaman and Garcia were slain only after they threatened the cowboys with guns, the Texans claimed.

Actually, thievery was no stranger to Little Sodom. Only a few months before the double killing, four of the town's inhabitants were lynched for cattle rustling. The hang-

The church is the best-preserved building in Loma Parda

ings occurred over a period of three weeks.

Some of the best accounts of life in the village come from old-timers who once lived in the town by the Mora. Isidro Montoya of Las Vegas was born there in 1869. His grandfather was knifed to death by Fort Union soldiers. His mother told him about a Loma Parda "policeman" who wanted to "get even" with a soldier. He lay in wait on a rooftop and shot the man to death. Tried before a justice of the peace for murder, he was acquitted.

Justice caught up with him anyhow. Some soldiers, unsatisfied with the verdict, seized the man and headed toward Fort Union and another trial. At the foot of Government

Canyon their attention was distracted by a "lone pine tree." There they stopped, threw a rope over a branch and left their prisoner swinging.

Mr. Montoya also remembers that the town had a pool hall and the dance halls even served champagne.

Roman C. DeBaca, another former resident, says the soldiers often got drunk and beat up the taxi-wagon drivers. He recounts the story of two residents with a grudge against some soldiers — apparently a not uncommon thing. They killed both men in front of a dance hall. Troopers from the fort stormed into Loma Parda to search for the slayers. They caught up with one at a stable, where he had hidden in some hay. The soldiers fired the hay but the man escaped, this time fleeing to the nearby hamlet of La Pardita. He was soon caught, however, and hanged. The fate of the other murderer is unknown.

Surely the grisliest recollection of "Little Sodom" is this notice from the post board at Fort Union:

A report has just come to us that a murder was committed on Sunday last — the 9th of October, 1871 . . . a man lies dead in the bushes close by, about one mile from the village near the *partida*. Horses were saddled and several men dispatched. . . . The dead man was found, devoid of all clothing, which seems to have been the motive. What a crime! To kill a man for the clothes on his back. The dead man was named Bergman. He belonged to the Eighth Cavalry band stationed at the fort. His head was beaten to jelly by stones. His clothes were sorely wanted.

On November 2, 1882, Private James Gray went into Little Sodom although it was off limits. He was ambushed and slain. A few days later some of his buddies disguised themselves in civilian clothes and attended a dance in the village. The found the man responsible for Gray's death, seized him and hanged him.

Naturally, such a place attracted its share of desperadoes. The *Las Vegas Optic* reported the story of a murderer named James Lafer who paid a visit to Loma Parda in 1888:

. . . In Loma Parda he is still remembered as the man who picked up a New Mexican woman in the street, placed her across his horse in front of him, and rode into the saloon, making the bartender set up drinks for the whole party, and because his horse would not drink, he shot him through the head, lifted the woman from the saddle before the horse fell, and walked out leaving the horse dead on the floor. . . .

But Little Sodom's days were numbered. The town declined along with Fort Union. By 1880, Precinct 13's population had dipped to 257. By 1885 it was down to 200.

In 1883 all but a small detail of troops were withdrawn from the fort and in 1891 it was abandoned to the elements. Loma Parda, which had boasted a post office since June 18, 1872, lost it on December 15, 1900. By 1910 even the name was gone from the census. Strangely, it still lingers on oil-company road maps although no one has lived there for twenty years.

A bridge across the Mora at the town washed away in 1948. Nobody bothered to replace it.

Today Loma Parda sleeps forgotten beneath the shade of several enormous cottonwood trees, lost in the backwash of time. Because of its isolation, few people visit it, except for working cowboys from the Eddleman Ranch, of which the town is a part. To reach it, you must turn off U.S. 85 to the northwest at an unmarked gravel road at the village of Watrous. After an eight-mile drive, another unmarked road wanders off northward. Follow this across the plains until it begins winding down a rugged canyon choked with piñon and juniper. It is too rough for low-clearance cars and a walk of a mile or so is necessary.

Even when you reach the bottom of the hill it is difficult to see Little Sodom, so masked is it by those giant trees. But the site is marked by a pair of empty concrete bridge piers.

You must ford the gurgling Mora and follow the ruts to "Main Street." The effect is other-worldly. The village looks as if it should be inhabited by something more substantial than the breeze riffling the leaves of the cottonwoods. This is a place where one should hear voices, the shouts of children at play.

There are buildings on both sides of the street. All but one have roofs intact. Glass still remains in many of the windows. A little adobe church keeps silent vigil, as if ready for the bell to ring, an organ to sound.

Up the street, sleeping soundly in the shade, are the ruins of the McMartins' store. Solidly built of stone it was — the masonry

is excellent. You can still discern its outline but the roof is gone and the walls have been used often as a quarry. Directly behind this building low mounds of rubble mark the grave of the "fancy house."

Diagonally opposite from the McMartins' store is a long, low adobe building that once housed Julian Baca's dance hall. It is empty. The doors and windows yawn.

Across from Baca's is still another adobe, perhaps the home of Toribio Garcia, the neighbor who gave up his life in a futile effort to help the dance-hall proprietor. Glass remains in the door but the roof is sagging. The adobe is eroding badly. Oddly, a yellow Spanish rose blooms brightly by the doorstep.

The atmosphere is completely out of tune with today. Adding to the effect on my visit was the soft, mournful hoot of an owl lost somewhere in the dense green foliage of the cottonwoods.

Little Sodom is dead and its sins are ashes vanished on the wings of the wind. Standing on its forgotten, unmourned and untended grave, it seems somehow fitting that the church is the best preserved building in the town.

The friendly, open faces of plains people (Mrs. Berle Talley, Claunch)

Mrs. Stella Smith: "I'll always come back; this will always be home"

4 | The "City" of Song

In strange contrast to the village of sin on the banks of the Rio Mora is Claunch, a hamlet lost in the pastel vastness of the southern Estancia Valley. Built by homesteaders, this town seems as remote from sin as it is from the twentieth century.

Claunch stands at the meeting place of two forgotten gravel roads snaking across the rolling prairie. The nearest towns of any consequence are Mountainair (population 1607), thirty-seven miles distant, and Carrizozo (population 1500), forty-two miles away. It takes nearly twenty miles of driving over washboard gravel road to get to Claunch.

The road is South Highway 10. On the north it leaves the paving at Gran Quivira, on the south at U.S. 54.

Once the town was the center of a prosperous bean-farming area, bustling with activity. Then the drought came and lingered year after cruel year. The prosperity dried up, along with the pintos. The homesteaders moved away.

Today only the prairie wind whistles through the empty corridors of the school built by the WPA. Most of Claunch's buildings are empty. A rusty gasoline pump stands forlorn and decaying beside a building that once was a combination store and post office. The post-office sign, still nailed to the porch roof, is weathered and faded.

But there is life remaining in Claunch, helped along on the wings of song. An American flag flutters bravely from a pole at the little general store and post office. Three church buildings line Highway 10. They are kept in good repair and show evidence of fairly frequent use. And several times a year the joyous sound of singing echoes across the prairie.

Claunch is the home of the Torrance County Singing Convention. It was near the town that the convention was started beneath a brush arbor back in 1916. A group of homesteaders thought it would be a good idea to get together four times a year and spend a Sunday singing gospel songs.

The conventions are just what the name implies: a Sunday gathering of people to sing gospel songs, see old friends, talk over old times. A gathering to partake of a feast of rejoicing. It is a custom with its roots buried deep in the soil that nurtured the hardy plainsmen who homesteaded this land, a custom born of the loneliness of the frontier, of the human need for companionship, of Christian faith.

It began with singing "schools" that soon became "conventions" in backwoods New England of the 1700s. The custom rolled west with the creaking prairie schooner, spreading across the frontier. It reached New Mexico with the ranchers and sodbusters and has been part of plains culture ever since.

In 1916, when the Torrance bean farmers decided to form a "convention," the land was still free to anyone man enough to plant his roots and claim it for his own. The sodbusters lacked a church, or even a school. There wasn't even a post office at the crossroads

where Claunch was later established. But the homesteaders formed their convention anyway, beneath a brush arbor on the wide prairie under the sparkling blue New Mexico sky. They gathered, and they sang, almost all of one bright summer day. And they spread a feast there beneath the arbor.

They have been gathering four times a year ever since, either at Moriarty, Mountainair or, most frequently, at Claunch, the convention cradle.

Only six or eight families still live at the crossroads today. But on a "singing Sunday" the place is likely to be jammed with cars and people. It is like a homecoming, a reunion of old friends who gather from near and far, from all over New Mexico, from Texas, sometimes Oklahoma, even Colorado; from larger towns, including even booming, citified Albuquerque, 106 miles away.

They come to relive, briefly, the old days. They come to see old friends. They come to feast on homecooked victuals fixed in the oldfashioned way. But mostly they come to raise their voices in song.

It was like that the summer Sunday I visited this farming hamlet. A Sunday when the yellow sun was friendly warm and the sky clear blue and dotted with puffy white cumulus clouds looking like so many dabs of cotton. A Sunday when just a breath of breeze roughed the bunch grass and Russian thistle grown green from uncommon rain.

They gathered in the simple white Assembly of God Church promptly at ten o'clock. Presiding was Harvey J. Austin of Albuquerque.

Tall, spare and soft-spoken, the blue-eyed Austin looks younger than his seventy-odd summers. He joined the Torrance convention in 1918, not long after he and his father homesteaded near the site of Claunch.

He still owns a ranch in the area.

Although not the kind of man who seeks public office, Austin has wound up being president of the Torrance singers every one of the last twenty-two years. As president, Austin leads only a few songs himself. Mostly he acts to "just keep things going."

A singing convention is, if anything, informal. Everybody comes to sing and *everybody* does. Everyone in the audience takes his turn at standing up front to lead. It is up to him (or her) to name the tune and the accompanist.

"Barney Cook, will you come up?" said Austin, smiling.

Cook, also of Albuquerque, stepped forward from his seat in the front pew. He asked Mrs. Ethel Whatley of Alamogordo to play the piano.

Mrs. Whatley, wearing spectacles, is a "typical housewife." She wears a baby-blue suit with hat. Her smile is warm and friendly and a little self-conscious.

"Let's sing Number Eight in *this* book," said Cook, holding up a red, white and green paperback songbook entitled "Winning Songs."

Mrs. Whatley struck a chord. The crowd joined in. The song was *The Great Convention in the Sky*, a spirited tune. The harmony was surprisingly good, the volume strong.

Everybody sang, including some youngsters who looked as if they had been specially scrubbed and polished for the occasion.

You watch the singers. Their faces are the friendly, open faces of plains people, farm folk. They range from glowing pink youth to lined old age. Many of the men have the lean, lank look you have come to associate with ranchers; their faces burnished leather-brown by the hot Southwest sun and the whispering wind. The same look

is on the faces of some of the women. Others would look equally at home at a church social in the Indiana or Kentucky farmlands.

The song ended on a rousing chorus. There was a ripple of applause. Cook, who looks like a country Sunday School teacher in collar and tie, raised his hand. Quickly, he flipped through the book, eying the pages through his rimless glasses. He led another number. Then Austin called up Steenie Russell of Carrizozo, an old-timer in these parts.

Russell is long and lean. His face is deeply tanned. He gives the appearance of a man who would look more at home on the back of a horse than at a singing convention.

Others took their turn. Songbooks were switched. New piano players come forward. Songs followed rapidly, one after another, full of joy and life and love. Even the titles are happy: *Joy is Coming* and *Then We'll Be Happy.* . . .

In a little while it was the turn of the Gloryland Quartet. This group, from Roswell, is impressively professional. Members are Joe Norris, O. A. and Nila Kinnison and Ed Holley. Pete Berry is the pianist. They donate their song to singing conventions like this one all over New Mexico's East Side. The night before the event at Claunch they gave a free concert in Mountainair. Grateful residents took up a collection of thirty-nine dollars and provided them with free lodging and meals. Someone else filled up the gas tank of the old bus they have converted into a traveling hotel.

At noon the convention moved down the road to another old church. One that once housed a Baptist congregation, it was later donated to the women of Claunch, who have turned it into a pleasant community center.

Here a feast had been spread. And it *was* a feast. No citified *hors d'oeuvres* but real, stomach-filling, honest-to-goodness *victuals*. Meat loaf, fried chicken, roast chicken, ham, beef roast and pork roast. Turkey, molded fruit salads, slaw, tossed salads. Vegetables like pickled beets, green beans, wax beans, mashed potatoes, potato salad, candied yams. Homemade yeast rolls and cornbread. Chocolate cake, angel food, vanilla cake, white cake, apple pie, cherry pie, blueberry pie and so on and on and on and on.

Austin introduced me to Ed Williams of Mountainair, convention vice president. The portly Williams has been with Williams-Howe Hardware there for twenty-odd years. His wife is convention secretary. The Williamses were looking forward to their early retirement. He explained:

"You see, I've got this camper on the back of a pickup truck and me and the missus are going to take it easy and do some travelin' and lots of fishin'."

We met Mrs. Stella Smith of Pueblo, Colorado. She and her husband ranched eight miles north of Claunch for many years when pinto beans were the big farm crop.

"Why, in those days there was a homestead on every six-hundred-and-forty-acre section," she remembered, her eyes far away. "Now it's more like one for every twenty."

The Smiths stayed on until a few years ago when Mr. Smith died suddenly of a heart attack. Mrs. Smith moved to Pueblo but she has hung onto the Torrance County land.

"I'll always come back," she said, her voice softly wistful. "This will always be home. Why, these folks are the best friends a person could have."

She paused for a moment. Then she smiled. "You just can't believe how good these folks were to help after my husband died!"

We could, indeed, believe it.

Steenie Russell told us about the start of the singing convention. He was there.

"We'd get together and sing at somebody's house," he said, remembering. "Finally, we formed a real singing convention — met in a brush arbor."

Mrs. Berle M. Talley of Claunch, a dignified-looking woman with a soft smile, told us about how Claunch got started. First there was a school. Finally, in 1928, a post office was established.

"We first named it Fairview, but they wouldn't let us use the name since there was another Fairview in the state," she said. "So we named it Claunch, after Old Man Claunch who owned a ranch near here."

It was all right with Old Man Claunch, until one day somebody started to set up a bar and call it the "Claunch Saloon." Then he objected, firmly. The saloon never opened.

I also met Mrs. Nora Stewart, known to everyone as "Mother" Stewart. She had lived here longer than anyone.

We learned that singing conventions are common among Texas plains folk in New Mexico's eastern counties. Meetings are held four times annually, from April to November. Once a year a state convention is held, usually in April. Sometimes the meetings draw as many as 1200 persons.

We learned later that a large industry has grown up, headquartered mainly in Dallas and Memphis, to serve the needs of singing conventions and singing schools. Conventions are active in practically every state. New songs are written and published regularly to serve them.

I also learned the secrets of "shaped notes." Examination of the songbooks revealed that the music is out of the ordinary. At least it is not what I have been used to.

A feast is spread in Claunch

The clef is the same but each note is different. The notes, "do," "re," "me," etc., are given different shapes. The system seems to work pretty well.

The purpose is to allow persons who are not able to read music to follow the tune. This, I learned, was the method used in the early-day singing schools to teach backwoodsmen.

Austin explained that convention routine is pretty much the same as it has been since the early days. The group sings for two hours in the morning, then breaks for lunch, and comes back for three hours or more of song in the afternoon.

Usually, the convention "year" begins with a convention at Claunch on the fourth Sunday of April. Another is usually held in June, another in August and the last in October.

After lunch, the Claunch sing resumed at the church down the road. More people showed up. President Austin greeted each individually, extending a handshake, a friendly smile and a word or two.

When the time finally came I found myself a little reluctant to go. There was something here you seldom see any more. A spirit far removed from modern computerized existence: something genuine, something honest in a world constantly regaled by the phony, the shoddy, the imitation. A spirit that seems somehow to fit this land of sparkling clean air and infinite distance and enormous blue sky.

Walking out to the car I heard the Torrance singers strike up another tune. A familiar one at last, among all those I had never heard before: *When the Roll Is Called Up Yonder.*

In a moment I was far up the dusty road, very much alone on the broad prairie, lost on a vast, rolling ocean of land, but the song followed me. I found myself humming its melody.

Bob Olinger looked from here into the muzzle of a shotgun held by Billy the Kid in the second-story window (restored courthouse, Lincoln)

5 | Bloody Lincoln Town

If song is the symbol of Claunch, then the sixgun should be the trademark for Lincoln Town. For Lincoln was the haunt of Billy the Kid, one of the West's most legended figures. It was in Lincoln that buck-toothed Billy blasted himself out a niche in frontier history through the medium of the struggle known as the Lincoln County War.

Now the guns are stilled and Lincoln is rich only in memories. Time lies easily on this village close beside the Rio Bonito thirty-two miles east of Carrizozo.

It is, above all, Western. And it is *old*. It wears the soft, mellow look of Old New Mexico. Most of the houses are made of adobe, their walls gently uneven as if the plaster were patted into shape by hand. Many have *portales*, the long, low porches associated with the early days. A sleepy place, a place for pausing. . . .

Lincoln and its setting seem to go together, like a paint horse and a Western saddle. This is high, rolling country; a landscape of mingled tans and gray-greens and nearby mountains brooding blue on the horizon. Scenic country. The kind so often painted by artist Peter Hurd, who lives down the road a piece at the village of San Patricio.

Peacefully pastoral today, Lincoln's past is misted by the acrid gray of gunsmoke, its ground stained with blood. Some of the blood was shed by the man known as William H. Bonney (his real name was Henry McCarty), who thereby became a hero and soon a legend.

The cocky gunman has inspired scores of books, hundreds of magazine articles and several movies, as well as a television series. He looms big in any history of frontier violence. In Lincoln County, his shadow is gigantic. Each August, Lincoln Countians faithfully re-enact his "greatest" exploit — a desperate escape from the Lincoln County Jail and the murder of his two guards.

While "Billy Bonney" was a single participant in the Lincoln County War of 1878, his fame has overshadowed the bloody conflict. The "war" itself has been woven into our frontier heritage in a more unobtrusive way, serving as the model for countless fictional Wild West plots.

Even the setting was primed for drama. In 1878 this was the largest county in the United States, a rich cattle empire sprawling over 27,000 square miles. One hundred and eighty miles long and 160 wide, the county was larger than some Eastern states. Its good grass and water attracted many Texas cattlemen who had been driven off their open range by homesteaders. Along with the ranchers and their bawling herds of Longhorns swarmed the misfits, the outlaws, the gamblers. Hundreds of them.

Any man "on the dodge" from Texas law could feel reasonably safe if he crossed the line into New Mexico. Texas had so many fugitives from justice it listed them in a regularly published book. In 1878 the book numbered 226 pages and listed 4402 fugitives, many wanted for murder.

New Mexico provided sanctuary. The territory had little law, except what a man enforced himself with the aid of a six-shooter. Practically every man carried a gun out of necessity. Liquor was plentiful. Minor disputes frequently wound up with one or both men lying dead or wounded in the dust.

Until the influx of the cattlemen and outlaws, Lincoln Town was a quiet place, snug in the valley of the Rio Bonito. The town was settled by Spanish-Americans, who named it Placitas, or "Little Square." This was later changed to Bonito, or "Pretty." In 1869, the Territorial Legislature, in a burst of patriotism, changed the name to Lincoln.

By the late 'seventies, the crack of gunfire was a fairly common sound in the little town. There had even been a hanging or two. And one grisly night some Texas hooligans killed four persons at a party, from apparently no more motive than one of pure cussedness.

Even if Lincoln was accustomed to violence, however, it was hardly prepared for the 1878 bloodbath. While the origins of the "war" are misty, the apparent cause was the plan of Alexander A. McSween and John H. Tunstall to open a mercantile business in Lincoln. The business posed a threat to the monopoly enjoyed by the Dolan and Riley Company, a monopoly which small ranchers claimed gouged them on prices and credit. J. J. Dolan, thirty, and John H. Riley, thirty-seven, both native Irish hotbloods, were not about to permit such a threat to the business they had just borrowed heavily to buy from L. G. Murphy, another Irishman.

McSween, thirty-five, was a Canadian-born lawyer who had moved to Lincoln in 1875. He was known as a peace-loving man

John H. Tunstall, the young Britisher whose murder triggered the Lincoln County War

who had studied for the ministry before switching to law. After moving to Lincoln, he met Tunstall in Santa Fe and invited him to visit him. The twenty-three-year-old English-born Tunstall was in America looking for places to invest his family's money. McSween became his adviser on financial matters. Tunstall bought a ranch in Lincoln County and in 1877 started building a store on Lincoln's Main Street. Tunstall and McSween planned a mercantile business, also a bank in partnership with famed rancher John S. Chisum.

Complicating the cause of the trouble was an insurance policy for $10,000 on the life of Emil Fritz, former partner of L. G. Murphy. Not long after his arrival in Lincoln, McSween had been hired by Murphy to collect on the policy. Murphy's successors, Dolan and Riley, accused McSween of stealing the $10,000 and later got Fritz's heirs to sue McSween.

Representing the heirs, McSween had filed a legal action seeking to examine the books of the Dolan-Riley Company and its predecessor in an effort to determine the value of Fritz's interest. Dolan, however, influenced Fritz's heirs to resist the request.

Dolan obviously wanted the books kept secret. Some authorities think they would have revealed evidence that the mercantile firm had bilked the government on sales of beef to the Indians on the nearby Jicarilla Apache Reservation and to the Army at Fort Stanton. No one knows because the books were never examined.

The legal question on the books hung fire in the courts, which were controlled by the "Santa Fe Ring," a reputed link between every district judge and district attorney in the territory. The alleged kingpin was Thomas B. Catron, U.S. district attorney in Santa Fe and a friend of the Murphy-Dolan-Riley crowd. He was also the holder of the Dolan-Riley mortgage.

By Christmastime of 1877, Lincoln was buzzing with preparations for the opening of the new Tunstall store. At that time Mr. and Mrs. McSween and their friend John Chisum took a trip to Las Vegas. As soon as they were out of town Dolan got the Fritz heirs to swear out a warrant accusing McSween of embezzling the $10,000 insurance money.

Word was sent to Santa Fe and immediately Catron had McSween and Chisum (who had nothing to do with the case) arrested in Las Vegas and thrown into jail. Chisum was released but McSween was arraigned and pleaded not guilty.

Meanwhile, McSween's partner, Tunstall, fired off an angry letter to *The Mesilla Independent*, accusing Sheriff William Brady, who was aligned with Dolan-Riley, of keeping $1500 in tax money that legally belonged to the state. The letter proved Tunstall's death warrant.

On February 5, 1878, the Fritz heirs, encouraged by Dolan, sued McSween to collect their $10,000. A judge at Las Cruces issued a writ of attachment against McSween. On the ninth, Brady served it, no doubt with great relish.

Although there was no evidence that McSween owned any interest in the stock in Tunstall's store, Brady attached everything there. The next day, he attached all of McSween's property in Lincoln.

Dolan and Riley no doubt rubbed their hands with satisfaction at the imminent end of a troublesome competitor. But they wanted to leave no crumbs for either Tunstall or McSween and there was still the Tunstall ranch in the Rio Feliz country about fifty miles from Lincoln. Once again, there was *no* evidence that McSween owned any interest in the ranch or its stock. But the writ gave the sheriff the authority to seize whatever property *might* belong to McSween. Brady moved.

This time, he did not serve the papers personally. Instead, he assigned the job to a part-time deputy, J. B. (Billy) Matthews, a full-time Dolan-Riley employee.

Matthews thereupon rounded up a "posse" of eighteen or twenty men, not a few of whom were known gunslicks and horse thieves bearing grudges against Tunstall and his men. Quickly, they rode to Tunstall's ranch and attached the property, livestock and equipment.

Tunstall wasn't there, having left that

Only authenticated photograph of Billy the Kid

morning to take some horses to Lincoln. Riding with him were his foreman, Richard M. Brewer, and three other cowhands, one of whom was Billy Bonney, as he called himself.

This marks The Kid's first appearance in the trouble. Barely eighteen, he had joined Tunstall's crew sometime in 1877. At that time his life had not been exactly chocolates and champagne although not nearly as lurid as legend has it. Born Henry McCarty, no one knows just where, he took the surname Antrim when his mother married a man of that name. When she died, young Henry soon got into trouble by stealing clothes from a Chinese in Silver City. Jailed, he escaped and fled to Arizona. There, in August, 1877, he shot and killed a blacksmith who was bullying him.

That October *The Mesilla Independent* mentioned him in connection with a gang of horse thieves. He next appeared in Lincoln County, using the name William H Bonney. Now, on February 18, 1878, the affable, friendly youngster was close by when the first guns roared in the Lincoln County War.

On the way back to Lincoln from the ranch, Matthews' posse encountered Tunstall and his men on the road and began firing indiscriminately at them. Tunstall and the others became separated. All but Tunstall rode for high ground where they could make a defense. Tunstall, apparently confused, rode toward the posse. Covered by a score of guns, Tunstall was ordered to dismount. He was then disarmed, shot twice, and his head bashed in with a rifle butt. Tunstall's four men held their position afar and didn't learn Tunstall's fate until the posse left.

A coroner's jury later put the blame for Tunstall's murder on Jesse Evans, Frank Baker, Tom Hill and William Morton, all notorious horse thieves.

News of the murder swept across Lincoln County with the speed of a spring duster whistling across the prairie. The McSween-Tunstall forces, backed by many small ranchers, demanded justice. Sheriff Brady refused to act but finally the McSween faction prevailed upon J. B. Wilson, a justice of the peace, to issue murder warrants for Tunstall's slayers.

Dick Brewer, Tunstall's foreman and owner of a ranch himself, watched and waited for two weeks. Convinced that Brady planned to do nothing, Brewer finally rode into Lincoln and got Wilson to deputize him. He had no trouble at all in rounding up a posse of eleven men, friends and former employees of Tunstall. Among them was young Billy Bonney.

The posse rode eastward toward the Pecos River, where they had heard their quarry had fled. There, in the river bottoms south of Roswell, they flushed Baker and Morton, who galloped off amid a volley of gunfire. The six-mile chase would have done credit to a Hollywood horse opera. It ended with Baker and Morton in custody.

On March 9, the posse, prisoners in tow, cantered into Roswell, where Morton was allowed to mail a letter to his cousin in Virginia. In it he expressed fear that he was going to be killed.

That same day the posse rode out of Roswell, no doubt pondering a serious problem. If they turned the men over to the Lincoln County authorities they feared both would be freed. Near Steel Springs on the ninth or tenth, Baker and Morton were allowed to "escape." Each man was shot eleven times. For good measure, William McCloskey, a member of the posse, was also shot: he was suspected of being Morton's secret friend.

Brewer and his posse now took to the hills, not knowing that their already slender legal tie had snapped. Somewhere in the timbered high country they heard the news that Governor Samuel Axtell had revoked the peace justice's appointment. He also restated his regard for Sheriff Brady. Obviously, the law was on the Dolan-Riley side.

This conviction no doubt played a part in the decision of five of Tunstall's followers to ride into Lincoln Town early on April Fool's Day. Apparently, they were Billy the Kid, John Middleton, Hendry Brown, Fred Wait and Jim French. Eyewitnesses said they put their horses in the corral behind the Tunstall store, then hid behind a plank gate leading from the corral to the street.

Just before nine a.m. Sheriff Brady and Deputy George Hindman, each armed with six-shooters and late-model Winchesters, came walking up the Main Street. Just behind the two strode J. B. (Billy) Matthews, chief deputy. Bringing up the rear were two more deputies, heavily armed.

The size of the armed party is indicative of Lincoln's state of mind. Brady's only errand was to post a notice at the courthouse postponing the April court term.

As the five reached the east end of the Tunstall store, the corral gate swung open. A volley of shots rang out. Brady fell, riddled by sixteen bullets. Hindman dropped at the same time, groaning. A deputy helped him up and started guiding him toward Stockton's Saloon. Another shot sounded. This time, Hindman crumpled in the dust, dead.

Matthews, meanwhile, a few steps behind the leaders, raced for the shelter of a house across the road. As he did so Billy the Kid and Fred Wait ran to Brady and Hindman, aiming to grab their shiny new Winchesters.

As they leaned over the dead men, Matthews opened fire from across the road. A slug caught Wait in the thigh but he managed to get back to cover along with the Kid — minus the Winchesters.

Billy and the three others got their horses and fled. Wait got to Dr. T. F. Early's back door and the physician dressed his wound. Sam Corbett, a McSween partisan, took the wounded man to his house and sawed a hole in the floor under a bed; there the outlaw lay, revolver in hand, when the house was searched.

Lincoln was aflame with excitement. Troops from nearby Fort Stanton were in town and helped search houses without legal warrants. The County Commission called a special session to authorize a reward of $200 each "dead or alive" for the killers.

Andrew L. Roberts, a pint-sized Ruidoso Valley resident nicknamed "Buckshot" because of an old arm wound, heard the news. Buckshot had ridden with the posse that slew Tunstall. Now he rode toward Lincoln to ask lawmen about the rewards. They were happy to oblige, adding that they had heard that Dick Brewer, the Kid and others might be found near Blazer's Mill.

Sniffing bounty money, Buckshot armed himself with rifle, sixshooter and ample ammunition, climbed aboard his mule and headed for Blazer's, fifty miles away. Buckshot had become quite adept with a Winchester, firing it from the hip since his old injury prevented him from raising it to his shoulder.

Although one might question Buckshot's judgment, not so his courage. About noon on April 4 he reached Blazer's. His quarry was waiting. There were twelve of them; they had arrived shortly before, seeking food in the long adobe building that served travelers. All were heavily armed. They were headed by Dick Brewer, who had led the killers of Baker and Morton. The group now called themselves Regulators, a kind of vigilante band, sworn to avenge the death of Tunstall.

The Regulators were waiting for dinner to be served. One, Frank Coe, standing in a door, recognized Buckshot when he rode up on his mule. Since he had been in on the Tunstall murder, the Regulators wanted him.

Buckshot undoubtedly saw the horses ridden by the others. Undaunted, he dismounted from his mule, drew his rifle from its boot and walked over to the front porch of the mill where Coe stood. The two sat down on the porch and Coe tried vainly to persuade Buckshot to surrender himself.

The others, who had agreed to give Coe a chance to talk Buckshot into peaceful surrender, grew impatient. They moved around the corner of the porch, six-shooters drawn. Billy the Kid was among them. Charlie Bowdre, his pistol aimed directly at Buckshot, ordered him to put up his hands.

Roberts, sitting there with his Winchester in his lap, was unbothered.

"Not much, Mary Ann," he said, pulling the trigger of the rifle.

Buckshot's rifle and Bowdre's pistol apparently went off at the same instant. Bowdre's shot buried itself in Roberts' stomach. Roberts' bullet glanced off Bowdre's belt buckle and knocked the six-gun out of George Coe's right hand, taking with it Coe's trigger finger.

Roberts, still seated on the porch, worked the lever of the Winchester rapidly, firing again and again. One shot wounded Regulator John Middleton in the chest. Bowdre and the others took cover.

Mortally wounded and in terrible pain,

Buckshot dragged himself through a door to a bedroom, pulled a mattress off the bed and lay down on it on his stomach. There, gun in hand, he did battle.

One of Roberts' shots killed Brewer instantly. Soon afterward his companions took their wounded and rode off. Buckshot Roberts died the next day and was buried on a knoll, side by side with Brewer.

In the wake of this sanguinary encounter, quiet settled over Lincoln County. A few weeks later, Judge Bristol convened a grand jury at Lincoln. A Dolan-Riley sympathizer, he did his best to put all the blame on McSween. But the jury favored McSween and gave him a clean slate. Murder indictments were returned, however, against Middleton, Brown and Billy the Kid for the Brady killing.

Four days later, on April 19, the Kid rode in to Lincoln to plead not guilty. Billy, however, wasn't around on the 22nd when a warrant was issued for his arrest.

From April 1 to the 27th the only law in Lincoln was that which every man carried on his hip. Finally, on the 27th, county commissioners named John Copeland, a McSween partisan, as sheriff. Dolan immediately rushed off to Santa Fe to complain to Governor Axtell, who just as quickly removed Copeland from office. George Peppin, Dolan's man, was named as his replacement. Peppin immediately imported some hired gunslingers from Dona Ana County, to enforce the "law."

Thus, as the summer sun began to warm the wide New Mexico landscape, the Lincoln tension stretched bowstring-taut. The place was an armed camp. Riders fought skirmishes here and there throughout the county. In late June, the *Las Vegas Gazette* reported three fights in San Patricio, near

Lincoln. "In one day, one man was severely wounded and several horses were killed." No one doubted that the war was heading rapidly toward a bloody showdown.

About July 1, Peppin sent a posse of eighteen men under Deputy T. B. Powell all the way to the Pecos seeking Brady's murderers. The target was the Chisum ranch at South Springs.

The posse surrounded the ranch house and opened fire. Chisum and his men returned it. Bullets sang throughout the day and through the night. The next morning Powell gave up and led his posse back to Lincoln.

Meanwhile, McSween was sorely troubled. Beset on every side by the Dolan-Riley forces, he realized his time was running out. Desperate, he rode to South Springs to seek Chisum's counsel. Chisum, himself a rugged fighter, no doubt told the lawyer he had no other alternative than to fight. In the end, that was McSween's decision. With a bodyguard of Chisum cowhands, he rode toward Lincoln and his moment of truth.

As he rode, his entourage grew. Some were gunmen. Many were ordinary farmers and ranchers who felt they had a stake in his fight. All were heavily armed. As the sun set on July 15, McSween and an "army" of forty-one men rode into Lincoln Town.

On the east edge of the village McSween split his forces. Some went to the Ellis and Montano houses. Others camped near town. Ten rode with McSween to bunk at his house immediately west of the Tunstall store. Among the latter was Billy Bonney.

Meanwhile, Sheriff Peppin had rounded up forty men, commissioning each a deputy. They included several notorious gunfighters, such as Jesse Evans, one of the slayers of Tunstall. Another was John Kinney, widely known Dona Ana County gunslick, with his handpicked band of fifteen gunmen.

The McSween and Peppin forces fortified themselves in various buildings up and down Lincoln's long main street. On the morning of July 16, the battle was joined. For three days bullets whined back and forth between the houses, continuing throughout the night. Casualties were few and by July 19 the battle was stalemated.

Desperate, Peppin sent a message to Colonel Nathan Dudley, commanding officer of Fort Stanton, nine miles away. He asked for a howitzer. Dudley rejected the request. Then the canny Peppin sent him a second message saying that a stray bullet from McSween's house on July 16 had nicked a Fort Stanton soldier, and Dudley responded quickly.

On the pretext of protecting the women and children of Lincoln, Dudley led a force of sixty cavalrymen into Lincoln, banners flying. With them they brought a Gatling gun and a howitzer.

Dudley quickly demonstrated whose side he was on. He and his staff persuaded Justice Wilson to issue warrants for McSween and others, charging assault on the wounded trooper, Benjamin Robinson. Armed with the warrants, Peppin moved at once to serve them.

In the gathering dusk, Peppin rode to Isaac Ellis's store on the east edge of town. He ordered the storekeeper to give him coal oil that he could use to burn out McSween. A little later a torch was touched to the McSween home.

As the flames leaped skyward Deputies Marion Turner and Bob Beckwith shouted to the defenders to surrender. The answer was a shot that dropped Beckwith dead in his tracks. Firing began again, heavier than ever. Against a backdrop of crackling flames, gray choking smoke and the rattle and sing of gunfire, the battle ended.

McSween, it is said, still unarmed and wearing a white shirt, walked out of the house and tried to surrender but was shot to death. Along with him died Vicente Romero, Harvey Morris and Francisco Zamora. McSween died with his boots on but without a gun.

Billy the Kid decided it was better to run than die. He managed to escape in the darkness amid a hail of bullets fired by Fort Stanton troopers. Mrs. McSween also survived the fight and was close by her husband soon after the end. The courageous woman had stood firm by her husband during the three-day battle. It was reported that she played the piano during lulls in the fighting.

For all practical purposes, this grim denouement ended the Lincoln County War. It did not, however, complete the killing. Four more men were to die as an indirect result before the bloody book was finally closed.

For awhile after the fiery July ruckus the government considered declaring martial law in Lincoln. Governor Axtell was removed and replaced by Lew Wallace, Civil War general who was later to gain enduring fame as author of the novel, *Ben Hur*. Peppin's gunfighters, meantime, managed to keep things quiet.

Governor Wallace soon issued an amnesty proclamation that pardoned any "misdemeanors and offenses" committed in Lincoln County between February 1 and the proclamation date of November 13.

All remained quiet in Lincoln, until February 18, 1879. On that date a one-armed lawyer, Huston Chapman, retained by the widow McSween to help in settling her hus-

Charlie Bowdre, one of Billy the Kid's buddies, and his wife

band's estate, was shot down on the street in Lincoln. The killers were William Campbell and Jesse Evans, both notorious Dolan gunfighters. A witness to the killing was, of all people, Billy the Kid.

Billy had come to Lincoln to "make friends" with J. J. Dolan and live in peace. He was standing close by when Campbell and Evans gunned down the hapless lawyer in front of the Lincoln Post Office.

The newest bloodshed caused Governor Wallace to interrupt his novel-writing long enough to make a hurried trip to Lincoln. There he managed to get both Campbell and Evans arrested and placed in the Fort Stanton guardhouse, from which they soon escaped.

Pat Garrett, slayer of Billy the Kid, seated at left; another lawman, John Poe, at right

Not long after the governor took a personal hand in Lincoln he received a letter from Billy the Kid, in which the outlaw expressed his desire to live in peace. Billy offered to turn state's evidence as a witness to the murder of Chapman in return for amnesty on the other charges he faced.

As a result of the letter, Wallace arranged a secret meeting with the outlaw at the home of Squire Wilson in Lincoln. Billy agreed to submit to arrest and tell a grand jury about the killing of Chapman. Wallace promised him protection from his enemies and explained how he might take advantage of the governor's amnesty proclamation.

Billy later submitted to arrest and was held for a time. A grand jury indicted 200 persons, most of them members of the Dolan crowd. Most of them later took refuge under Wallace's amnesty proclamation and got off. But the district attorney at Mesilla refused to allow Billy Bonney to claim amnesty. Jesse Evans and his friend Campbell weren't recaptured after they fled Fort Stanton — at least not by New Mexico authorities. Evans later served two years on a murder charge in Texas, but escaped.

The Kid himself escaped to live as an outlaw for more than two years, killing at least one man during a brawl in a Puerto de Luna saloon and being a party to another murder.

Six-foot, four-inch Sheriff Pat Garrett halted his depredations in a siege of a ruined rock house in the snow at Stinking Springs on December 23, 1880. Tried at Mesilla for the murder of Buckshot Roberts, Billy was freed on a technicality, but he was convicted and sentenced to hang for Brady's murder.

Pathetically, the little outlaw wrote several notes to Governor Wallace but the governor ignored them. The hanging was set for May 13 at Lincoln and the outlaw was brought by Deputy Robert Olinger from Mesilla. Olinger had ridden with the Dolan crowd during the war.

Since the war had ended, changes had taken place in Lincoln. The Dolan-Riley combine had gone bankrupt and the big store had now become the Lincoln County Courthouse. An upstairs room had been turned into a jail cell.

On April 28 Deputy Bob Olinger took five other prisoners across the street to the Wortley Hotel dining room for some lunch, leaving the Kid guarded by Olinger's assistant, J. W. Bell. Somehow the Kid got hold of a sixshooter, probably hidden by a friend in the courthouse privy. With it, Billy shot and killed Bell on the courthouse stairway.

Someone called Olinger, who left his prisoners at the Wortley and ran to the courthouse. From an upstairs window, the Kid let go both barrels of Bell's shotgun, killing Olinger instantly.

Evidence of Billy's popularity among the Lincoln townfolk is the fact that no one bothered him in the next hour or so while he tried to remove his manacles. Finally, he shook hands all around and rode off leisurely. He remained at large for another two months before two bullets from Garrett's Colt cut him down in a darkened room at Fort Sumner.

The legend of Billy the Kid has been growing ever since. You feel it forcefully in Lincoln today. The courthouse has been restored and is now a museum. You can walk up the creaky enclosed stairway where Bob Bell's last view of this world was the muzzle of Billy's Colt. You can walk across the broad boards of the old courtroom upstairs and peer out the window where Billy looked down the shotgun sight at Bob Olinger. He could almost be there, standing at your elbow, his buckteeth gleaming in a friendly grin.

Across the street, back slightly from the highway, is the restored Wortley Hotel. Its architecture is like the frontier style so favored by those who built Lincoln — high hip roof and *portal* extending ninety-two feet across the front.

The Wortley's nine lodging rooms and dining room served many persons from its establishment in 1872. Destroyed by fire in 1934, it was rebuilt recently on the old foundation, an exact replica of the original. Rooms are furnished in the frontier style, even to brass bedsteads. In the dining room country-style meals are served on old-time round oak tables. Having lunch at the Wortley is like stepping backward a pace in time.

One can also walk beneath the *portal* of the old Tunstall store and go inside, where the Old Lincoln County Memorial Commission operates another museum. The interior is a little musty with age. The broad planks of the floor are worn smooth and shiny. It is quiet here. Even visitors talk in subdued voices. Here are rough board counters, unpainted shelves. Here is a teller's cage for the Tunstall-McSween-Chisum bank that never got going. Here are a few items of merchandise from bygone years.

Next door to the museum, but under the same roof, is the post office, the door of which is usually open. Rows of lockboxes are still in use. So is the ornate postal window.

Out in the street there is where Brady and his chief deputy were shot down in the dust that April day so long ago. You can turn here and walk to the rear of the Tunstall store through the same passageway that was barred by a plank gate in 1878. Behind the store, where the corral once stood, bunch grass flourishes. If you walk to the back of the lot you can look down on the trickle of water that is the Rio Bonito. It is a peaceful scene, with a few milk cows grazing contentedly in the shade of a cottonwood tree.

And if you're not careful, you'll step on two small brass markers perhaps three feet apart, set flush with the ground, hidden in the tall grass. One marks the last resting place of Alexander McSween. The other is the grave of John Henry Tunstall. One wonders if they slumber soundly.

A crumbling adobe wall frames the skeleton of a store building in White Oaks

6 | The City Greed Destroyed

The grave of a city destroyed by greed lies only thirty airline miles northwest of Lincoln Town. The miners called it White Oaks, after the trees they found in the gulch leading off Baxter Mountain. The town quickly bloomed into a city of 4000 people. It thrived until the townsfolk demanded too much from a railroad.

It all began because John J. Baxter got thirsty. Baxter was a frustrated Forty-niner. On the rebound from the California gold fields he found himself in the dusty New Mexican hamlet of San Antonio, a hundred miles west of White Oaks.

San Antonio later was to become known as the birthplace of hotel tycoon Conrad Hilton. But in 1878 it was a community without distinction — except for the *cantina* that dispensed various refreshments. John J. Baxter found it most inviting. He stopped there first.

Once the Missourian had one drink under his belt and another in his hand he returned to his favorite subject — gold. He'd been too late in California. Now he asked about it at every opportunity.

The Mexican tending bar was helpful. It was many years ago, he recalled, but there was a place far to the east across the *malpais* (lava flow) where the Spaniards had panned for gold. Baxter grew as excited as a novice hunter who has sighted his first twelve-point buck. Where was the gold?

The native laughed at the *gringo's* greed. "*Si.*" He could draw a map, he said.

Baxter tarried only long enough to replenish his bourbon supply before loading up his mule and heading east.

The *malpais* is a jagged wasteland now ogled by travelers on U.S. 380 between San Antonio and Carrizozo. It was a tough trip for Baxter and his mule, the sharp rocks tearing at their feet like so many daggers, but they made it. Baxter found the gulch, a grove of white-oak trees and a spring. Also a mountain. But more important, he found gold.

Not much gold, true, but enough for an optimist. Most of it was in the sand in the bed of the gulch, but there was some in the rock on the mountain. Baxter filed a claim there, dug out a few hundred dollars' worth of dust, then moved on to a more likely-looking spot.

He dug some more. Other prospectors began to drift into the gulch and around the mountain, which by now was known as Baxter's Mountain. They camped by the grove and soon began calling it White Oaks.

Baxter began to fidget. Maybe it was the people. Maybe it was an itchy foot. Pretty soon he chucked it all to head for greener fields around Silver City. As a kind of footnote, he got himself shot during an Indian raid on the Gila River in 1885 and later returned to Baxter's Gulch to find a booming city. By then, his original claim was worth a fortune — but not, of course, to Baxter.

Other miners lacked Baxter's wanderlust. They stuck around. John V. Winters and John E. Wilson found some gold in the gulch gravel just as Baxter had. Their labors some weeks produced as much as thirty dollars in gold dust.

Then Tom Wilson, a kind of mystery man, showed up. Nobody knew much about him and nobody asked. Winters liked the newcomer and took him on as a partner.

It was Tom Wilson who strolled up the mountain one day to eat his lunch, sat down on a rock and noticed some crystals. He broke off some pieces and found several bits of wire gold. Excited, Wilson got his partner and the two dug deep enough into the mountain to expose a vein of gold. They staked a claim.

That night Wilson told Winters that his share of the claim was for sale. What would Winters give him for it? Winters quickly fumbled through his meager belongings. He finally came up with forty dollars' worth of gold dust, two dollars in silver, a bottle of whisky and a broken pistol. Wilson accepted. The next morning he saddled his horse and rode off to the west and into limbo.

Who was he? Why did he give up his interest in what was to become the rich Homestake Mine? Some say he was fleeing Texas law. That is only a guess. Winters was untroubled by Wilson's motives. He kept right on digging, and four feet down struck ore that assayed $15,000 to $40,000 in gold to the ton!

Winters died soon afterward, leaving his heirs to fight in the courts over his bonanza. They sold out to James Seigfurst for $50,000. Seigfurst took enough gold out in his first year to pay for the mine, build a mill and pay him a $10,000 profit. In the spring of 1880, $35,000 worth of gold was taken out of the North Homestake in two days. Up until 1904, the mine yielded $525,000.

The news of Winters' strike rolled with the speed of a prairie fire fanned by a desert wind. Prospectors thronged to Baxter's Gulch; among them was Abe Whiteman.

Abe staked a claim up the gulch from the North Homestake and called it the "Old Abe." As fiddle-footed as Baxter and Wilson before him, Abe wearied before he even proved up the claim and sold it to William Watson for a dollar.

Watson struck a bonanza so rich that during the first year it occasionally produced more than $30,000 in gold in a single week. The Old Abe tapped the richest vein of all in 1890. By 1904, the Old Abe — by then the deepest mine in New Mexico at 13,750 feet — had produced to the tune of $875,000.

White Oaks saw its share of other strikes. The South Homestake produced $600,000 before the ore petered out. The Little Mack, the Comstock and the Rip Van Winkle were other big producers.

Such strikes brought miners swarming into Baxter Gulch by the hundreds. With them came the usual quota of gamblers, saloonkeepers, prostitutes and other camp followers. They laid out a townsite among the piñon and juniper trees. The lots brought high prices. Tents went up first, to be followed shortly by shacks and then more prominent buildings. Before long, all kinds of structures lined White Oaks Avenue and Jicarilla and Livingston streets.

The Pioneer was the first saloon in town. It took a brave man and a cast-iron stomach to partake of its pleasures for long. They say the Pioneer dispensed three different grades of whisky, each at a different price, but all from the same barrel.

It wasn't long until Henry J. Patterson came along to open the Star Saloon. The next thing anybody knew, Henry introduced "culture" to the burgeoning boom town with a place called "Starr's Opera House."

Prospectors bound for the White Oaks mines, photographed in Las Vegas

A traveling band of performers known as the Mitchell Dramatic Troupe staged the first performance. The town was overcome by culture. Everybody in the place got deliriously drunk, including some of the members of the Mitchell Dramatic Troupe. The leading actors and the manager lost every nickel they owned at Henry's roulette wheel. They were stranded in White Oaks and had to keep performing until they could get enough money to leave.

White Oaks residents dated the official founding of the town as August 15, 1879, but there were only tents for houses until nearly a year later. The first real house wasn't finished until July 17, 1880, an event that launched another uproarious celebration. The town got so drunk the jackrabbits looked like pink elephants. It lasted for days.

Daily stagecoaches began bringing mail from Socorro to Fort Stanton via White Oaks in October, 1880. In December, J. H. Wise launched *The White Oaks Golden Era*, a weekly that was to last four years. Three other newspapers were published during White Oaks' years of prosperity. These included *The Lincoln County Leader* (1882-94), *The New Mexico Interpreter* (1885-91) and *The Old Abe Eagle* (1885-1905).

White Oaks developed its own "suburbs" that some might consider slums. Buffalo still roamed the plains during the early years, and hidehunters made the town their headquarters. They created their own section, called "Hidetown," a slum of dirty brown shacks and green hides that were spread upon the ground. The stench was something like the combined odor of a couple of slaughterhouses and an open sewer.

There was also "Hogtown," a tenderloin jammed with gin-mills, gambling dens and whorehouses. Most of the shooting origi-

nated in this part of town, as liquored-up miners let off a little steam.

White Oaks was fairly respectable on the whole. Of course, there were killings. Joel Fowler, a gunman, shot down three suspected cattle rustlers not far out of town.

Because of the lateness of its birth White Oaks escaped the Lincoln County War crossfire; but some of the "veterans" of the war were frequent visitors. Billy the Kid, along with desperadoes like Dave Rudabaugh and Tom O'Folliard, dropped into town occasionally.

Residents said it was Billy's interest in horse stealing that brought him to White Oaks so often. He wasn't the only horse thief who hit the town. On June 10, 1882, *The Red River Chronicle* reported that a band of White Oaks vigilantes removed a horse thief from jail and "hung him."

By the fall of 1880 White Oaks had 800 permanent residents and by the following January it had a thousand. Before long, it had three churches, a fine $10,000 brick schoolhouse that was the town's pride, two hotels and a host of saloons. A durable two-story building was erected to house the Exchange Bank.

White Oaks' population soared to 4000 by 1887 and the town was bursting its breeches. *The Interpreter* asked if it wasn't time that White Oaks Avenue had sidewalks for its entire length. Nothing was said about paving the street.

The town attracted many ambitious people. Some of them later became famous. Emerson Hough practiced law there; he later became a novelist and used his White Oaks background in his books.

Two other White Oaks lawyers were W. C. McDonald and Harvey B. Fergusson. McDonald became the first governor of New

Mexico following statehood and Fergusson went on to become a United States Congressman.

The residents of White Oaks thought the boom was going to last forever. The future couldn't have been brighter, what with the Old Abe getting richer practically by the day. White Oaks even had coal. About the only thing the town lacked was a railroad.

This was an era of railroad building and promotion. Rail connections were a tremendous asset to any community. Such a link was needed by White Oaks to ease the transportation of its mineral wealth. Since the mining camp also had deposits of coal, the residents figured practically any railroad would be happy to lay rails into the town.

The residents tried and tried without success until 1888, when action appeared likely. The Kansas City, El Paso and Mexican Railway, known in the territory as "The White Oaks Road," prepared to drive steel up Baxter Gulch.

Now greed began to take over among the folks of White Oaks. Property owners got together to consider right-of-way for the railroad and land for a depot. They all decided they had the railroad in a bind. They reasoned that the railroad *had* to come to White Oaks, so why not make the top dollar out of the land? They set a high price and when the railroad told them it was unreasonable they refused to back down. The railroad's answer was to bypass the mining town entirely. The tracks would go through the nearby village of Carrizozo instead.

The businessmen, dumbfounded, begged the rail promoters to come to White Oaks on their own terms but it was too late. The company's answer was "No." The rails never came up Baxter Gulch. White Oaks had to be satisfied with a stage connection with the

A Victorian masterpiece in White Oaks

railroad at the little town of Carrizozo.

White Oaks businessmen rationalized, telling themselves the loss of the rails would make no difference to the bustling boom town. It was only a little while after the railroad fiasco that miners struck the main vein in the Old Abe, to pour out a river of precious metal.

The late Dave Jackson knew White Oaks in its salad days as well as its soup-kitchen times. He used to say that the heart went out of the place when the railroad was lost. It lost its gold soon afterward. The veins began to dwindle in the 'nineties. When the rich ore disappeared White Oaks died.

In contrast, Carrizozo thrived as trading center for the great Lincoln County stock range. Eventually it became the county seat. It had the railroad.

At White Oaks, sporadic mining continued but has amounted to little since 1930, when a fire closed the Old Abe forever. The post office gave up the ghost as recently as 1954, when the population had shrunk to eight families. Today there are ten occupied houses in town. Some residents work in Carrizozo, some are retired and a few own ranches.

Most of them like the solitude offered by the ghost-town atmosphere, and access to the outside world is easy. A good gravel road, State Highway 349, turns east off U.S. Highway 54 a few miles north of Carrizozo. Crossing the Southern Pacific tracks, it wanders across a dun-colored plain sprinkled with grotesquely shaped "yucca" trees.

In early summer or even midsummer the yucca is one of the Southwest's most spectacular plants. The thick, palmlike trunk is topped by a cluster of spiked green leaves with points so sharp they are called "Spanish Dagger" or "Spanish Bayonet." From each cluster a tall shoot springs skyward. From it dangle dozens of delicate white blooms like so many bells. If you drive the road to White Oaks when the yuccas are blooming you'll decide that New Mexico used good judgment in naming it the state flower. Desert dwellers cut off the bloom-filled spikes and lay them on graves as decorations on Memorial Day.

After awhile New Mexico 349 leaves the yucca and enters country thick with piñon and juniper and scrub oak. When you near the 6400-foot altitude of White Oaks you begin to see faint traces of mining activity.

They are only scars that time is just now beginning to erase. Sometimes it is a tunnel, etched coal black on the side of a hill. Sometimes it is a dump of tailings, streaked with mottled gray and yellow.

Eight miles east of U.S. 54 you reach the first sight of White Oaks. Appropriately, it is the cemetery. They called it "Cedarvale," according to the somewhat faded sign over the gate, and it is almost buried by the scrub. But the fence is kept up and someone now and then must repaint the sign. The graves inside the fence are overgrown with prickly pear and tumbleweeds but many are decorated with plastic flowers.

Among those resting here is Susan McSween, who played the piano during that bloody siege during the Lincoln County War. Some years later, she remarried and settled at White Oaks. After her second husband died she ran the ranch practically singlehanded. She died in the 1930s.

It is only a half mile or so from the cemetery to the grave of White Oaks. You pass an old brick house, its porch decorated with lathe-turned wood, Victorian style. The place has been taken over by the tumbleweed and feathery *chamisa* and *cholla* cactus.

The rest of the town is a contrast between utter decay and well maintained homes. Ruins are everywhere. Here, an adobe wall crumbles into dust. There, debris litters a foundation. A big two-story brick building testifies that this was once a prosperous city. Its windows are boarded over on the first floor. The upstairs windows gape. The plaster has peeled from the walls and the rain and the wind are working on the mortar between the bricks. Someone has painted signs on some of the bare boards barring windows and doors:

LOOK BUT

DO NOT ENTER

Another says:

KEEP OUT   DANGEROUS

You notice that in spite of all this most of the occupied homes boast TV antennas.

Signs have been painted on some of the boards that bar windows and doors

Monument to one man's vanity — Hoyle's Folly, White Oaks

On a hill just across Baxter Gulch to the north looms a substantial brick schoolhouse, once White Oaks' pride. The most imposing landmark left is the red-brick mansion known as "Hoyle's Folly." The L. E. Kirkpatrick family bought it several years ago when it was a shambles and have been restoring it ever since.

It is a Victorian masterpiece. The builder spent $42,000 on it in 1887. The foundation goes down nine feet to bedrock. Stonemasons came all the way from St. Louis to cut the twenty-five cornerstones, all iden-

tical. Stained-glass windows were brought by freight wagon from Corning, New York. A giant window in the front of the house was imported from France. Floors are hardwood. Fireplace mantels are hand-carved.

Dave Jackson told Mrs. Kirkpatrick the fantastic story of the house and how it got its name. Jackson knew builder Matthew Hoyle. He was the successful foreman of a gold mine who made up in arrogance what he lacked in stature and appearance. Hoyle was a self-made man who had grubbed his way to some prominence in the Western mining camps. Throughout his struggle he had harbored a love for a young girl he had known in the East.

Somewhere along the road to success, Hoyle got the idea that the girl shared his love. He decided he would build a love nest — a mansion worthy of his sweetheart. He attacked the project as if he had the wealth of the Old Abe and the North Homestake combined. It took two and a half years to build and cost every penny he had been able to save. At that, before he could finish it, he had to get a mortgage with the Exchange Bank of White Oaks for $1500.

Finally, the dream palace was completed and Hoyle headed eastward, wearing his heart on his soiled sleeve. He confessed his love to the girl and told her about the mansion he had built in far-off New Mexico. The girl rejected him. The overbearing Hoyle was shattered. His world was suddenly in shards. It was more than he could bear. Hoyle vanished.

The bank, meanwhile, tried its best to locate him. But Hoyle was gone for good. The mansion on the hill stood vacant and lonely for a long time. Then, one day, Hoyle's brother brought his tubercular wife, Ida, to White Oaks. The bank let them rent "Hoyle's Folly." The couple moved in, hoping that the high, dry New Mexico country would cure the ailing wife.

However, Mrs. Hoyle died in "Hoyle's Folly." Later, Hoyle himself died in a mysterious fall down a mineshaft.

The Kirkpatricks like the old place and have no fear that it is haunted. They would like to see it become a museum and if it ever does they plan to move to a smaller home.

Like many another resident of lonely Western ghost towns they harbor flickering hopes that White Oaks will bloom again. After all, men with a hunger for riches once again are scratching at Baxter Mountain. Who can say what lies buried beneath the next ledge?

Gravestones in the village cemetery, Los Alamos

7 | Den of the Forty Thieves

Los Alamos, a forgotten village in the wide grasslands four miles east of Las Vegas, shares its name with the birthplace of the atomic bomb. It stopped being a town a long time ago and is now the headquarters for a cattle ranch. It is a peaceful place marked by a grove of cottonwoods on the banks of the Sapello River. The trees gave the spot its name.

Tranquil today, it is hardly the place one would associate with murder and robbery; but seventy-five years ago, this was the last hideout of Vicente Silva and his notorious "forty thieves."

Silva was less publicized than hoodlums like the Daltons and Jesse James but he matched them in viciousness. So shocking were his crimes that his name became a synonym for cruelty.

Like a hundred other New Mexico villages Los Alamos was born to serve the needs of native farmers. It died when trading shifted to much larger Las Vegas. Few people would have noted its passing had it not been for Silva.

Silva's appearance belied his cussedness. He wore a full beard and was considered quite handsome. What he lacked in education he more than made up for in charm. Born in Bernalillo County, he moved to the roaring cattle town of Las Vegas in 1875, where he soon made himself a respected businessman, active in local politics.

At the time Las Vegas was New Mexico Territory's most prosperous city and also one of its wildest. It had become the trading center and shipping point for a livestock empire made possible by the vast grasslands that gave the town its name. Thousands of cattle and sheep grazed on the meadows. Wool was shipped out on the Santa Fe Trail. Hundreds of cowboys flocked into town to give it a reputation throughout the West as a riproaring place. Gunplay and murder were common.

Silva saw the possibilities. In an imposing two-story building on the plaza he opened a saloon he called "The Imperial," soon adding a gambling casino and a dance hall.

The railroad arrived in town four years after Silva to signal the end of the Santa Fe and even greater prosperity for Silva. He kept the Imperial open 'round the clock. There was no disgrace in operating a saloon in the frontier West — at least so long as it was successful. Silva's was certainly that. Over the years, his stature grew. He had a wife, Dona Telesfora, and a foundling daughter adopted in 1885.

But Silva grew dissatisfied with his saloon profits. In the late 'eighties he began organizing a gang, secretly rounding up some of the meanest cutthroats available in northern New Mexico. Each member was forced to take a blood oath of secrecy. A kind of military discipline was put in effect. Officers were selected.

Silva seemed to think of everything — even the police. He enlisted several members of the Las Vegas police force to protect the hoodlums. A Spanish-American who loved bombast, he picked a memorable name for his band: The Society of Bandits of New Mexico. There were about forty members.

Wasting little time, Silva launched a crime wave such as had never before been seen in lawless Las Vegas, which was as used to crime as it was to cattle. Robbery, murder and assault became common. Las Vegans couldn't walk through the plaza after dark without danger of being assaulted. Cattle and horse stealing increased. No one suspected that the hundreds of crimes were part of an organized plot.

Viciousness marked many of the band's dark deeds. Typical was the murder of an unidentified man. His naked body was found in an *arroyo* outside of town, the remains mutilated, the face skinned to prevent identification, and all the limbs amputated.

Jacob Stutzman was another victim. An old and respected Las Vegas tailor, Stutzman was murdered by three Silva hoodlums. They did such a good job of hiding the tailor's corpse that it was never found.

The gang also murdered Abraham Aboulafia, a Syrian merchant. Las Vegans found his corpse one morning, a knife buried in its back. He had been robbed. No one suspected the Silva agent, a member of the police force, who had committed the crime.

Carpio Sais, director and treasurer of the Sabinoso schools, came to Las Vegas to get money granted to found schools in his district. He was given $170 and started back for home, never to be seen again. Another Silva victim, he was murdered beneath the bridge over the Gallinas River in Las Vegas.

Many similar crimes were recorded, the details unknown until the gang broke up and some of the members confessed. Silva, meanwhile, continued to keep up his front as a saloonkeeper, meeting secretly with his hoodlums at night in upstairs rooms at The Imperial to split the loot.

When it was not safe to meet at the saloon, Silva summoned his gangsters to a hideout at the little village of Los Alamos. They met at the home of a trusted member of the society, Manuel Gonzales y Baca, called by his cronies *El Mellado*, "Toothless."

Silva secretly bought Monte de Largo Ranch, with its headquarters well hidden in the San Pedro Mountains near the mining camp of San Pedro. The ranch provided a haven for cattle and horses the gang stole. The rustlers drove them there for rebranding with Silva's VS brand. Ricardo Romero, Silva's first lieutenant, was in charge. Gang members called him *"El Romo,"* "The Flat Nose."

As the crime wave continued in Las Vegas law-abiding citizens made repeated petitions to the territorial governor for help. They got no response. This was the situation when Captain Jose Santos Esquibel decided to do some investigating on his own.

The captain had lost many horses to rustlers from his ranch at Cuervo in Guadalupe County, fifty miles east of Las Vegas. Now he began to question Patricio Maes about the stolen stock. Maes, a member of the Silva gang, told him the animals were at Monte Largo.

Refugio Esquibel, the captain's son, took a cowboy to the ranch where they spotted the stolen horses. Some had already been branded with Silva's VS brand. They rounded them up and drove them to Las Vegas, where the captain was waiting. The captain rode immediately to The Imperial Saloon and confronted Silva with the evidence. Caught by surprise, Silva was unable to explain things. Esquibel left, with a promise to take the case to district court. Silva was

shaken. Obviously the blood oath of secrecy had been violated. Something must be done. He sent word to all of his men to assemble at the Imperial, then summoned some of his trusted aides to do some detective work. This they completed by the appointed night of October 22, 1892.

The wind was howling, whipping up an early blizzard as Silva's gang gathered at the Imperial. The crowd in the saloon was even larger than customary that night. Silva's announcement to the crowd that the saloon, casino and dance hall would close at midnight fell like a thunderclap. Barflies shook their heads in disbelief. Silva's place had never been known to close its doors before. When the clock tolled twelve, however, Silva drove his patrons into the storm. Only members of the Society of Bandits of New Mexico remained.

They gathered in a large room on the second floor to hear Silva declare that one of them had violated the blood oath of secrecy. Silva said he would leave the punishment up to the society. Then he paused dramatically, studying the surprised faces of his organization, raised his hand and pointed his finger at Patricio Maes.

"There is the traitor!"

He waited a moment, then gestured to still the angry babble. But he was fair, the saloonkeeper said. He would give the informer a better chance than he had given his fellows in crime. Maes would stand trial, just as if he were facing a court of law.

Silva then picked out one member of the gang to sit as judge, another as attorney for the accused and made himself prosecutor. The gang leader charged Maes with placing the entire society in danger by revealing to Captain Esquibel that the gang had stolen his horses. He read a letter he said was signed by Maes saying that Maes was quitting the People's Party (a political party controlled by Silva) and joining the Republican Party and the Society of Mutual Protection, a Vigilante group.

"No!" shouted the accused. He was innocent: he never wrote such a letter, he said.

The parody of a trial continued. At the end more than half of those present voted to spare Maes' life but to punish him. The decision sparked a violent argument that Silva finally quieted by ordering liquor brought from downstairs. Once peace was restored, Silva eloquently pleaded to the gang to put Maes to death. It would protect the rest of them, he said, and shouted:

"Which of you wants to go to the penitentiary?"

The new vote was unanimous for the death penalty. The "court" then sentenced Maes to be hanged from the bridge over the Gallinas River.

The informer sank to his knees, pleading hysterically for mercy. Silva had prepared for the verdict in advance. A rope suddenly appeared, produced by Remigio Sandoval, otherwise known as "The Hawk." Martin Gonzales y Blea, known as *El Moro*, "The Moor," fashioned a noose and slipped it over Maes' neck.

Silva's macabre imagination displayed itself now. Gang members donned masks and formed ranks, four abreast, to escort the quivering Maes. They marched down the stairway and into the street with their sobbing victim, then out into the night and down the street through the wind-driven snow.

The cold wind whipped their masks and clothing as they marched unseen through the pitch-black night. Honest citizens were in bed.

At the bridge, Maes mumbled a terrified prayer while the masked men tied the rope securely to a steel railing. Then Silva and "The Hawk" grasped his struggling form and roughly threw him over the side. There was a thud. The rope had broken and Maes had landed in the river bottom, unconscious. The executioners scrambled down and found that enough rope remained to finish the job. Quickly they hoisted Maes' still figure, tossed the rope up to the others, who pulled it up and tied it to the bridge, leaving Maes dangling.

At daybreak, Silva reported to police that a man's body was hanging from the bridge. He had seen it, he said, while passing by.

Police, as usual, found no clues and Silva thought he was safe until he got word that Captain Esquibel planned to get the grand jury to indict him on a charge of horse stealing. The jury was to convene on November 7. On November 4, Silva fled to Los Alamos. When the grand jury convened it did as expected, leaving Silva a fugitive.

Silva now directed his gang from the little village on the Sapello, and occasionally from a cave near the town of Coyote. Life as a fugitive distressed the bearded bandit. He chafed at long periods of inactivity and isolation. As the long winter faded in the warmth of spring, he looked around for something to occupy his time.

William Franks" store in Los Alamos caught his eye. It carried a large line that ranged from dry goods and hardware to food. It looked like easy pickings.

Just before midnight on April 6, 1893, Silva and several members of the gang broke into the store and carted the safe away, then returned to strip the place of everything they could load on the wagon. Afterward, Silva gathered all of Franks' books, accounts and papers and touched a match to them, costing Franks $10,000 in due bills and IOUs. In the cave at Coyote the hoodlums pried open the safe to find only forty dollars in cash, some postage stamps and a few IOUs.

Silva's twisted brain had been seeking a scapegoat for his sudden turn of fortune. He found two in his wife and her young brother, Gabriel Sandoval, whom Silva had always disliked. For some time Silva had carried on a torrid romance with Flor de La Pena (Flower of the Rock), who lived on the outskirts of Las Vegas. He told her he intended to eliminate both his wife and her brother.

He had launched his plot on January 23 by having his adopted daughter, Emma, kidnaped from school. Next, he had two members of his gang on the police force lure Sandoval to a lonely spot on the edge of town. There Silva knifed him to death and had his body dumped into an abandoned privy.

After the raid on the Franks store proved so disappointing Silva brooded on his problems. About a month later, he sent word to his wife that both Sandoval and the daughter were safe. (The daughter was, in fact, safe in Taos.) He asked his wife to meet him after dark on the edge of town and he would take her to see her loved ones. The distraught woman agreed.

On May 19, 1893, Silva met her at a rendezvous near Las Vegas, and in a buggy drove her to Los Alamos. When they arrived at the house of "Toothless," Silva asked the five members of the gang present to step outside so he could talk with his wife.

When they were alone, Silva demanded the $200 she had brought with her, as well as her jewelry. Then he plunged a knife into her breast and summoned his men.

Silva did not know that his villainy was getting too much for his cronies to stomach. The five men had discussed this matter while Silva was doing away with Dona Telesfora. They had also speculated upon the amount of money the bandit leader carried in his always bulging money belt.

Silva showed the five his wife lying dead on the bloody floor. He unbuckled his money belt and extracted several bills, then handed each man ten dollars. If the five sets of dark eyes seemed to flash with interest at the money belt, he didn't notice it.

He ordered the five to wrap his wife's body in blankets and shawls. Then he led them to a gully just south of the village. The arroyo was called *Triste,* meaning "Sorrowful Place."

Here, shielded by darkness, the bandits dumped Mrs. Silva into the arroyo, kicked the banks over her and started back to Los Alamos.

They had gone perhaps twenty-five paces when Antonio Jose de Valdez, better known as "Monkey Legs," softly drew his .45 pistol, placed its muzzle only inches from Silva's shaggy head and the shot smashed into his brain.

The five men gathered around their fallen leader, stripped him of his money belt and other valuables, then rolled his body into the same arroyo where they had just deposited his wife and kicked in the banks over it.

Back in Los Alamos, the murderers examined their loot, dividing about $10,000 in cash. Then they separated.

No one but members of the gang was aware that Silva and his wife were dead. The authorities continued to search for the saloonkeeper as a horse thief, completely unaware of his other activities. But although Silva was dead, his influence lingered.

Less than a week later, Cecilio Lucero, a member of the society, committed a gruesome double murder at the village of Vegoso, six miles from Las Vegas. Lucero lived at the home of a cousin, Benigno Martinez, who owned a flock of about 2000 sheep. On May 25, 1893, Lucero suddenly shot to death his cousin and then Juan Gallegos, a herdsman. Afterward, he pounded in their heads with a rock and tied their feet to long ropes fastened to a burro.

The next morning, the beast walked into Las Vegas dragging the mutilated victims behind him. Lucero was quickly arrested and brought to town. A few nights later a mob of 300 Las Vegans smashed into jail, removed him and strung him up to a pole.

Silva's death did little to slow the crime wave. The difference was that now the individual gangsters staged their crimes on their own, without the skillful planning of their late leader. Finally the harassed territorial governor issued a proclamation of amnesty, offering a pardon to any accessory who would testify against his fellows.

"Toothless" became the stool pigeon. He broke in March, 1894 while in jail awaiting trial on a rustling charge. Summoning the police, "Toothless" dictated a detailed account of the gang's activities to a stenographer, including the murder of Gabriel Sandoval. He was careful not to mention the murders of Silva and his wife.

The day following the confession, workmen exhumed Sandoval's body. Police immediately launched a territory-wide manhunt for Silva and his companions. As news of the sensational story got around, three other gang members accepted the amnesty and corroborated the testimony of their partner in evil. All still kept silent about the murder of Silva.

Rewards for Silva soon totaled $3000. He was reported seen in many places. A man in Colorado was even arrested and extradited as Vicente Silva, but was released when he was identified.

The crime wave continued. German Maestas, twenty-six-year-old member of the Society, hunted down a Los Alamos sheepherder who had stolen his wife's love. With the aid of Jesus Vialpondo, he shot the shepherd to death but was quickly captured, convicted and hanged.

Vialpondo continued at large, committing several robberies. His career ended after he and a companion murdered a young man who had discovered a theft they had committed, then burned his body. Both were hanged in Santa Fe in 1895.

The truth about the deaths of Silva and his wife did not come out until March, 1895, nearly two years after the murders. On March 17, both bodies were exhumed from their lonely graves near Los Alamos.

Today there are few reminders of the brutal criminal around the headquarters of the Ruby Ranch, which occupies the village site. The prosperous spread is owned by Willard Kirkpatrick of Post, Texas. Foreman is Everett (Buster) White, a husky, sun-tanned stockman.

A good gravel road leads to the Ruby ranch, leaving the north side of U.S. Highway 85 about four miles east of Las Vegas. Four miles later the road tops a hillock and you come to a large stucco gate, with RUBY RANCH emblazoned on it in big letters. A half mile inside the gate is Los Alamos.

It bears no resemblance to the village that once occupied the site. Except for the abandoned church across the road from the ranch house, it looks like many another Western cattle ranch.

A cluster of giant silver maples shades the house occupied by Mr. and Mrs. White, a rambling old pitched-roof adobe that looks like a horse-opera homestead. It is authentic West, from long, shaded porch to the two-foot-thick walls. As timeless as the building seems, only one portion is a real relic of Silva days.

The garage at one end of the L-shaped house was the Franks store, looted by Silva and his men that dark spring night in 1893. It houses farm equipment now but scraps of history stick to the inside walls in the form of faded blue and white wallpaper.

Out behind the house, gravestones mark the village cemetery. Headstones pre-date the death of the Silvas.

Farther away, a concrete bridge spans the Sapello beneath some cottonwood trees. It is a bridge to nowhere, a relic of yesterday on an abandoned road.

So faint is the memory of Silva and his crimes here that Ruby Ranch residents are unable to point out the site of the house used by the gang as a hide-out, the scene of the last act in the drama.

Many house foundations are hidden by the tall grass that billows in the breeze. It might have been any one of them.

Los Alamos garage that once housed a store looted by Silva and his men in 1893. Right, A concrete bridge crossing the Sapello beneath some cottonwood trees

Small Catholic chapel in Rayado

8 | A Meeting Place of Giants

Rayado sleeps on the banks of the Rio Rayado at the eastern foot of the Sangre de Cristo Mountains. Tall cottonwoods shelter several buildings scattered around gravel New Mexico Highway 21 which leads here from Cimarron. The place gets its name from the river, which is hardly more than a brook. How the stream got its name is another question: the English translation is "streaked."

Principal landmark is a rambling L-shaped adobe house with a tin pitched roof and a porch that extends across its entire front. It is painted and well kept. Out back are several farm buildings.

Across the road a small Catholic chapel, as neatly kept as the house, hides in deep shade. Southward down the road are more farm buildings, a "trading post" operated during summer by the Boy Scouts and an enormous flat-roofed adobe house with the log rafters the Spanish call *vigas* protruding from the walls.

Like Los Alamos, Rayado lost its village status a long time ago. Now it is part of the Boy Scouts' sprawling Philmont Ranch but it will never lose its links with history. This was a meeting place of giants.

The L-shaped adobe, for instance, is the

house from which Lucien Bonaparte Maxwell began building his land empire in the late 1840s. The flat-roofed adobe is a Boy Scout reconstruction of the house built by the famous Kit Carson, scout, mountain man and Indian fighter.

Carson was a native of Kentucky who was lured by the Western wilderness at the age of fourteen. He ran away from a man to whom he had been apprenticed and joined a caravan bound west on the Santa Fe Trail. Arriving in New Mexico in 1826 he quickly learned to shift for himself in hostile country, becoming a skilled trapper and hunter. In 1842 he guided Colonel John C. Frémont on an important expedition across uncharted wilderness to the Pacific Coast.

Carson developed a hankering to settle on his own ranch in 1845 and chose the valley of the Rio Rayado as a place to build a home. His location was a spot on the Santa Fe Trail. This was wilderness, part of a poorly defined Mexican land grant owned by Guadalupe Miranda and Carlos Beaubien. Miranda was a Mexican, Beaubien a French-Canadian.

The twenty-six-year-old Indian fighter built himself a spacious adobe house on the site of Rayado and cultivated some fifteen acres in garden and feed. Before he could harvest his first crop the wilderness called. In August, 1845, Carson got an urgent message from Colonel Frémont and took off to guide another expedition to the Pacific Coast.

Later he returned to Rayado and others came with him. They built up a settlement beside the stream.

Lucien Bonaparte Maxwell strode into the picture in 1849. Few frontier characters were as colorful as the burly, cigar-chewing Maxwell. Son of a prosperous Missouri trader, Maxwell longed for the freedom of

Kit Carson, who founded the settlement on the Rio Rayado

the wild. Like Carson he ran away from home to go West and become a Rocky Mountain trapper, a dead shot and a skillful woodsman. He also came to know Carson, who was already building himself a legendary reputation.

Maxwell settled in Taos, then headquarters for the trapping industry in the Rockies. In 1842 he married the beautiful Luz Beaubien, belle of Taos, who was only thirteen years old. The child bride was the daughter of Carlos Beaubien, the same French-Canadian who owned half of the land grant on which Kit Carson had settled. Whether Maxwell knew about it at the time of the marriage is a question. He soon found out and bought out Miranda's interest; later he inherited the other half from his wife's father.

His friend Carson, meanwhile, kept urging him to join him on the Rayado. Maxwell finally yielded, built himself a big house and started carving himself a niche in American history. A small military outpost was set up there to protect settlers against the Indians.

When Maxwell settled on the Rayado, he thought his land grant contained somewhere between 32,000 and 97,000 acres. It was not until later that he found out he was America's greatest land baron, ruler of an empire of 1,700,000 acres.

Maxwell stayed on the Rayado for eight years, then moved his headquarters to the Cimarron River, eleven or twelve miles to the north. He built a mansion there that soon became the talk of the frontier (Chapter Nine).

Maxwell ruled his empire for another twelve years, holding it in an iron grip even when a gold strike brought thousands of squatters onto the grant to scrape for riches in the Moreno Valley (Chapter Ten).

Maxwell sold out to a syndicate in 1869, ending his connection with the Rayado-Cimarron country. The new owners lacked Maxwell's savvy and caused a long war with settlers over land ownership, both in and out of court.

The sixgun was law in the Rayado coun-

The old Maxwell house at Rayado

try in the 'seventies and 'eighties. One night gunfighter Clay Allison led a band of cowboys to the village in search of Doctor Longwell. A brawler and a bully, Allison bore the physician a grudge.

Allison and his cohorts rode up to the Longwell house carrying a rope and demanding to see the doctor. Mrs. Longwell was ready for them: she said the doctor was sick in bed — with smallpox. It was possibly the only time in his spectacular career that Allison backed down. He and his friends wasted no time in heading down the road.

Rayado continued to live throughout the latter years of the century because of the Santa Fe Trail, which provided a direct route between Cimarron and Fort Union. However, traffic on the trail dwindled as the fort declined, and so did the village by the river. Only a few Spanish-American families continued to live there.

Kit Carson's house fell into ruin. A youngster named Fred Lambert from Cimarron used to play within its tumbledown walls. Fred still lives in Cimarron (Chapter Nine).

Rayado slumbered until 1922 when a new kind of giant strode onto the scene, a giant cut from the same yardgoods that provided Carson and Maxwell. Waite Phillips was a native of the Iowa farmbelt transplanted to Oklahoma's red clay, a rugged individualist and modern-day empire builder. He had created his own kingdom, producing oil wells, pipelines, refineries and market outlets.

Phillips was enchanted by the Rayado-Cimarron country just as Carson and Maxwell had been before him. He started buying giant chunks of the old Maxwell land grant until he owned an enormous spread of mountain and forest and plain. In 1927 Phillips and his wife took an architect on an extended tour of Europe to get ideas for a home on their New Mexico ranch. They absorbed much from the land around the Mediterranean.

They completed their house in 1928 and the Phillips family spent six months of each year there until 1941. The mansion was a showplace, filled with objects of art from all over the world.

First-floor ceilings were hand-illuminated by an Italian artist Phillips brought to New Mexico for that purpose. The piano was made especially for the living room, its case decorated by the same artist. A ground-floor trophy room was crammed with mementoes of hunts.

Phillips called his ranch "Philmonte," a combination of his own last name and the Spanish *monte*, for mountain. The mansion, about halfway between Cimarron and Rayado, he called Villa Philmonte.

Phillips and his son, Elliott, roamed the mountains at every opportunity, hunting and fishing and hiking. The more they got to know the country the more they wondered how they might share their discovery with others. Phillips reached a decision in 1938.

He wrote to the National Council of the Boy Scouts of America, inviting council members to come to Villa Philmonte to discuss a gift of land. They arrived in September. Among them was Ray H. Bryan, now the head of Philmont Scout Ranch.

Phillips led them on a week-long horseback inspection of his ranch. Then he gave the scouts 35,000 acres and $61,000 to develop a scout camp.

The scouts combined "Phillips" and "good turn" to come up with "Philturn Rocky Mountain Scout Camp," which opened in 1939. Later they decided to use Phillip's original name of Philmont, minus the final "e."

Ray Bryan, closely associated with Philmont's pioneer years, vividly remembers its challenge. "This was a camp without precedent," he said. "We had absolutely no pattern. We had to devise a program, decide what we were going to do with it."

One hundred and ninety-six scouts camped at Philmont that first summer. Phillips was a frequent visitor, spending hours chatting with the scouts. What he saw pleased him. He was convinced the boys were realizing the benefits he had foreseen.

In 1941 Phillips gave the scouts an additional 91,000 acres of his ranch, including the mansion and its furnishings. He turned over to the scouts the twenty-three-story Philtower Building in Tulsa to help support the ranch. The gift was worth an estimated $5,250,000. Its value today is closer to $10,000,000.

Phillips died in 1964 and left the scouts another million dollars, the income from which supplies scholarships to the camp for indigent boys. Convinced that his ranch was in good hands, he attached no strings to the gift. He made only one request: if the scouts ever sold Philmont, two paintings at Villa Philmonte were to remain in Colfax County. Portraits of Mr. and Mrs. Carlos Beaubien, original owners of the Maxwell Grant, they hang in the mansion dining room.

The scouts have preserved the house and furnishings. Bedrooms are used to house special guests. The house may be visited with permission from ranch headquarters.

Today scouts and their leaders come here from all over the world. Philmont is actually three separate operations, each closely linked with the other.

A Volunteer Training Center is designed for scout leaders. Seven thousand people use it annually, spending twelve days in outdoor training.

The camping division is the largest single part of the ranch, annually playing host to about 16,000 scouts. More than 150,000 boys have camped at Philmont since the camp was started.

The third section is a working cattle and sheep ranch, with a basic cattle herd of 350 and about 250 sheep. It covers 60,000 acres.

Phillips suggested that the scouts maintain a ranch and to help them get started he provided a basic herd of registered champion Herefords. The ranch pays its own way. Philmont pays more than $6000 property tax each year on the profit-making end of its operations.

The ranch's chief mission, however, is to give boys an experience in the wilderness. You become instantly aware of that when you drive into camp headquarters. A "Philmont" sign spans the gate on tall log posts. Hiking boots hang indecorously from it, their worn and pitted soles showing. It is a Philmont tradition. Scouts toss their worn-out boots up there as silent testimony to the ruggedness of Philmont's "road."

The check-in station looks like an oversize Greyhound parking lot on any summer day, with buses from every section of the country thundering in and out. Scouts are everywhere. Leaders meet with staff counselors at the station to plan their twelve-day stay.

Scout directors try to let each boy develop his own itinerary from a large choice. The scouts may pick from such varied programs as camping, hiking, fishing, mountain climbing, archeology, historical reconstruction, conservation and so on.

Scouts can also learn the care it takes to reconstruct portions of the past. Kit Carson's ranch house at Rayado is a monument to their skill. Now a museum, open to visitors, it is an excellent example of Spanish colonial architecture. Whether it is the Carson ranch house reconstructed is another matter. Fred Lambert, who played in the ruins as a boy, remembers that the house was some distance from this one, across the road and closer to the river.

An anonymous donor gave the scouts an additional 10,000 acres of the Maxwell Grant in 1963, a tract on Baldy Mountain. The scouts have begun to restore the old mining camp of Baldy Town on the flanks of the mountain. Scouts may learn something about mining in the abandoned mines on Baldy or pan placer gold from a stream.

About 500 employes are required to operate Philmont during the summer. The annual staff payroll tops $400,000. Twenty-three staffed camps are scattered over the mountains, each with a director, program counselor and quartermaster. Many other smaller camps dot the ranch.

It takes seventy-five vehicles of various types to run the ranch. A two-way radio setup gives instant communication with even the most remote camp sites. Headquarters can locate any of the scores of campers in a short time, no matter how far off they happen to be in the mountains. Chaplains from various faiths conduct church services, frequently following scouts to remote camp sites.

The impact of Philmont on city-bred youngsters is remarkable. Youngsters who have been no closer to the West than their television screen get a taste of the real thing. They see deer and antelope ranging the mountains, even watch Philmont's seventy-five-animal buffalo herd thunder alive from the pages of the past.

They get a chance to fend for themselves against the wilderness, almost like their ancestors. Philmont counselors insist that the boys come away from their twelve-day experience a little closer to manhood than before.

A bronze plaque in the gazebo at Villa Philmonte bears an inscription that reads:

. . . Donated for the purpose of perpetuating faith, self reliance, integrity, freedom — principles used to build this great country by the American pioneer. So that these future citizens may through thoughtful adult guidance and by the inspiration of nature visualize and form a code of living to diligently maintain these high ideals and our proper destiny.

WAITE PHILLIPS, *December 31, 1941*

Phillips would be most pleased with what is being done with his great gift to the American people. Probably old Lucien Maxwell and Kit Carson would be pleased also.

Kit Carson provided a watchtower on his house at Rayado

A view of Lucien Maxwell's house at Cimarron, taken after one of the fires that destroyed most of it

9 | Wild Wonderful Cimarron

The literal translation from the Spanish for the word *cimarron* is wild, untamed, unbroken. It is an appropriate name for Cimarron, New Mexico, twelve miles north of Rayado. For Cimarron was indeed wild — so wild that it got a reputation all across the frontier for gunplay and violence. Few towns loom so luridly lawless. No one managed to tame it in those days.

What man failed to do, time has managed — softly, surely and most probably permanently. Today, Cimarron is finally tranquil. The most exciting thing to ruffle its slumber is the throaty roar of bus diesels

in the high-country summer. Nobody complains, for the buses bring thousands of Boy Scouts to Philmont Ranch and dollars to the merchants of Cimarron.

There are actually two Cimarrons, and it is easy to confuse new and old. "New" town dates from 1905 and straddles U.S. Highway 64 just north of the Cimarron River, a stream noted for the beauty of its palisaded canyon a few miles west on the road to Taos. "New" Cimarron wears a look of age. Much of it, thickly encrusted with Victorian gingerbread, surrounds a little plaza that contains an oddly primitive concrete statue of Lucien

Maxwell with a rifle across his knees. The rest of "New" town is scattered up and down U.S. 64, most of it modern and undistinguished.

"Old" Cimarron hides from the tourist beneath many elm and cottonwood trees south of the river on New Mexico Highway 21. N.M. 21 is the original route of the Santa Fe Trail. Old Cimarron was a division point. One leg ran south to Fort Union and Las Vegas and the other headed west up Cimarron Canyon to Taos.

Less than a mile separates old and new Cimarron in distance, but in time the space is a hundred years. Little remains to tell you that old Cimarron was once actually a town. There is the big, comfortable-looking two-story Don Diego Hotel just east of the road. Another building, next door to the hotel, shows the mark of years. Across the street is an old dance hall that has been turned into a garage.

A towering gray stone building of three stories is by far the most prominent landmark. It could have been built last week, so unblemished is it by time. It is actually one of Cimarron's oldest, built in 1864 by Lucien Maxwell as a grist mill.

You can find other relics of the past around if you pry. One house, for example, pre-dates the village. This building is on a side street east of Highway 21. It was built in 1847 by a wagon-freighting firm that operated on the Santa Fe Trail. It is the oldest house in town. It served the Dahl Brothers as a warehouse.

Maxwell decided to move his headquarters to Cimarron from Rayado about ten years after the Dahls built the warehouse. Maxwell was then living in adobe splendor at Rayado. But the site on the Cimarron was more strategically located at the juncture of the two legs of the trail.

The house Maxwell built at Cimarron put his other place to shame. Three stories high and covering a city block, it quickly became a frontier landmark. There were rooms for billiards, gambling and dancing. It housed spacious servants' quarters and a section especially for the women of the household.

The land baron loved people and he loved to gamble. There was always room for one more guest at his house. Thousands of dollars changed hands in the Maxwell game rooms. Maxwell "banked" his money in an unlocked bureau drawer in his bedroom. He was never robbed.

Primitive concrete statue of Lucien Maxwell in the plaza, "New Town," Cimarron

Maxwell anecdotes are legion. He owned several racehorses that he would run at the drop of a *peso*. But one animal, better than all the rest, was Maxwell's particular joy. When a man challenged him to a race, he leaped at the opportunity. Maxwell was convinced the horse couldn't lose and practically cleaned out his bureau drawer to back up his belief. Other Cimarron residents believed the same thing and put up their own money.

Then Maxwell heard a rumor that his jockey was planning to throw the race. The land baron bided his time until just before the race, then summoned the jockey. He pointed to a white rock beside the track about fifty feet from the finish line and explained that he expected the jockey to be in the lead when he reached the rock. If not, Maxwell pledged, he would blow the jockey's head off with a rifle shot an instant later.

Maxwell's horse won — easily.

The land owner loved beautiful furniture and furnished his mansion with the best he could find, all laboriously freighted over the Santa Fe Trail. In business, Maxwell spurned papers in favor of a handshake and a verbal agreement. He was known for his generosity and started many in the ranching business by giving them livestock and a small ranch to be run on shares.

Five hundred people worked in Maxwell's fields. He had several thousand acres of land under cultivation and ran thousands of cattle and sheep on his ranges.

Cimarron thrived along with Maxwell. The grist mill was an asset to both. It generated business for the town and attracted scores of Indians who came from miles around to watch the groaning machinery make flour out of grain.

A quirk of fate has linked Maxwell's name with that of Billy the Kid. Maxwell had bought a Navajo girl to present to his wife as a personal servant. The child, Deluvina, became practically a member of the Maxwell family and after Maxwell's death she remained with the household of his son, Pete, at the Maxwell ranch at Fort Sumner. Many people believe that Deluvina was Billy's sweetheart and that he had gone to Fort Sumner to see her the night Pat Garrett's bullet cut him down. But if Deluvina was, she kept her secret until her death in 1927 at the age of eighty-one.

Maxwell's connection with Cimarron ended in 1870. He sold out and moved to Fort Sumner to spend the rest of his days longing for the northern New Mexico high country.

The town he built continued to prosper. It became a gunslingers' mecca. Almost from the moment of its birth the town became a frontier hotspot. Within a few years it boasted fifteen saloons, four hotels, a post office and a newspaper.

Gunfire crackled frequently during the 'seventies and 'eighties, the two most colorful decades in Cimarron's history. Part of it was provoked by the Colfax County War which erupted after the English syndicate to which Maxwell sold his grant tried to assert ownership. A tornado of resentment swept the county, producing a murder and a couple of lynchings. The trouble lasted for a generation.

Cimarron's social center shifted from the Maxwell house across the street to the St. James Hotel (now the Don Diego) after Maxwell moved away. Twenty-six recorded killings took place in the hotel saloon in one ten-year period. The hotel hosted some of the worst badmen and some of the best "goodmen" the West ever produced.

Cimmaron as it appeared in the 1870s

Henry Lambert, a little Frenchman, built the hotel. Lambert was born in Nantes, France, in 1838 and wound up in the United States in 1860 after a career as a sailor and cook. He became chef to General Ulysses S. Grant in 1862 and before the year was out had moved to the White House as President Lincoln's chef.

The Frenchman came to New Mexico in 1863, lured by a gold rush on the Maxwell Land Grant. At the boom camp of Elizabethtown, he quickly learned there was more gold to be found by cooking in the kitchen than by scraping at the hills with a pick.

Lambert opened a hotel in E'Town but moved to Cimarron when the gold fever began to cool. He built an adobe hotel that quickly became a favorite frontier gathering place.

Clay Allison, a rancher known throughout the West for his gunfighting prowess, was a frequent patron. A handsome man with hard eyes and nerves to match, he had a gunpowder temper and had never been bested in a gunbattle. Few persons got in Clay's way when he was drinking, which was often.

The gunfight staged by Allison and Pancho Griego in the St. James Saloon is still remembered in the Cimarron country. Griego's reputation almost matched Allison's. An incident at the St. James on June 6, 1875, had enhanced it.

Griego was dealing monte for a group of

Negro soldiers when an argument flared. Pancho knocked the money to the floor and as the soldiers broke for the door he drew his gun and fired. His bullets killed two of the soldiers. He dispatched the third with his Bowie knife.

Sometime later, Pancho decided to take on the redoubtable Allison. Standing at the bar in the St. James, Pancho hinted to Allison that he blamed him for the recent lynching death of one Cruz Vega. He began to fan himself with his sombrero, holding it in his left hand to shield his right as it slid his six-shooter out of its holster.

But Allison had stayed alive by paying attention to small details. He detected Griego's stealth and before the Mexican could fire, Allison shot him dead with two well placed bullets.

David Crockett, nephew of the original frontiersman, and a gunslinging pal named Gus Heffron shot three other Negro soldiers to death in the same saloon. Crockett was a bully, noted for his habit of stirring his coffee with the barrel of a sixgun. He and Heffron were standing at the bar when the three soldiers came in and asked for drinks. Henry Lambert refused, but offered to sell them liquor in flasks that they could take outside and drink. The soldiers objected, an argument flared and Crockett and Heffron got involved.

Both started shooting. The Negroes couldn't get the leather covers on their holsters unfastened in time to return the fire. Crockett and Heffron killed all three, putting three bullets in each.

The two pleaded self-defense and escaped punishment. A posse later shot Crockett to death and seriously wounded Heffron when the two created a disturbance on the streets of Cimarron.

The *Las Vegas Gazette* explained that the two had been good citizens, "but they got it into their heads they should act as desperadoes and outlaws; they would get drunk and ride through the streets of *Cimarron*, enter stores and even private dwellings, riding horseback, break showcases in stores, compel clerks to black their boots at point of shotgun and pistol . . ."

Henry Lambert, in a futile bid to keep peace, posted a sign on the wall of the St. James Saloon:

GENTS WILL PLEASE LEAVE
THEIR SIX-GUNS
BEHIND THE BAR WHILE
IN TOWN!

This Will Lessen The
Customary Collections
For Burials

Henry's son Fred lives today in Cimarron in a green and white house trailer just across the street from his father's old hotel. Fred was a lawman in the Cimarron country for forty years with a reputation for getting his man. He is retired now and since his wife's death a few years ago, lives quietly with a couple of pet dogs.

Fred's blue eyes soften when he talks about the old days. He vividly remembers Buffalo Bill Cody, a close friend of his father. He was a handsome, flamboyant figure, whose long locks fell around his shoulders.

"I can see him now, reared back in a chair smoking a long black cigar," Fred said.

Cody used to give the Lambert children tricycles and other toys for Christmas. He came to Cimarron frequently and gathered Indians for his Wild West show near here. Cody later looked at land south of town, toward Rayado, where he thought about raising "catalo," a hybrid of bison and cow. The Philmont Boy Scout buffalo herd now ranges the same land.

Buffalo Bill is only a small part of Fred's memories of the frontier past. By 1887, when he came into the picture, some of the gunsmoke had dissipated — but not all.

As a small boy, Fred used to sweep out the saloon. He will never forget the morning he came face to face with a stray corpse behind the bar, victim of a shootout the night before. Nor will he forget that night down the street at Swink's Dancehall, which is now a garage. He stood only an arm's length from violent death.

A bully accosted Fred and four other teenage boys and took them to the dance hall where a Spanish-American dance was in progress. The Spanish and Anglo populations of Cimarron ordinarily kept their social affairs strictly segregated, neither interfering with the other. But shortly before some Anglo cowboys had "hurrawed" a Spanish dance. The bully and his friends were venting their revenge on the most convenient Anglos.

The bully lined them up in a row at Swink's in the flickering yellow light of oil lamps. Fred and his friends had only one gun among them, a venerable .44, loaded with the only three cartridges they could find. The gun was thrust in the belt of the youth standing next to Fred.

The rhythmic Spanish music stopped. The room grew tense. The bully stepped forward and swung his pistol barrel hard against the face of the boy with the gun in his belt.

"He went down to one knee," Fred remembered. "And the instant his knee touched the floor his right hand came up, gun blazing."

The bully dropped, three bullets in his heart.

"Somebody shot out the lights and everybody raced for the street," said Fred. The five boys led the pack.

The boy who fired the shots was fined $100 on a charge of carrying a deadly weapon. He was still living near Raton as this was written.

Fred, commissioned by telephone as a special deputy sheriff at the age of fifteen, promptly captured two men and a woman wanted for murder. He found his quarry in a buckboard after crossing the Cimarron River. The man whipped up his Winchester but accidentally caught the barrel against the dashboard of the wagon. It deflected his aim and the shot hit the dust between the front feet of Fred's horse. Fred fired in that instant, hitting the gunman's hand. The fight ended. It was the start of a distinguished career for Fred.

Barred windows on the old jail in Cimarron

Fred Lambert, a law officer in the Cimarron country for 40 years

Fred Lambert doesn't look the stereotype of the frontier marshal. He is a little guy who loves people and who seems more at home with a brush and easel than with a gun. He is a prolific and talented artist and his trailer is filled with oil paintings and pen-and-ink drawings. Fred is also a writer, who has published much poetry and now has a book in print on the Maxwell Land Grant. He regularly contributes articles on the West to magazines.

He keeps his Colt's single-action revolvers as spotless as in the days when he wore them. Both are on .45 frames, chambered for .32-20 shells, the same type he used in his Winchester.

Fred speaks softly and evenly, his eyes perceptive and alert. He has a fine sense of humor and the sensitivity of an artist but underneath lies an edge of toughness. He seems content to live just across the street from his yesterday.

The situation is similar for yet another resident of old Cimarron, Mrs. Mary Lail. At eighty-three, she is the oldest native of the town. She lives in the oldest house, the same one built by the Dahl Brothers.

My first visit with her was on a bright day in early November. Someone had pointed out her house to me, close beside an unpaved side street that was once the Santa Fe Trail. The trail veered sharply downhill to ford the river just at the end of the house.

She appeared quickly when I knocked on the door, white-haired and motherly in a print cotton housedress. Smiling, she invited us inside. Almost instantly we were friends.

On the porch, a giant tortoise lumbered over to rub a red, green and yellow painted shell against my ankle. "That's Arizona Gene," she laughed. "Had to paint him so I can find him when he gets out."

She led us inside, pointing out the sixteen-inch-thick walls of the adobe, showing us books and furniture and pictures dating from frontier days. Soon we were in a quiet, comfortable country kitchen. Over the sink a window looked out toward the river not a hundred yards away. A jelly jar half filled with water sat on the sill. In it was a single wildflower, a bright yellow splash of fading autumn.

A piercing shriek came from the living room, shattering the quiet. It was "Joe," Mrs. Lail's talking Mynah bird. It uttered a phrase so clear it made us marvel.

"Surely you've got time for a cup of coffee," smiled Mrs. Lail and without waiting for an answer got out some cups and saucers. Cookies followed quickly.

"A few people come to see me," she said. "After all, I am the oldest native in the oldest house in Cimarron."

Mrs. Mary Lail, oldest resident of Cimarron

She is not embarrassed by her years, for she has a great zest for life and such an overwhelming love for children that she has raised thirty of them. Only four were her own. She kept the others for varying lengths of time. Some were babies who needed homes briefly. Others lived with her for years. She considered all her children. Her own are all dead. So is her husband.

She told us about the house and about Cimarron, regretting its lurid reputation and remembering little about the bloodshed. Her fondest recollections are those when as a little girl she was allowed to baby-sit for some of the women at the dances at Swink's.

She has lived in this house since 1906. She is sensitive and intelligent, loves literature and poetry and is proud of her large library. She has been writing poetry most of her life and has sold some of it as lyrics to song publishers.

Mrs. Lail told us about her poetry and her "children" as we sat there drinking coffee in the quiet kitchen. Her eyes went far away and she began to recite a poem she had written, right here in the kitchen, some years ago.

Has anyone seen three children or four,
playing around my kitchen door?
It was only a little while ago —
It can't be fifty years I know —
That they tumbled and laughed in glee
Out there beneath that old tree.
I was too tired that summer day
To go out with them in the shade to play.

She paused, her blue eyes filled with tears. She wiped her eye, then continued, her voice choked with emotion.

Has anyone seen three children or four,
Wandering away from my kitchen door?
Oh, if you have, Oh! Please, I pray
Go call them back, ere they go astray.

Be sure and tell them that I now am free
To play with them beneath the old elm
    tree.
But silence answers, 'too late, too late,'
God has called them in and closed the
    gate.
If I could see three children or four
Come romping in at my kitchen door
I know that I would shout with joy
Much louder than the noisiest boy.
And then, because I was their mother,
I'd start to cry like any other.
I'd take the cookies from their shelf
And tell each boy to help himself
If they made tracks on my kitchen floor
I'd wish they'd make a million more.
I'd hang my apron on its hook
And go with them down to the brook.
I'd help untangle fishing lines
And look for birds' nests in the vines.
We'd stroll along the stream for hours,
Just piling sand and picking flowers.
I'd climb with them, up to the loft,
Where they have hid, to smoke, so oft.
I'd even try one cigarette,
Although their fumes upset me yet.
A real companion they'd find in me —
I should not say 'I,' it would be 'us,' or
    'we.'
Oh, I'd give this world, once more to see
Those romping forms 'neath the old elm
    tree.
But alas! I waited all too long.
For now those precious forms are gone.

It was very quiet in the kitchen when Mrs. Lail finished. Out in the yard, the breeze sighed in the branches of the big elm. I got up from the table and walked to the window, looking to the river, sparkling so brightly in the sunshine.

The past of Cimarron seemed very close at hand and not very violent at all.

A battered skillet still hangs on the ramshackle porch of a ruined house (Elizabethtown)

10 | The Town That Died Twice

Elizabethtown is a ghost city with a past linked closely to Cimarron. Its ruins roost high atop a hill in the wide, green Moreno Valley five miles north of Eagle Nest on New Mexico 38.

Packrats scurry through the high bunch grass that fills the streets. Birds roost in the perfectly arched stone windows of the town hall. A battered skillet still hangs disconsolately on the ramshackle porch of a house falling down. A gate that looks ready to crumble clings to rusted hinges on a post of a fence that has long since disappeared.

It is silent here, except for the ever present wind whispering through the grass or the far-off cawing of a crow wheeling against the sky. The years and the elements have been unkind to E'Town. The few buildings that have managed to withstand their ravages show signs of weakening. The town is but a skeleton, the boards of the buildings the familiar ghost-town hues of cinnamon and burned toast.

If you stand in the wreckage of the town and look to the east you can see 12,549-foot Baldy Mountain, the magnet that created E'Town and also destroyed it.

You must go backward in time more than

a century to find the beginning — back to 1866 when a grateful Indian brought a chunk of "pretty rock" to Captain William Moore and William Kroenig at Fort Union. Captain Moore had once found the same Indian badly wounded and on the verge of death. He gave him water and took him to Fort Union where he was nursed back to health.

The "pretty rocks" were rich copper-ore specimens that Captain Moore and Kroenig spotted instantly. They quickly sent two men to accompany the Indian to the scene of his find, a spot high on the slopes of Baldy. They found lots more "pretty rock" lying about. When Moore and Kroenig heard the news they sent Lawrence F. Bronson, Peter Kinsinger and a man named Kelley to Baldy to do the necessary work to certify the claim before winter set in.

The trio reached Baldy well into October, when shimmering yellow aspen covered the mountain. They found a creek flowing off the western face and started climbing. They made camp on the banks of Willow Creek as dusk fell. Bronson and Kinsinger pitched in and started cooking supper while Kelley dug a gold pan out of his saddlebag to pass the time panning the creek gravel.

He scooped out some gravel and made a couple of idle passes with the pan, then screamed with excitement for his companions. They came running. Kelley extended the pan. A couple of gold flakes glittered in the fading light.

They forgot all about supper in their haste to start exploring their own little gold field. They spent the next few days panning gold, chipping rock from promising outcrops and digging ditches, ignoring the copper strike altogether. It was too late in the season to do more.

Then they carved the words DISCOV-ERY TREE on a promising ponderosa that overlooked their campsite and retreated down the mountain. They returned to Fort Union, pledging they would keep the secret to themselves.

It took only a few days for the word to get out. It traveled with unlikely haste, reaching all the way to Colorado, where hundreds of miners were at the moment bemoaning the collapse of a gold rush.

These miners and others barely waited for the snow to melt off Baldy's flanks in the spring of '67 before going to the diggings. A horde reached Maxwell's place at Cimarron even before the snow was gone, panting to be on the move to Baldy. By summer, 300 men had quit their posts at Fort Union to head for the mountain.

Bronson and his companions were among the feverish swarm on Baldy that spring. They laid off five claims from their "Discovery Tree" and washed out fourteen ounces of gold during the summer.

Goldseekers found color at places like Spanish Bar, Michigan Gulch, Pine Tree Ravine, St. Louis Gulch, Nigger Gulch and Humbug Gulch. Four hundred claims had been filed within an eight-mile radius of old Baldy by July and a steam sawmill was belching smoke and whirring out 4000 feet of lumber a day. The lumber found a ready market, even at the staggering price of fifty dollars per thousand feet. Many miners were building sluice boxes in the gulches to better separate the gold flakes from the sand, a more efficient method than the pan.

James A. McKenna, who visited the E'Town gold fields a few years later, gave this description:

The sluice-box was built of plain rough lumber like a trough with both ends left open. Slats, or riffles, which were blocks of wood, rails,

House in Elizabethtown

poles, iron bars, and often sacking, matting, or hides with the hair up, were laid crosswise on the bottom . . . being further apart at the end . . . than at the beginning. The riffles caught the free gold. Mercury was sometimes put into the grooves to help catch the gold, especially if it was light in weight . . .

But the hundreds flocking to the Moreno needed many things besides lumber.

Captain Moore, whose good-Samaritan act was responsible for the whole thing, saw the need. He opened a store on the hill overlooking the valley in June of '67. Business flourished. Within weeks, log cabins began sprouting all over the hill around the store.

Obviously, some organization was needed. Moore and his neighbors hired T. G. Rowe, a surveyor, to plat a town. He laid out a city checkerboard style, with wide avenues between blocks of lots. The settlers decided to call it Elizabethtown in honor of Captain Moore's daughter, Elizabeth Caterina, born April 3, 1863. Soon five mercantile businesses were thriving on the hilltop and by July twenty buildings had been completed and that many more were under construction.

Most of the population of E'Town vanished just as soon as the high-country cold set in, but some stuck around, managing to keep warm at places like the May Flower Saloon, the Arbor Saloon, a billiard parlor and a gambling den. And by that winter another establishment had opened its doors to a grateful town. The bagnio offered two "girls" of undetermined age.

Territorial promoters meanwhile watched E'Town's success with open-eyed envy. They enlisted the support of Lucien Maxwell, on whose land the gold rush was occurring, and platted a rival townsite six miles south. They

Elizabethtown, first incorporated town in New Mexico Territory

Street scene, Elizabethtown, during its boom

named it after Maxwell's daughter, Virginia.

The town was started in early 1868 but boasted only forty inhabitants by April. The men behind it poured forth a steady stream of flowery promotion about Virginia City's potential. It was all to no avail: by the end of July, nobody was left.

An E'Town resident commented about it in the Santa Fe *New Mexican*: "Virginia City moved up here yesterday — come up on a burro; says it is too lonesome down there, and can't stand it; had to go three miles to speak to anyone, so it concluded to come up here."

Other promoters started a "town" two miles up Grouse Gulch, calling it "Mountain City." It proved to be more mountain than

city and by 1870 its two saloons had moved to Elizabethtown.

Lucien B. Maxwell watched the influx of goldseekers to the Moreno with great interest. After all, the gold rush was taking place on *his* land. He probably remembered what had happened to John A. Sutter, whose land empire was ruined by the California rush of '49.

Realizing that he couldn't fight the inevitable, Maxwell entered actively into the gold rush, filing many placer claims. With Moore, Kroenig and others, he formed the Copper Mining Company to work the copper find that sparked the rush. Work started in 1867 and Maxwell's luck held true to form. Three hundred feet into the mountain, his

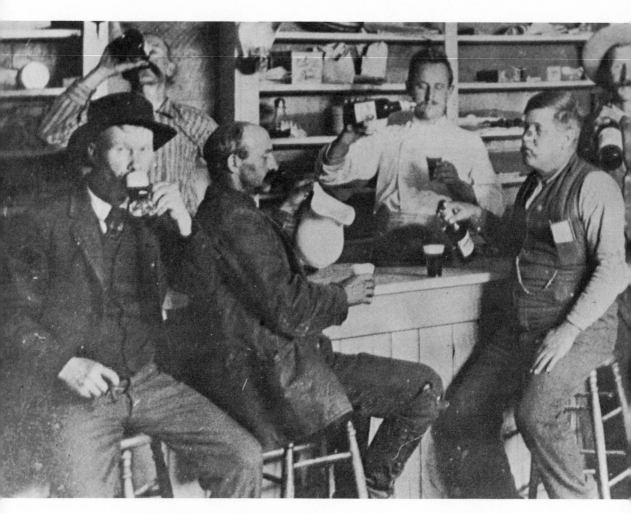

Scene in an Elizabethtown saloon

miners struck a vein of gold-bearing quartz ten feet wide!

Maxwell learned the next year about another hardrock strike on Ute Creek and filed on it. This claim turned into the rich Aztec Mine — the initial assays of which showed a yield of $19,455.37 in gold and $189.88 in silver per ton. The land-grant baron didn't miss a single dollar. He set up a sawmill and improved the road between Cimarron and Elizabethtown, then set up a profitable toll gate to snag the goldseekers heading for the Moreno.

Maxwell even managed to get along with the squatters swarming all over his land. He charged many of them rentals for placer and quartz claims and got away with it. The charges were reasonable: twelve dollars a year in advance for a placer or gulch claim, and half the proceeds of a lode claim.

Maxwell also plowed considerable money back into the gold field. Water shortages constantly harassed the placer miners. Maxwell invested heavily in Nicholas S. Davis' scheme to build a forty-one-mile system of ditches and flumes to bring water from Red River to the Moreno.

It was an engineering marvel for the day. The aqueduct was started in the spring of '68 and completed a year later. Flumes carried water over gulches and valleys. The longest measured 2800 feet and hung seventy-nine feet above a gully. Some parts of the flumes are still visible on the old Red River Pass road. But the big project was a failure, delivering less than a seventh of the water it was supposed to bring.

E'Town thrived anyway. More than a hundred buildings sprawled helter-skelter over the hilltop by the spring of 1868. The population hit and passed 500. Before the year was out an estimated 3000 persons were working in the gold fields and most of them lived in E'Town.

It was a real boom town, with lots selling at prices ranging between $800 and $1200 and sugar going for forty cents a pound. Twenty stores and saloons were fighting off customers that summer of '68. The Moreno Hotel was built and eighty-three invited guests toasted its opening in champagne on June 1. The town got a couple of short-lived newspapers, *The Moreno Lantern* and the *National Press and Telegraph*.

E'Town's growth was so phenomenal that by 1870 it became the first incorporated town in New Mexico Territory, with a mayor, a council and practically all the other frills of civilization. Next, it became the seat of a new county, carved out of Mora County and named in honor of Vice President-elect Schuyler Colfax.

It was an exciting and hazardous place to live. A visitor wrote that the town had many saloons ranging in length from 100 to 200 feet. The bar was always located in front, with gambling tables and dance hall in the rear.

The male dancer compensated for his privilege of dancing by going up to the bar after each dance, where he and his partner partook of the luxuries kept there. . . . The frequent visits produced a lot of conviviality, stirring up the wilder men, who always had hung to their belts this six-shooter law and very often declared the law unto themselves, playing at such amusements as shooting out the lights in the halls and then shooting quite promiscuously until a stampede resulted. . . .

Badmen of every stripe frequented Elizabethtown. As early as 1868 townspeople had to organize a militia to protect themselves, not only against the gunslingers but against wandering bands of Utes and Jicarilla Apaches who looked upon the area as their own hunting grounds.

Army troops stopped the Indian trouble in 1868. Elizabethtown's own residents soon took up where the savages left off. The gunplay got so bad that the E'Town residents formed a vigilance committee.

The vigilantes dispatched some badmen with gunfire and hanged others. They took a Mexican charged with murder away from the sheriff and hanged him to a tree. He had been granted a change of venue to Mora County. The vigilantes left him swinging with a card attached to the cadaver reading: *So much for change of venue.*

The bloody climax to one of the West's grisliest chapters of crime occurring in E'Town during the gold boom was the story of Charles Kennedy. Kennedy, a big, husky full-bearded man, had built a cabin at the foot of Palo Flechado Pass, twenty miles from E'Town on the road to Taos. He lived there in comparative solitude with his Ute wife and her young son. Few people paid much attention to the taciturn man. He made infrequent trips to town for supplies and when he did he always kept to himself while his wife stayed in their spring wagon and spoke to no one.

E'Town paid him no mind until one cold night in late September, 1870. A crowd of miners and others, including the renowned Clay Allison, were insulating themselves against the chill at John Pearson's saloon. Kennedy's wife suddenly fell in through the door, footsore and bleeding, and gasped out a story so horrible it made the most hardened man in the place cringe.

She said Kennedy had been luring travelers to his cabin for the past two years. He would offer them dinner and once they sat down at his table murdered them with either a gun or ax. Then he would rob them of their valuables and kick the body into a small cellar to remain until he had time to burn or bury it.

She said that a day or so before Kennedy had slain a Ute Indian and put him in a temporary tomb under the cabin floor. Tonight, said the Indian woman, Kennedy lured a prospective victim to the cabin. While he was eating he asked the Kennedys if there were many Indians around.

"Can't you smell the one Papa put under the floor?" asked the little boy.

Kennedy was enraged. He shot his guest dead and bashed the child's brains out against the fireplace. Then he threw both into the cellar, threatened the Ute woman with similar treatment if she ever told, locked the doors and drank himself to sleep. The terrified woman waited until Kennedy was in a stupor, then climbed painfully up through the chimney to flee to Elizabethtown.

Allison and the miners saddled up and headed for the Palo Flechado, where they found the murderer still dead drunk. They searched the place and found human bones and a body under the fireplace.

Kennedy's examining trial was held October 3, 1870. Jose Cortez testified that he had seen Kennedy shoot a whiskered Anglo who had stopped at his cabin for the night. The court ordered Kennedy held for action by the grand jury.

Three days later some Taos Indians brought a human skull into town they said they had found near the Kennedy place. That was enough for the miners. They crashed into the jail, seized Kennedy and forced him to select a "jury" of twelve men from the mob. Another was named as Kennedy's counsel and proved so convincing that he talked two of the jurors into hanging up the verdict so the accused could get a proper trial.

The mob withdrew, but only until the following night, when they tied a stout piece of hemp around Kennedy's neck and dragged him through the streets to the slaughterhouse where they strung him up.

Clay Allison, who always seemed to be around when anything violent was happening, was there when the execution took place. He cut off Kennedy's head, put it in a sack, and carried it all the way to Cimarron, where he dumped it on the bar in front of Henry Lambert.

"Hang it up outside," ordered Allison. It would be an object lesson to wrongdoers, the suddenly moral Allison explained.

Lambert protested, but Allison's intention was clear. The Frenchman finally shrugged and staked the head on the corral fence at the St. James, where it stayed for months and eventually mummified. It disappeared one night, never to be seen again.

Kennedy was just one criminal in E'Town's lurid career. "Coal Oil Jimmy" Buckley stirred up some excitement in 1871, leading a couple of other hoodlums in a series of stagecoach holdups on the road to Cimarron.

The posting of a $3000 "dead or alive" reward cut Jimmy's career short. Soon afterward, a couple of Jimmy's friends brought in "Coal Oil Jimmy" and his chief partner in crime — dead. The friends had pretended to join the outlaws, then waited until the right moment and shot both down in cold blood.

The Colfax County War also stirred some excitement in Elizabethtown. After the Maxwell Land Grant was sold, the new English owners tried to crack down on some of the squatters up and down the Moreno Valley.

Irate settlers reacted by setting fire to the homes of some grant people in Elizabethtown and troops had to be sent from Cimarron to quell the riot. More rioting broke out the following spring.

Elizabethtown's doom was already in the cards. The richest placer and lode deposits had begun to play out. The water shortage prevented hydraulic mining on the necessary scale.

The Maxwell Land Grant Company had filed ejectment suits against a number of settlers on the grant but these proved to be merely more nails in the E'Town coffin. Many who were barely eking out a living decided it wasn't worth the effort. The town, crowded by thousands in 1870, began to slip. By 1875, except for a few stores, E'Town was virtually a ghost.

Freight wagons in Elizabethtown during the boom of the early '70s

An Eastern newspaperman visited the Moreno Valley in 1881 and gave a graphic picture of the once lively town:

It makes one lonesome to walk the streets of Elizabethtown. Although not an old place, it is deserted and instead of the crowded streets or crowded houses, rum shops, gambling saloons, and hourly knock downs of a few short years ago, a sort of graveyard stillness, deserted buildings and general tumbledown appearance is everywhere observed.

E'Town and the Moreno lived on in a kind of limbo for nearly a quarter of a century, to be resurrected in the 'nineties, when a promotion drive by the land-grant company stirred new interest in the area. Well capitalized operators opened many old mines. Prospectors and miners once again swarmed into the valley to rejuvenate Elizabethtown. It actually appeared for a time that E'Town might be on the way toward gaining some permanency. A monster dredging machine assembled aboard a barge in the Moreno River boosted the optimism.

H. J. Reiling of Chicago, who had recently developed a gold dredge, was the father of the idea. He figured New Mexico's gravel would be a good place to give his dredge a try. He built a dam on the Moreno to back up enough water to float the huge machine, then bought 200,000 feet of lumber to build the boat. He hauled 35,000 pounds of equipment to E'Town over wagon roads from the railroad at Cimarron. The boat was christened the *Eleanor* amid much fanfare on August 20, 1901.

It was a success from the start, taking out as much as $750 to $1,000 in gold dust daily. Elizabethtown basked in the rays of the *Eleanor's* reflected glory.

Reiling was encouraged and determined

to see what he could do with a dredge in Colorado. He mortgaged the *Eleanor* to get the money. The very next year was unprofitable on the Moreno and the company was bankrupt by the end of 1905. Charles Springer and J. Van Houten of the Maxwell Land Grant Company bought the dredge in June, 1906 but she never operated again.

Now a new disaster struck Elizabethtown in the form of fire. The blaze destroyed many buildings in the business section. The *Eleanor* was left to rust and sink deeper into the sands of the trickling Moreno until it finally disappeared. Nature had reclaimed that part of the valley.

The passing years brought sporadic revivals of hardrock mining on Mount Baldy, where for a time, the mining town of Baldy was reborn. But after World War II, even the Maxwell Land Grant owners gave up and sold the last 10,000 acres on Baldy, including the mineral rights.

A member of the National Council of the Boy Scouts of America bought that tract and presented it to the scouts with the request that his name not be revealed. The Aztec Mine, which had produced more than $4,000,000 in gold since 1868, was part of the property.

Elizabethtown today is an object lesson in the transitory nature of the works of man. You can see few of them as you look across the Moreno Valley toward Mount Baldy. There is the highway, of course, a narrow black ribbon in the foreground, dotted by the occasional moving shape of a car. Around are the bleak ruins of a once bustling city.

Other than that, you see little enduring evidence of man. You are mostly aware of the broad, gray-green sweep of the valley and the distant cone of Baldy and the eternal sky.

Elizabethtown's town hall, long abandoned to the elements

Overleaf: *The ruins of Elizabethtown, with Baldy Mountain in the distance*

A decaying two-story hotel guards the junction like a castle

11 | Valley of Shadow

Tragedy haunts the valley of the Vermejo, fifty miles east of Elizabethtown. The coal town of Dawson lived and died here. And while the village itself has vanished, the memory of two of America's worst mine disasters will shadow the valley forever. Nearly 400 men died in the two calamities that occurred only ten years apart.

Colfax, an almost abandoned ranch town, marks the gateway to the Valley of Shadow where U.S. Highway 64 and New Mexico 234 meet, about eleven miles east of Cimarron. An imposing but decaying two-story hotel guards the junction like a castle, its windows gaping black and empty. Life has drifted away and only the skeleton remains, staring somberly southward toward the sagebrush-covered hills.

Driving northward along the Vermejo toward Dawson you can understand why J. B. Dawson settled here. It is a pretty valley, marked by low bluffs on each side, their contours softened by bunch grass and scattered piñon and juniper trees.

Dawson came this way in the 1860s, looking for a place to homestead. He found it at a point five and a half miles upstream from the site of Colfax. It offered good graze and a hillside coal seam. The coal was handy for cooking and heating and Dawson had so much he could sell some to his neighbors.

When Dawson found that his ranch was on the Maxwell Land Grant he paid the company $3700 for a deed, then found out he had bought 20,000 acres. He ranched the land with a partner, Charles Springer, until 1901, when a firm incorporated as Dawson Fuel Company bought the property for $400,000.

The company built a hundred cottages for 500 people, linked the spot with the Rock Island Lines via a 137-mile-long railroad, erected coke ovens and started mining coal. The first trainload moved down the Vermejo in August, 1902.

The coal seams were rich and mining expanded rapidly. Slavs, Greeks and Italians flocked to the valley. By 1905, 124 coke ovens were belching fire and a prosperous city was blooming.

Death, as always in coal mining, stayed close at hand. Fire broke out in No. 1 Mine in September, 1903. It was followed by explosions but 500 miners escaped. Men worked for a week to control the fire and when it was over three were dead.

Such accidents were expected, however. Dawson continued to grow. It finally attracted the attention of the giant Phelps Dodge Corporation, which bought the mines and tried to make Dawson a model city. The firm built schools and churches and improved miners' homes. In the process the company developed some community spirit. Dawson's football team became a New Mexico powerhouse.

Phelps Dodge also strove to make the mines as safe as possible. The company did such a good job with Stag Canyon Mine No. 2 that it attracted the eyes of coal-mining

experts who described it as "the highest achievement in modern equipment and safety appliances that exists in the world." The statement came in 1913, a year after shipping experts said the *Titanic* was "unsinkable."

The New Mexico Inspector of Mines completed two weeks of inspection of the Dawson pits on October 20, 1913. He reported that Stag Canyon Mine No. 2 was totally "free from traces of gas, and in splendid general condition."

Wednesday, October 22, dawned bright and clear at Dawson. Two hundred and eighty miners reported for work at Stag Canyon Mine No. 2. Work went on as usual until a little after three p.m. Two miners stood at the main entry waiting for tram cars. They were the only men on the day shift not inside the mine. They saw William McDermott, general mine superintendent, walk through the portal into the mine. A few minutes later a roar shuddered through the mountain.

"The first sound was like a sharp high-powered rifle shot, immediately followed by a prolonged muffled roar, and a distant vibration of the earth for several hundred feet," the *Raton Range* was to report the next day.

Seconds later flame flared out of the tunnel mouth for a distance of a hundred feet. Dense smoke followed. Rock, dirt and debris cascaded over the two miners in the entry, burying both. One managed to claw his way out but the other died in the rubble.

Two miles way the same rumble shook the weatherboarded homes in Dawson, sending fear racing through everyone in town. Housewives rushed into the street, frantically grabbing children, then raced for the narrow dirt road that snaked upcanyon to the mine.

General Manager T. H. O'Brien was working practically next door when he felt the rumble. Realizing at once what had happened, he pushed the electric button that started the mine siren keening its warning through the bright afternoon, summoning men from three other mines. Then he raced for the portal of Mine No. 2.

It was hidden by clouds of dense, oily gray smoke. The stench of coal dust was heavy in the air. Suddenly, O'Brien was surrounded by miners from other tunnels, their faces and overalls black with soot, their carbide cap lamps burning.

O'Brien barked orders that were superfluous. The men knew what to do. They started to dig away the rubble from the entry at once.

With the main entry blocked, O'Brien headed for the main airshaft, which contained a ladder for use as an escapeway. There he found dense smoke billowing skyward and he knew that the giant ventilating fans had stopped.

O'Brien now donned an oxygen mask and led miners into Mine No. 5, where he knew a tunnel led to Mine No. 2. Tons of rock had sealed the passageways.

By now the first pathetic trickle of people from Dawson had arrived at the main entry. Some had run all the way. Women, their faces blanched with fear, clustered around the portal. Some carried babies, others tugged at toddlers. As the crowd grew, ropes were strung to keep the people from interfering with the rescue work.

Rescuers worked frenziedly, knowing that many men might still be alive in the mine. Darkness fell and great arc lights were brought to bathe the scene in garish detail. The men finally cleared a path into the tunnel to permit "helmet men" — miners wearing oxygen masks — to burrow their way through the debris in the mine.

By ten p.m. they had penetrated only a hundred feet. They found five men sick and dazed from their injuries and the fumes, but alive. A cheer rippled across the waiting crowd as the five were brought out. By two a.m. the next day the rescue teams had found two more miners alive and had brought out the bodies of fourteen.

Phelps Dodge, meanwhile, loaded a train in Douglas, Arizona, with doctors and nurses and sent it speeding to Dawson. J. C. Roberts, chief of the U.S. Mine Rescue Station for the district, arrived to take command of the rescue effort.

By Friday, twenty-three men had been rescued. Miners were going into the pit in shifts of fifteen each, wearing unwieldy, primitive oxygen helmets that allowed them enough air to work two hours. They had to walk 3000 feet into the mine before they could start digging.

O'Brien worked harder than any of his men. He kept at it with hardly a pause until Friday afternoon; then he collapsed.

The interior of the mine was a chamber of horrors. Rescuers found one dead man "leaning against a wall with both hands elevated to his face, as though he was striving to ward off a sudden and unexpected blow." They found another dead man standing erect with a pick still in his hand, just as he had struck his last blow into the coal.

Hope flared briefly just after five o'clock on Friday afternoon when rescuers found a battered mine mule alive several thousand feet in the pit. Jose Fernandez they found in a room nearby, bruised and unconscious, barely alive. He was the last man to come out alive.

By Saturday, officials abandoned hope

for the 261 men still in the pit. That same morning, James Lerdi and William Persa, two "helmet men," were caught in a shower of coal dust and tore off their oxygen masks. Both died instantly from the gas, the only casualties among the rescue teams.

Brief funeral services were held over the thirty-six black coffins of the first miners brought out of their tomb. All were buried in separate graves in the cemetery on the south edge of town.

When the slow, plodding task of recovery ended, the toll stood at 263, the second worst mine-disaster toll in U. S. history.

Phelps Dodge gave each widow $500, then later added $1500, plus another $200 for each child. The company relocated any family that wished to return to Europe.

The State Mine Inspector discovered the cause of the disaster nearly a month afterward. A miner had violated mine rules by setting off a dynamite charge while men were in the pit. The charge was overloaded and forced coal into the mine for about forty feet. This ignited coal dust that swept through the entire pit.

The mine was cleaned and production was quickly restored. Dawson continued to thrive, with little fear of repetition of the frightful day in 1913. But history repeated, on Thursday, February 8, 1923, less than ten years after Stag Canyon. The scene this time was Mine No. 1.

One hundred and forty men reported for work that typical brisk but sunny winter day at Mine No. 1. Two veterans were among them, Felini Martini and Charles Candale. They were assigned to work in the deepest part of the pit, far back in an area called Crosscut No. 4 North.

Young Albert English, Jr., a foreman, was officially assigned to another mine but offered to work in No. 1 to replace a man who went home ill. His father, Albert English, Sr., was working in the same mine.

Nobody in the pit that day was concerned about the fact that a cold snap had frozen some water pipes that fed a system used to sprinkle tunnels to keep down dust. Volatile coal dust is a constant menace underground. Dawson rules required that all dust caused by coal-cutting machines had to be removed before blasting. No blasting took place until all miners had left the pit.

Eighteen men had checked out of the mine by two-thirty p.m., most because of illness. At that moment, a train of thirty-five cars laden with fine coal and coal dust, had started on its way toward the mine entry. Fifteen hundred feet away from the portal the train suddenly jumped the track and the locomotive smashed into timbers supporting the tunnel roof.

The heavy beams crashed with a roar. Coal cars piled into one another like so many dominoes, overturning and spewing thick, choking coal dust into the air.

The wire that fed power to the trains was hooked to the timbers. It fell against the steel side of a coal car, creating a flashing blue arc of electricity. The coal dust ignited with a roar, the blast gaining in ferocity as it spread. The sprinkler system was off, so the blast reached the deepest part of the pit.

Far back in Crosscut No. 4 North, Felini Martini and Charles Candale felt the ground quiver, then the horrible distant rumble that rose in a steady crescendo as the blast moved through the mine toward them.

They fell to the ground, praying, burying their heads in their arms. The roar continued as tons of rock and coal and timbers cascaded down throughout the mine. Both knew that if the blast didn't get them the black damp probably would. Any explosion can open pockets of lethal gas.

The air was already thick with choking coal dust. The two miners, desperate, soaked their sweaters in water from their canteens and buried their faces in them.

At the moment of the blast, Scott Dupont, general inside superintendent, was about to enter the portal. He stepped back to get out of the way of a rail car he heard approaching in the tunnel.

A tongue of flame and a cloud of smoke erupted from the entry. The concussion knocked Dupont down, the flame singeing his hair. He struggled to his knees and crawled away. The following day, in spite of his injuries, he led a rescue team into the mine.

Dupont's step backward probably saved his life. The force of the blast was so great it crumbled the heavy reinforced concrete facing around the portal as you might crush a piece of stale bread into crumbs. Only a black scar remained on the side of the mountain after the explosion.

This blast was also felt in Dawson, causing a rush for the mine. School closed immediately. Families and children raced on foot and by car up the narrow road. A witness remembered later only the screams and cries of the women and children as they ran to the mine.

Guards once again had to keep women from entering the mine to see about their loved ones. Rescuers, however, this time had it slightly easier: the ventilating fans were undamaged and quickly cleared the air in the wrecked tunnels, making possible work without cumbersome oxygen masks. However, this time it quickly became obvious that the blast had probably killed everyone underground.

Fred English, seventeen, star forward on the Dawson High School basketball team, was on one of the rescue crews. Both his brother and father were inside the mine. Young English was among the rescuers who brought out the torn body of Albert E. English, Sr. The brother was not found until later; he also was dead.

Meanwhile, deep in the mine, Martini and Candale lay in their pitchblack tomb, their faces pressed against the wet sweaters. They heard voices in another crosscut — faint, but still voices. Neither dared say a word.

"All night long we heard voices in another crosscut near us," Martini recalled later. "But we were afraid. We did not talk."

Guards at the mine entry were trying to restrain Martini's hysterical wife from entering the tunnel to hunt for her husband.

Martini and Candale lost track of time. After many hours, the voices stopped. The two miners decided to try to get out. They started through the darkness, still pressing their faces against the sodden sweaters. Minutes later they stumbled over the bodies of four men, apparently the source of the voices they had heard during that endless night.

They struggled on, feeling their way along rough tunnel walls until their hands were torn and bleeding, stumbling over giant boulders and ripped timbers. At last rescuers found them. They had been in the pit of death for nineteen hours. Their saving spurred rescue teams with renewed hope but it soon became apparent that the two men were the only survivors. One-hundred and twenty men were dead.

A temporary morgue was set up in the Dawson Opera House and a coroner's jury was impaneled. T. L. Kinney, a Dawson justice of the peace, was coroner. Ten years before, when he was mayor, he had organized a rest station for rescuers.

The dead were buried in separate graves after brief funeral services. Phelps Dodge once again paid compensation to miners' families and offered relocation. The company later erected an iron cross on each grave.

The final victim was removed from the mine twelve days after the blast. Cleanup work started at once. The mine later resumed production.

Dawson continued to thrive in spite of the disasters. Mining continued until April 30, 1950, when ever increasing competition from natural gas and oil ended the need for Dawson's coal.

The final act in Dawson's rather grim story took place soon afterward when Phelps Dodge sold practically the entire town to National Iron and Metal Company of Phoenix, but retained the land and a few buildings.

The firm salvaged most of the structures and machinery for scrap. The remains were hauled away by train and then the rails themselves were taken up to follow the town into oblivion.

Little remains to show a town ever existed here. A few buildings still stand, serving as headquarters and living quarters for the Diamond D, Phelps Dodge's 65,000-acre ranch.

Several families who work on the ranch

Abandoned coke ovens at Dawson

Lofty smokestacks protrude from the crumbling bricks of coke ovens — Dawson today

The cemetery at Dawson: row after row of silvery-gray crosses

live here. Joe Cruz is among them, a little man who has been a cowpoke for most of his life. He came to Dawson thirty-four years ago to punch Diamond D Cattle. The miners are gone but Joe remains, with a ready smile and a family of twelve children to lend their laughter to this lonesome valley.

Standing in the corral, Joe pointed out the old building used as a morgue at the time of the two disasters. It is now used to store ranch equipment. Off across the valley two lofty smokestacks protrude from crumbling coke ovens. But the row houses of the company town have vanished and only concrete sidewalks and streets with weeds growing in the cracks testify that a town once existed.

There was hope for a time, a few years ago, that Dawson might, like the legendary

Phoenix, be reborn from its ashes. This occurred when Kaiser Steel began searching the area for a source of coal for its big mill at Fontana, California. But Kaiser passed over Dawson and its enormous remaining coal reserves and instead went eighteen miles beyond Dawson to a place called York Canyon to open a completely new mine.

The Sante Fe Railway later laid rails up the Vermejo again, straight across the Diamond D's alfalfa field at Dawson, and on to York Canyon. Once again coal trains are moving through Dawson but they come from York Canyon. Coal is loaded aboard a special train that highballs to Fontana without a stop.

Standing on the south side of Dawson, a big sign points to CEMETERY, indicating that many people pass this way to pay their respects to loved ones. If you drive up the hill you will see the graveyard, almost like a military cemetery, with row after row of silvery-gray iron crosses. The paint sparkles with freshness. Phelps Dodge sees to that, repainting the markers every year. The company also keeps the grass cut.

Foreign-sounding names are written on most of the markers. A majority of them bear the death dates of 1913 and 1923. Plastic flowers lying on many graves testify that some will always remember Dawson and the Valley of Shadow.

Joe Cruz of Dawson

Abandoned church in Cabezon, with Cabezon Peak in background

12 | Village by the Giant's Head

Nearly 150 miles southwest of the lush Cimarron country, a black peak thrusts skyward from the wrinkled desert like the crown of a giant sombrero. Geologists call it a volcanic plug, the neck of an old volcano exposed by the elements that have eroded away the cinder cone. The Spanish, who called it *Cabezon* — "Big Head," founded a village almost at the foot of the mountain, near a steep-walled desert stream called the Rio Puerco or Muddy River.

The village lived for nearly two centuries, only to become a ghost town which even in death gives an appearance of life. You must approach closely to detect the decay. It is an old village, with its roots planted deep in the eighteenth century.

Its story reaches back in time, many years before the village was even thought of. Back to the Indians who wandered this harsh land. To them, the mountain was a symbol. Each tribe had a name for it. To the Jemez it was *Wasema'a*. The Isletans called it *Tchi'kui-enad*. The wandering Navajos called it *Tsenajin*, or Black Peak, a very special mountain indeed.

For to the Navajos, in their primitive way, *Tsenajin* was not a mountain at all, and certainly not the dead throat of a once fiery volcano. It was the head of a giant killed by their folk heroes, the Twin Brothers. The Brothers supposedly slew the giant on the sacred Navajo mountain to the southwest, the one we know as Mount Taylor. The Navajos figured that if the peak was the giant's head, then the lava at the base must be the creature's clotted blood.

The Giant's Head marked the eastern boundary of the Navajo tribal world. They reacted with alarmed mistrust when Spanish settlers began to drift west of that point. But the Spanish had viewed New Mexico as their own special province since the 1500s. Their settlements sprang up everywhere, often merely a *rancheria*, an adobe hut and some corrals. Sometimes two or three families built their homes together for protection and this formed the nucleus of a village.

Naturally, the Spanish were drawn to the valleys, where water was most accessible in an arid land. They came to the Puerco, a 140-mile-long channel draining a 5860-square mile area of New Mexico. The Puerco even then was muddy and often dry. A friar visited the area in 1776 and found its water "as dirty as the gutters of the streets." But it was still water. The Spanish settled up and down the river, without regard to any claims the Navajos had. Some of them settled near the base of the peak the Navajos considered sacred — probably in the 1760s.

Jack Rittenhouse of Santa Fe, the leading historian of Cabezon, has found the record of a marriage at a place called *El Puesto del Cerro Cabezon* as early as 1772. The Montoya family had applied for and received a land grant at Cabezon as early as 1767.

The Navajos watched the Spanish come in. Then they struck, and continued to attack the Puerco settlements until the colonists fled for their lives. They stayed away only a few years before returning, only to be driven off once again.

Finally, Colonel Kit Carson and the United States Army subdued the Navajos once and for all in 1863. Only then did the Puerco valley really open up for permanent settlement. Several Spanish families moved back to Cabezon in 1872 and this time the settlement stuck for nearly a hundred years.

Meanwhile, New Mexico had been annexed to the United States. Holders of Spanish land grants had to have them approved by the U.S. government. They called the grant at Cabezon the Bosque Grande Grant. It contained more than 3200 acres.

The Spanish had located the village strategically, at the crossing of two main trails. One ran from Zuni Pueblo (south of Gallup) to Jemez Pueblo in the northeast. The second ran from Albuquerque to the Jemez Mountain town of Nacimiento, now known as Cuba on New Mexico Highway 44.

The first trail was an ancient Indian route. After the U.S. Army built Fort Wingate near Gallup in 1868, this trail became the line of the direct road from Santa Fe to the fort. By 1875, a stage line called the Star Line Mail and Transportation Company was running stagecoaches over it.

The stages made stops at Pena Blanca, San Ysidro, Cabezon, Willow Springs, San Mateo, San Antonio Springs, Bacon Springs and Fort Wingate. The line continued west from the fort to Prescott, Arizona Territory, 507 miles from old Santa Fe. Stages covered the seventy-six miles between Santa Fe and Cabezon in about nine and a half hours during normal weather.

For a time, the Atlantic & Pacific Railroad (later the Santa Fe) considered swinging the tracks southwesterly just south of Santa Fe along the same general route as the trail through Cabezon. However, they dropped the plan, the road swung south to Albuquerque, then west, and Cabezon lost its chance of permanence.

In 1874, a German immigrant named William Kanzenbach came to Cabezon and opened a store and saloon. Four years later, he was joined by a partner, Rudolph Haberland, who became the village's first postmaster. The two ran into money problems and got mired in debt to Charles Ilfeld Company of Albuquerque, the leading territorial wholesaler. Ilfeld took over the trading post in 1888 and sold it to John Pflueger and Richard F. Heller. The two bought the place on time and found that business boomed. They had it paid for within six months.

Boards weathering under the sun—Heller store, Cabezon

Spanish-Americans ran the other stores and saloons in the isolated little town at the foot of the Giant's Head. Pflueger and Heller were among the few outsiders who were ever accepted by the Spanish inhabitants of the village. Cabezon had a reputation over the years as a place hostile to outsiders.

The trade with the Navajos was profitable. The partners, Pflueger and Heller, took in sheep from the Indians on purchases and soon had a herd of 10,000, along with a couple of thousand cattle. It frequently took forty wagons to carry their year's wool clip to Albuquerque and market.

Pflueger sold out to Heller in 1894 and moved to Lamy. Heller stayed with Cabezon until the village had almost ceased to exist. In 1910 he built a new store with fancy turned posts on the front porch and a good corrugated tin roof. Heller lived just across the street from the store in a fourteen-room adobe house that often served as a free hotel for travelers. The house was a gracious spot of culture in the grim and isolated frontier village.

Heller's fortune declined in later years along with the town. He died in March, 1947, and Mrs. Heller stayed on to run the store and the post office until the following year. Then she closed it and moved to Albuquerque, where she died a few years ago.

Because the Puerco valley was so isolated, the area was a favorite haunt for outlaws. Many used Cabezon as a hangout. Descriptions of the village in the early days say its saloons were frequented by evil-looking men who wore pistols at their hips.

It was in 1884 that Candido and Manuel Castillo's notorious rustler band raided Kanzenbach and Haberland's cattle herd in the Puerco bottomlands at Cabezon. Juan Romero of Casa Salazar tried to stop them and was shot and killed for his trouble. Kanzenbach quickly organized a posse that chased the rustlers in a running gun battle, but the outlaws escaped.

Rewards were posted and more posses joined the hunt. One group was led by Bernalillo County Deputy Sheriff Jesus Montano. The posse tracked the two gang leaders high into the snow-covered Jemez Mountains. But Candido, bearded and long-haired, was always on the alert. The possemen found themselves looking down the business end of a Winchester aimed at them from the shelter of a tall ponderosa pine.

"*Vamos!*" the bandit commanded.

The five complied quickly, heading for the town of Espanola on the Rio Grande, a spot where they figured the two must head to get supplies. There they camped in a corral behind Amadao Lucero's store to wait for the rustlers. They found Lucero cooperative, and lay in wait behind the store on Good Friday (April 11), 1884. The Luceros were coming to eat supper.

The Castillos showed up and, unsuspecting, sat down at the table. Deputy Montano quietly posted two men at the front door, then went himself to the back door where he had a clear view of the badmen.

The deputy aimed carefully at Candido's head but found the kerosene lamp on the table directly in his line of sight. He motioned furtively to Lucero, who moved the lamp out of the way.

Candido, meanwhile, finished his food and rolled a cigarette, then stepped over the lamp to light it. Montano fired, hitting Candido in the side. The outlaw grabbed for his own six-shooter but collapsed before he could fire at his unseen enemy. Deputy Montano, meanwhile, fired at Manuel Castillo, who, apparently wounded also, still managed to get Candido to his feet and out the front door.

The sight of the two rustlers walking toward them was too much for the men guarding the front door. They opened up with a fusillade at the bandits, but none of the fifty shots they fired took effect. Both men escaped into the night. Next morning the posse tracked the Castillos by bloodstains in the snow. They led to a spot near the Denver & Rio Grande narrow gauge tracks, then ended abruptly.

Both Castillos were members of the Penitente Brotherhood, a secret religious sect that is still strong in northern New Mexico. The Penitentes are noted for their secret Holy Week rites that include a re-enactment of the crucifixion. The Castillos had come upon a Good Friday procession of the brotherhood and the Penitentes took care of their own. Montano sought aid from Rio Arriba County officials but got nowhere. They also were Penitentes.

Jose Lovato later told the deputy he had seen Candido's dead body on Easter Sunday at a house on the road to Chama. He showed the deputy where the body was buried but when Montano opened the grave the body had been removed.

Cabezon was also the scene of an ax murder. A postal inspector came to town to check a reported small shortage in the Cabezon post office, which was run by Postmaster Emiliano Sandoval. The inspector got no answers at all until he questioned Juan Valdez, who lived on the edge of the village. Valdez shrugged. The postmaster had the keys, the opportunity and he lived close by, he said.

The next night, as Juan lay sleeping in his house with his two sons on nearby pallets, several Cabezon residents rode up to the front door and dismounted. Each carried an ax. They stepped softly into Valdez' room. When they left Valdez had lost his head.

County officials moved quickly, charging the postmaster, Albino Gurule and Antonio Gonzales with murder. Gonzales had an alibi and was freed. Police held the other two for awhile, but they were eventually cleared and returned to the town at the foot of the Giant's Head.

Cabezon's people existed largely on their herds of sheep and cattle, which in time-honored tradition ranged freely over the country. There were too many cattle and sheep for the land to support. In the 1930s the United States government moved to do something about overgrazing and soil conservation through the Taylor Grazing Act. It allowed the government to regulate the number of livestock that could graze on a particular area.

The valley of the Puerco is almost classic testimony to the evils of overgrazing. Because of it destructive floods were common. When the government set grazing quotas it just about put the herders of Cabezon out of business.

The village had hit its peak in 1930, the year a big gas line was laid between Farmington and Albuquerque. It passed just a few miles north of the town and Cabezon was used to house many of the workers.

Mrs. Salomon Lovato of Albuquerque grew up in the village and remembers that summer well. "There were so many people that they were living in tents," she recalled. "There weren't enough houses for them."

Rodolfo Tachia, who ran a store in Cabezon, was Mrs. Lovato's fathers. Business boomed for him that summer. But things slipped back to normal the next year when the gas-line workers were gone.

Then the grazing restrictions were slapped on and the poor people of Cabezon began to drift away — to places like Albuquerque,

Ghosts rustle through empty houses (Cabezon)

where they could find work. Some, however, hung on to the very last. Even these stalwarts surrendered to the inevitable by the early 1950s. Cabezon was abandoned. A few former residents returned on weekends to look after their homes.

About 250 people lived in the village during the early 'thirties. About seventy children attended classes in the school, which had two teachers. Most of the people were poor but it was a happy place.

Lack of water always handicaped the town. Wells in Cabezon produce no potable water. It could be used only to irrigate garden vegetables. Residents depended on cisterns. They hauled the rest of the water into town themselves, traveling eight miles south to Guadalupe to get water at a spring.

The residents impounded enough water to irrigate alfalfa and vegetables by means of two earthen dams on the Puerco above the village. They planted vegetables in those bottomlands, mostly chili. Floods destroyed both dams in the early forties and they were never rebuilt.

Cabezon was seen a few years ago by millions on television after the Corvair people used it as a ghost-town setting for a commercial. It made a good ghost-town background, and still does.

Houses and stores line the winding street for perhaps a quarter mile. Walking down it, one gets an eerie feeling. Windows stare back sightlessly. Even the hardy tamarisk

Flock of sheep in the shadow of Cabezon Peak in the 1880s

Cabezon today

trees have died from lack of water. The pigeons have fled the cotes so thoughtfully provided by Richard Heller above the porch of his store. A beautiful little adobe church surrenders silently to the weather.

Heller helped build the little church, *La Iglesia de San Jose,* in 1894. Many Cabezon residents rest in its cemetery. The bell has been missing since the time a few years ago when Benny Lucero caught two persons stealing it. He took it to the nearby village of San Luis for safe-keeping.

Lucero grew up here. Now he works and lives in Albuquerque and revisits the town frequently in an effort to keep up the old home place. He squatted in the shade of an adobe wall and talked with me about the old days, his brown eyes faraway. He looked across the street to the vacant homes, to the giant thumb of Cabezon Peak and talked about the stores and the people moving in the dusty street and the *fiestas.*

The principal feast day was November 29, anniversary of the church dedication. The villagers built *farolitos,* tiny fires of piñon sticks, up and down the main street the night before *fiesta.* Then, out of the church moved a procession carrying the statue of San Jose. Later the figure was taken back to the church and *mariachi* musicians played gay music and got the *fiesta* formally under way. It usually lasted three or four days.

As I listened to Lucero a cloud drifted across the sun and cast a shadow over the Giant's Head. Lucero went on talking about the old days, his voice soft, idly making marks in the powdery dust with the end of a stick.

He keeps a .30-06 rifle handy in his pickup and tries to guard the town against the vandals who come in the summer. Their only purpose seems to be to destroy what is left. They have come regularly for many years. One group systematically broke every windowpane still remaining in town. Another began digging up the floor of the church looking for buried treasure. Others broke into the locked houses and stole anything they could find.

In 1964 the Sandoval County Commission put a gate across the road just outside of town and fastened it with a padlock. Now, to see the place you must get permission and a key, or climb the fence and walk in.

It is sad to look at the vacant houses and the adobe walls that are eroding so rapidly. Why, one wonders, would anyone want to destroy a town that nature is already demolishing, melding the soil of the houses into the mother earth from which they came?

There is no answer. Overhead the cloud drifts away from the face of the yellow sun and the shadow disappears from the Giant's Head as if someone had suddenly turned on a spotlight.

Kelly as it appeared during its boom days in the 1880s

13 | Town on the Magic Mountain

As at Cabezon, a mountain looms as the dominant feature in the life and death of Kelly, another ghost town a hundred air miles to the south.

The mountain produced the riches that brought wealth seekers swarming to this isolated spot in central New Mexico. And it was the mountain — as it always is for mining towns — that eventually shut off the flow of wealth and left the place deserted. But the mountain played yet another role in Kelly's stormy life — that of protector. It saved the brawling boom camp from almost constant harassment by savage Apaches.

The Spanish who settled New Mexico had an exotic imagination and a romantic gift for names. They could look at a natural feature of the landscape and come up with a name at once musical and descriptive. When they arrived in this part of New Mexico and saw a strangely shaped peak they saw in it a resemblance to Mary Magdalene.

Modern man may find the resemblance obscure, but it was quite real to the Spanish. They called their mountain Magdalena. When a town developed at the base they called that Magdalena too.

The Anglos who later rushed to the mountain to reap its riches were singularly lacking in romance. When a town blossomed high up on the mountainside they chose the prosaic name of Kelly. Although the miners weren't imaginative they were happy to accept the rare benefits the mountain bestowed.

The Apaches, who roamed across New Mexico Territory raiding ranches and towns, *never once violated the sanctity of Magdalena's flanks.* They thought the mountain was enchanted.

Witnesses swore that the Indians pursued white men to the very foot of the mountain but never went beyond a certain point. *Never* did an Indian kill a white man on the slopes of the Magic Mountain.

Maybe it was some of the same magic that led Pete Kinsinger to find a chunk of interesting looking ore on the mountainside. That was during the Civil War. Since Kinsinger was in the army and lacked time to prospect properly, he stuck the rock away in his saddlebag.

When the war ended Kinsinger gave the rock to Col. J. S. Hutchason, known among the mining fraternity as "Old Hutch." Kinsinger wasn't interested in the Magdalena area, heading instead for the Moreno Valley to be in on the excitement that created Elizabethtown (Chapter Ten).

With the war safely over in 1866, "Old Hutch" decided to take a fling at the Magdalena country. He and a Mexican named Barado Fidey began searching the hills and soon located some rich lead outcrops.

It was springtime. Old Hutch staked a claim, which he dubbed "Juanita." The reason for this sudden burst of romance isn't clear, unless Old Hutch suddenly remembered a charming señorita. Or maybe it was because it was spring. Continuing to prowl

the mountain, three weeks later he staked another claim, which he called "Graphic." No romance there.

Soon he began to mine both claims, which produced oxidized lead-zinc ore. He laboriously built a crude adobe furnace to smelt it. The lead was then shipped east over the Santa Fe Trail.

The discovery wasn't enough to make Old Hutch rich. In truth, it barely made him a living. But Hutch was an incurable optimist. He kept scratching away at the mountain.

He found another vein near his Juanita and being a generous man he showed it to Andy Kelly, who ran a small sawmill at South Camp. Kelly staked a claim and did a little work on it. But he lacked Hutch's patience and, most important, his optimism. The ground was as tough as hardtack, the sun was hot and the sawmill business beckoned.

Old Hutch, meanwhile, kept a fatherly eye on Kelly and when he failed to do enough work to keep the claim alive, Hutch jumped it. It was a lucky leap.

The Kelly-claim ore was low-grade carbonates averaging per ton fifty to sixty per cent lead, ten ounces of silver and a smidgeon of copper. The word traveled fast, as always. Prospectors began drifting up Magdalena's flanks to examine the prospects. They kept coming, slowly, until by 1870 so many were in the neighborhood they decided they ought to have a town.

Perhaps some innate kindness impelled the miners to honor the sawmill operator who was too pessimistic to keep digging. Maybe they thought that since he'd got nothing else from the mine, why not honor him by naming the town after him? Or maybe they figured it was a good joke on Kelly. History doesn't say.

Anyway, the town of Kelly was born amid the cholla cactus and the scrub evergreens on the side of the Magic Mountain. It flourished.

There was no great boom, at first, just a steady growth. The camp followers, quite as optimistic as the miners, came also. And in fairness it must be said that *some* of them were honest storekeepers and businessmen.

The boom didn't really get under way until six years later, when Colonel E. W. Eaton leased the Juanita from Old Hutch and soon struck rich silver pay dirt. Old Hutch's primitive smelter was the only one available, so ore preparation continued to be slow. The pigs of mineral were freighted all the way to Kansas City, over the Santa Fe Trail. Not all of the wagons made it. Once they came down off the Magic Mountain they were fair game for the Apaches.

Old Hutch finally sold out in the late 'seventies. He sold the Graphic for $30,000 to Hanson and Dawsey and the Kelly to Gustav Billings for $45,000. It was a fortune. But as time proved, he gave up too soon.

Billings soon built a smelter at Socorro, nearly a hundred miles to the west. It operated for twelve years. Kelly was long the territory's leading lead producer.

The boom continued and in 1885, when the railroad reached Magdalena at the foot of the mountain, Kelly soared. By now the town boasted many rooming houses, a couple of churches, seven saloons, two hotels, three stores and a couple of dancehalls. Things were so busy for a time that the hotels rented beds in shifts with an eight-hour limit to the shift.

Kelly was a riproaring boom town and wanted the whole world to know it. The saloons rocked twenty-four hours a day, the chips clinked, the cards turned, the roulette wheels spun and the glasses emptied.

Guns roared with fair frequency. As if there wasn't enough hell produced right in Kelly, Magdalena cowboys came to town occasionally to bring in a little more. They rode up and down Kelly's precipitous main street like so many wild Indians, whooping with joy and firing their sixguns at random.

That was one way to celebrate. Jonas Nelson, a man of imagination, showed Kelly how it *really* ought to do it.

Jonas was an optimist and a hard worker. He snapped up the lease on a mine called the Hardscrabble, then discovered that his finances weren't equal to his optimism and he was limited to a short-term lease. He even lacked enough tools to keep a full crew working full time. But Jonas solved the problem. He put the miners to work in relays just as fast as they could go. It *had* to pay off.

It did. It wasn't long until Jonas located a rich vein of silver-lead ore. By the time the lease ran out, the frenzied digging had produced a virtual mountain of ore.

Jonas was overjoyed. He almost collapsed when he saw the size of the check from the smelter. Many men would have made haste to stuff the profits into a sock and make tracks for the big city. But not a man with imagination. Not a man like Jonas. To him it seemed as if he ought to have a party. A *real* party.

Jonas ordered a special train from Los Angeles. It carried a sultan's selection of liquors, gastronomic delicacies of every sort and, of course, lots of pretty girls.

Dropping such an abundance of luxuries into a place like Kelly had a traumatic effect. The celebration was enough to drive the nails right through the board sidewalks. Practically everybody in camp got roaring, hilariously drunk on Jonas's whisky, champagne and other beverages, Jonas included.

The party went on for days and when it finally ended and everybody sobered up, Jonas found himself not only hung over but stone-broke as well.

History's final disposition of Jonas is unrecorded. Its disposition of Kelly is another matter.

Many mines were now producing, including the Anchor, the Grand Tower, the Iron Mask, the Stonewall and even the Alhambra. Transportation remained a headache. The rails finally reached Magdalena and a valiant effort was launched to run a spur line the three miles up the mountain to Kelly. But the engineers could get the tracks up only part way and ore wagons pulled by sixteen horses had to be used to haul the ore out to the railhead.

The boom continued until 1893, when silver was devalued and panic closed mines throughout the West. Billing closed his Socorro smelter that year. It looked like curtains for Kelly, but lead and zinc kept things moving. A new smelter erected at the Graphic in 1896 operated until 1904. There was obviously plenty of wealth remaining in the mountain. It was reported officially that up to January 1, 1904 the Kelly and Graphic mines produced lead-silver ore worth $5,800,000.

The Hardscrabble, which was sold in 1868 for twenty-five dollars, produced $325,000 up until 1904. By 1903, the district had produced a total of $8,700,000 in lead and silver. But that was only the beginning. Kelly got a second boost.

Part way up the hill a little church stands lonely and forlorn

Cony T. Brown, of Socorro, was responsible. Brown was a man with curiosity. He visited Kelly in the 'nineties and noticed many greenish-colored rocks sprinkled throughout the mine dumps. He wondered what they were and nobody seemed to know. Kelly residents took them for granted. Brown stuck a few rocks in his pockets and when he returned to Socorro had them assayed. He was astonished by the report.

The rocks were valuable zinc carbonate called Smithsonite, named after James Smithson, British mineralogist whose fortune endowed the Smithsonian Institution in Washington, D.C. Geologists say that the Kelly Smithsonite is the most beautiful found in the world. It is used as a pigment for paints and coating materials.

Brown told a friend, J. B. Fitch, about his discovery, and the two at once leased the Graphic mine. The first thing they did was to ship all the green rock from the mine dump, then start mining the rock from the mountain.

Residents of Kelly looked on in astonishment, shaking their heads: obviously Brown and Fitch were *loco*. They stopped shaking when they discovered the truth. Instead, they started scurrying among the hills to find green rocks. They combed every dump in town for the ore.

New companies moved into Kelly to redevelop old and played-out mines. Sherwin-Williams Paint Company bought out Brown and Fitch in 1904 for $150,000. Gustav Billing sold the Kelly mine that same year to Tri-Bullion Smelting and Development Company for $200,000. This firm then built a smelter at Kelly. Zinc mining continued, pushing Kelly to the forefront as New Mexico's leading producer of that metal.

The town hit its peak in 1905 with 3000 people crowding the camp. Old-timers rubbed their eyes in disbelief. Mineral production between 1904 and 1928 tripled that of previous years, hitting a total of $21,-667,950.

It didn't take too long to milk the mountain dry this time. Empire Zinc dismantled the big smelter at the head of Main Street in 1922 and sent the machinery to Cañon City, Colorado. The mines were practically exhausted. Work continued through the 'twenties but at a much reduced rate. It reached a crawl by 1931, when only a single carload of Smithsonite was shipped.

Life flashed faintly afterward, but it proved to be merely death throes. American Smelting and Refining bought out Sherwin-Williams in the 'forties and had a go at the mountain. It didn't last. The last lonely inhabitant, Pablo Tafoya, moved away. Kelly was dead.

Little remains today but a few broken buildings. If you want to view the cadaver, it is easy to reach. New Mexico 114 leads to the townsite; it is unpaved but a passable road.

The village of Magdalena, one of the last holdouts of the Old West, is the starting place. This town is an anachronism, a living relic of the 'eighties and the days when thousands of bawling Longhorns were driven to the railhead here.

Bravely false-fronted, Magdalena straddles U.S. 60 twenty-seven miles west of Socorro as proudly as a cowboy astride a paint horse. The town stands at the eastern edge of the San Augustine Plains, a vast expanse of high grassland extending for nearly a hundred miles across this part of the state.

One of the few remaining cattle drives occurs here every autumn, when George D.

A giant concrete foundation marks the site of the smelter, with the rustling remains of a mine tipple nearby (Kelly)

Farr of Datil drives a herd of hundreds of steers to the Magdalena railhead. Most ranchers have foregone the trail for trucks but Farr drives his cattle a distance of seventy miles, actually fattening them along the way.

If you want to see some Old West, you should visit Magdalena, then turn south on 114 to Kelly. The road climbs quickly through the foothills and country thick with scrub evergreens, stubby yucca and spidery cholla.

The three-mile journey to Kelly is a trip backward in time. Just beyond the end of the old spur track that never made the grade you arrive in Kelly — or what's left of it. The road bends sharply to the right at the edge of "town," then almost as quickly cuts to the left. You should stop here and climb the hill

directly in front of you where the tumble-down gate and the barbed-wire fence mark Kelly's Boothill.

Piñon and juniper are rapidly reclaiming the ground from those who slumber here. Unpainted, handcarved fences erected to protect the dead from marauding animals tilt precariously. So do the headstones and the crosses. Many grave markers, marvelous examples of the woodcarver's art, hide among the evergreens. The wind and sand have turned the ancient wooden crosses chalk-gray and ebony.

The rubble that is Kelly lies just up Main Street. A little church stands lonely and forlorn part way up the hill. But it is intact, with windows and doors and fresh whitewash on the adobe and a padlock on the front door. Sentiment preserves the chapel. The church figures large in Kelly for one day of the year

There are marvelous examples of the wood carver's art in the Kelly cemetery

High on the Magic Mountain is a good place to savor the view (Kelly)

— June 24 — when folks gather from miles around for a *fiesta*. These people preserve the church.

The site of the smelter is marked by a giant concrete foundation at the head of the street. The remains of a mine tipple rust nearby.

Destruction is all around you. Foundations are everywhere as silent reminders of life but the houses they once supported have vanished. You see the oddly assorted litter of ghost towns everywhere — rusty cans, blackened and twisted shoe soles, sometimes an entire shoe, a crumbling bedspring or the crushed top of an oldfashioned trunk.

If you climb up the mountain you will find tunnels burrowing into the depths of the mountain and occasional bits of rusting machinery. Exploring the old mine shafts and tunnels is not advised because of their dangerous condition. But if you walk up the mountain to a point above the smelter you'll find a magnificent view.

The rooftops of Magdalena are far below you. Beyond them is a staggering spread of plain and mountain and sky, a pastel landscape typically New Mexico.

It is a good place to understand the magic of the mountain.

Elfego Baca and a jail door, relic of his days as a lawman

14 | Miracle at Milligan's Plaza

U.S. 60 reaches westward from Magdalena across the San Augustine Plains like a black steel ruler laid on a table the color of sage. This is land to give the word *plains* real meaning. The country is flat to the limit of your vision, without a house or a line of fence — except along the highway — to mar its monotony.

The only shape to speak of lies far off, on the horizon, where blue mountains crouch. Hurtling in your car across the emptiness you become briefly aware of small things — a windmill standing bravely against the sky, as if defying the loneliness; stock tanks or

wandering Herefords.

Sixty-one miles from Magdalena you arrive at Datil, a crossroads hamlet marked by a Chevron station and a Texaco competitor just across the road. Thence you follow New Mexico 12, which veers southwest along the very edge of the San Augustines. If you didn't appreciate their vastness before, you will now, for it is sixty-nine lonely miles before you reach a town of any consequence.

That town is Reserve, a place once nicknamed Milligan's Plaza. It is a singular town. If Magdalena is "West," then Reserve must be "Far West." It has the look and the feeling. Hollywood could come here and set up cameras to film a horse opera without making anything but cursory changes in the town's appearance.

Streets are dusty and the buildings false-fronted in the best frontier tradition. Here and there amid the pickup trucks parked anglewise "downtown" you'll see a horse fastened to a hitchrail.

The inhabitants' faces are those common to the West, the skin burnished brown and tough by the wind and the sun, the eyes with a permanent squint. Their clothes are faded Levi's and Western shirts and scuffed cowboy boots with the heels worn over, and many walk with the rolling gait of lifelong horsemen.

Reserve is the heart of a vast cattle and timber empire. At 5700 feet altitude it is surrounded by many stately ponderosa pines and is within the Gila National Forest. It is also the county seat of Catron County, which is larger than some Eastern states.

The town has two notable qualities that have endeared it to *aficionados* of the Old West. One of these is the fact that it is ninety miles from a railroad, which is probably a record. The other — and far better known feature — is Elfego Baca. Reserve was the stage on which this cocky little Spanish-American blasted himself into a Western legend by the artful use of a pair of six-shooters.

If Baca was not the greatest gunfighter, he was unquestionably the luckiest, a fact that has been duly recorded time and time again. The late Walt Disney took this fact into account in the television series he wove around the Baca character, appropriately entitled "The Nine Lives of Elfego Baca." Characteristically, Hollywood overlooked the possibilities of Reserve as the scene for some of the action. Instead, Disney chose the town of Cerrillos (Chapter Two), south of Santa Fe.

Disney couldn't have selected a better character. Baca was only nineteen at the time of his flirtation with fate at this spot. What he lacked in years, he made up for in guts, or what others called just plain cussedness. If so, it came naturally. A native of Socorro, young Baca had been raised in Kansas among Anglo boys and had to learn quite early in life how best to defend himself.

Fate decreed that the Baca clan would move back to the wide open land of New Mexico. There Papa Baca soon got himself into a gunfight with a couple of *gringo* cowhands and laid both to rest in Boot Hill. As a result the elder Baca went behind bars for a number of years. Meantime, young Elfego continued to learn how to be ornery in a country noted for that quality. He also became adept in the use of six-shooters.

Even in 1884, long before television and Hollywood started romanticizing the West, the Western legend was already developing. The dime novel and the Police Gazette were already glorifying such as Billy the Kid and Wyatt Earp. The influence of such publications wasn't limited to the effete East. The kids out West read them too, including Elfego Baca, who set out to follow the example set by the heroes he read about.

Elfego liked to play the role of the brave Western lawman, fighting for the rights of the downtrodden. He began strapping on a pair of Colt's revolvers in the best fashion of Western gunslingers and pinning a mail-order deputy sheriff's badge on his shirt.

In October, 1884, young Baca was earning his keep working for a Socorro merchant of the same last name but no relation. A Spanish-American deputy — a real one —

came into the store one day and told Elfego his troubles. The deputy, Pedro Sarracino, was an officer in Frisco, or San Francisco Plaza on the Francisco River in western Socorro County. It is now known as Reserve. There were actually three towns strung up and down the river, Upper, Lower and Middle Plazas. They date from the late 1860s, when Spanish-Americans began farming the area.

Deputy Sarracino explained that there was no problem with the Spanish-Americans. But Texas cattlemen had moved in at about the same time as the farmers to take advantage of the rich grazing land. Their cowboys made life miserable for the natives, frequently making them "dance" to the tune played by a six-gun. People were even occasionally killed in the process.

Frankly, the deputy admitted, he was powerless to stop the terror. He told Baca the harrowing story of a native everyone called "El Burro," who had the misfortune of being captured by the Texans. They stretched him out on a store counter and castrated him as they might a calf. Another native protested and they used him for target practice.

Elfego was furious. He offered to return to Frisco with the deputy. Anyway, he said, he had some politicking to do in that area. Elfego then strapped on his guns, stuck his mail-order star in the pocket of his Prince Albert coat and returned with Sarracino to Frisco. He stayed with the deputy in the lower plaza, then started his electioneering. Before long, he found himself in the upper plaza, which was usually called "Milligan's Plaza" after a store and saloon run by a man named Milligan.

Milligan dispensed a potent firewater, which at the moment of Baca's visit caused a cowboy named McCarty, who worked for a rancher named Slaughter, to begin shooting up the town. As the bullets flew, Baca hunted up the local justice of the peace, Selso Lopez, to ask why he and his friends permitted such things. Selso shrugged, pointing out that there were many *gringos* around and if he arrested the cowboy his friends would make "serious" trouble for the poor people of Frisco.

Elfego figured it was already pretty serious. He told the J.P. that if McCarty were allowed to get away with this it would only invite more of the same. Thereupon, he pinned on his tin star, loosened his pistols in their holsters, marched out and "arrested" McCarty. He then brought his drunken prisoner before Justice Lopez and the bar of justice.

The J.P., who after all had to *live* in Frisco, flatly refused to hear the case. He was, frankly, terrified of the trouble young Baca was bringing down on his head. But Baca was adamant. If the J.P. wouldn't hear the case, he said, he felt it was his duty to take McCarty to the county seat at Socorro for trial. Since it was too late to start for Socorro that night, he escorted his prisoner down to the Middle Plaza to spend the night.

What the would-be lawman didn't know was that the minute he "arrested" McCarty, riders had dashed from the Upper Plaza in practically every direction to tell their brother Texans. By the time they got out of town the "arrest" by the lone teen-ager had turned into a full-scale rebellion by the Mexicans. This was something the Texans feared. As the word reached the cowboys out on the range they began heading for Frisco.

A Slaughter foreman named Perham led one group to the Middle Plaza and demanded that Baca release McCarty. Elfego's reply was a jaunty wave of his pistol and a declaration that he'd give them to the count of three to "get out of town." He promptly began to count. When he reached "Three" he pulled the trigger.

Utter confusion ensued. It was almost as if one of the steers they pushed around all day suddenly stood up on its hind legs and dropped a lariat around a cowboy. Such an attitude on the part of a "Mexican" was unheard of!

During the melee a cowboy took one of Elfego's bullets in his knee. Perham's horse reared and fell on him, crushing and mortally wounding the foreman. The cowboys beat a hasty and ignominious retreat.

Early the next morning, a group of cool heads among the Americans took action to avert serious trouble. This group, led by J. H. Cook, visited Justice Lopez and convinced him to try McCarty. Then they convinced Baca to bring his prisoner to the Upper Plaza for the trial. Baca complied.

The trial was over in minutes, with the J.P. fining the offending cowboy five dollars. It should have ended the matter, but didn't. As Baca stepped outside the justice's office, he was greeted by a virtual army of Slaughter cowboys, mounted and spoiling for a fight.

"Good morning, Mr. Wilson," said Baca.

"Good morning, you dirty Mexican blankety-blank," replied Wilson.

One of the cowboys fired a shot. Elfego whipped out his pistols and backed away through an alley and down a little lane. He saw only one place in which to seek cover — a tiny *jacal*, a Mexican hut made by driving logs upright into the ground and plastering the openings between them with mud. Inside were a native woman and two children.

"*Vamos!*" cried Elfego, hurrying the three outside. Quickly, he shut the flimsy door and waited. It didn't take long for the Slaughter outfit to ride up, breathing fire. Off his horse jumped Jim Herne, a Texan. He hauled his rifle out of its boot and headed for the hut, a determined look on his face.

"I'll get him out of there," he shouted to the others.

Herne didn't make good on his claim. He was greeted by two bullets fired by young Baca and fell to the ground, very dead. A couple of his friends dragged the body away.

There were eighty Texans in the Slaughter outfit. Baffled for the moment by one nineteen-year-old "Mexican," they withdrew to hold a council of war. Then they surrounded the hut and began to shoot. The time was nine a.m. on a bright October morning. Elfego didn't think he would live to see another.

In the first place, the *jacal* was hardly the place for a lone man to stand off eighty others who were hell-bent on killing him. Its construction was flimsy at best. The stakes that formed the walls weren't very close together and the dried mud between them was no protection against a bullet. One thing in Elfego's favor was the floor, which had been dug out so it was about a foot below ground level. By lying flat during Texas volleys, Baca could stay alive.

For some reason, the Texans chose to fire by volley instead of by sniping. Baca, meanwhile, either lay flat or sat low in the corner. He noticed a large plaster-of-paris reproduction of a saint. He put his hat on it, then placed it by one of the small windows. It gave the cowboys something to shoot at.

When Elfego had something to shoot at, he did so, with deadly effect. When the battle ended, the Texans had lost four men killed and a number of others wounded. After awhile, the cowboys tied ropes between the houses nearby and hung blankets over them so they could move freely about without being seen by the sharpshooting Elfego.

The battle went on all day. About six p.m., a Texas barrage cut part of the stakes that held up the roof and the collapse pinned Elfego under a great load of debris. For two hours, he lay beneath the rubble, listening to the bullets sing over his head.

Finally, as darkness fell, the young man dug himself out and stirred up the coals that were still hot in the little cook stove. He found some meat, made some tortillas and coffee and had a bite to eat. He told a biographer in later years that he really wasn't hungry.

About midnight the attackers tried a stick of dynamite. The blast wrecked half the hut, but left Baca intact in the one remaining corner. Things quieted down somewhat then, the cowboys probably figuring they had done the upstart in. Just in case, they weren't going to come close enough to make certain. They'd wait until morning.

At dawn, they were sadly surprised to see a curl of smoke coming from the hut's chimney. Elfego was cooking breakfast. Thereupon, all hell really broke loose, as the Texans let go with every cartridge they could lay hands on.

At midmorning, one fellow tried to advance close to the hut behind a cast-iron shield fashioned out of a cookstove. He made good progress until he poked the top of his head over the shield and Elfego promptly scraped it with a bullet.

The show continued all day, with a rooting section. The word had traveled to all three of the plazas and the Spanish-American natives lined the hills around the Upper Plaza to watch the festivities. None went to the aid of their embattled *compadre*.

As six p.m. approached on the second day Mr. Cook and his "cool heads" again decided that something should be done about this shameful affair. Cook enlisted the aid of Francisquito Naranjo. The two, accompanied by an American deputy sheriff named Ross, approached the *jacal*. Naranjo called out to Baca.

"Come on out!" he shouted. "It's all right."

The besieged Elfego could hardly believe his ears. He peered out, then returned the shout and leaped through the window, a six-shooter in each hand. Wisely, he ordered the three men to line up before him.

When the Texans saw their quarry suddenly out in the open, it was almost too much for them. They advanced and only an inspired speech by Cook warning them that they were breaking the law saved the day.

There was much grumbling and more talk but the stalemate was finally unstuck. Baca agreed to return to Socorro escorted by the cowboys and turn himself over for trial. He insisted on keeping his guns, though, and there wasn't much the Texans could do about it.

That very night the Texans and their prisoner started for Socorro in odd fashion. In the lead rode the Texans, followed by the buckboard driven by Deputy Ross. On the back seat, behind everybody, rode Elfego Baca, pistols in hand.

The "miracle" of Milligan's Plaza has become a kind of legend in the area. Elfego Baca had survived thirty-three hours in that hut with eighty men firing everything they could muster at him, including dynamite.

Testimony at Baca's trial was that more than 4000 bullets were fired into that little stake-and-adobe shack. The bullets hit practically everything inside except Baca. Knives, forks and spoons had bullet holes in them.

Elfego Baca, hero of the battle of Reserve, in Albuquerque many years later. Right, *Esquiel Romero playing the mandolin*

A broom was shown as evidence containing eight bullet holes in the handle. The door to the hut, smaller than an ordinary door, contained 367 bullet holes.

Some of the Texans understandably thought their Spanish foe had a charmed life. One testified quite seriously at Baca's trial that he was convinced that if he took a gun and fired it at Baca's chest from only five feet away it would have absolutely no effect.

Anyone who could survive something like that had little to fear from the courts. Baca was tried twice for murder and acquitted. He then went on to a colorful and somewhat unorthodox career as a lawman and lawyer. Death came to him quietly — with his boots off — in Albuquerque in 1945 when he was eighty.

In many places, an incident like that thirty-three-hour epic battle would prove to be a great commercial attraction. But not in Reserve. This cow-and-lumber town could not care less and in a way that is one of its charms.

Baca still lives strongest in the memory of the Spanish-American population of Reserve. Typical is Esequiel Romero, a seventy-two-year-old veteran of World War I.

The sound of music led me to Mr. Romero, who was playing a spirited Spanish tune on a mandolin inside a service station next door to the quaint old Catron County courthouse.

He was sitting there, all alone, entertaining himself with the mandolin. He wore neat khaki clothing. A battered Panama hat covered his gray hair. There was a twinkle in his brown eyes and a friendly smile on his lips.

Romero's mother came to Reserve when it was Upper Frisco Plaza in 1867 from Socorro. She was one of the many pioneers from the Socorro area lured to the area by its mountains and trees and streams.

Romero motioned to the two-story adobe courthouse next door.

"That used to be a hotel," he said. "They'd dance to sunup there every night."

Romero was one of the musicians at the dances held at the hotel for awhile. During his childhood, he remembers, there were many fights among the cowboys and the native population — and he was born twelve years after Baca had battled the Slaughter cowboys.

Romero showed us where the *jacal* stood that sheltered Baca during his epic stand — just behind the courthouse that fronts on Reserve's Main Street. There are only a few fruit trees there now. Time has erased all traces of the place.

Romero is retired after a lifetime spent deep in the underground darkness of the mines. He worked in the Madrid coal mines, in the silver mines of Mogollon and in Nevada and California. On the day of our visit he was "minding" the station for his brother, who was away.

A closer link with the Baca period is Florenzo Jiron, at eighty-two, the oldest resident in Reserve. Even he was born two years after the Baca incident.

He lives in a house a short distance south of the service station on Main Street, a home fenced in front by old wagon wheels. Gray-haired and grizzled, Jiron sat down on some firewood he had cut himself and told us the stories he had heard while still a child about Elfego Baca.

The cowboy who started the ruckus that faroff day in the Upper Plaza was named Charlie McCarty, he remembered.

"He fired at anything that moved after he got drunk at Milligan's," he said. "He shot a horse, some pigs and then a man."

Jiron's father was in the group at the scene when Baca finally came out of the hut, he said. There is frank admiration in his voice when he speaks of Elfego Baca.

"He was a good man — a good man — one of the best lawyers we ever had in Socorro County," he declares.

Perhaps those few words do a better job of summing up the Elfego Baca of history than Hollywood can ever do.

Florenzo Jiron, a link with the Baca per

Arch Straight's all-white 14-horse freight team transported much of the equipment for the first mines in the Cooney Mining District (Mogollon)

15 | A Town That Wouldn't Die

Mogollon clings to life buried in a canyon about forty miles south of Reserve. It was born in one of New Mexico's richest silver strikes and became a ghost town when the boom died. A few determined souls remained, keeping the town alive. Now the sparks of life flicker a bit brighter each year as the solitude and scenery lure a few more residents.

Its isolation is Mogollon's chief attraction. To reach it, you must turn east off U.S. 180 thirty-four miles south of Reserve onto New Mexico Highway 78. It is a good road, although some parts of it are not for the faint-of-heart flatlander. But it's blacktopped and perfectly safe if you exercise caution.

The road snakes its way upward into the mountains soon after leaving U.S. 180 and each curve hides a spectacular view of the Mogollon Mountains. Eight breathtaking miles later it tops out on a ridge to start a twisting plunge down into Silver Creek Canyon. The gorge is choked with vegetation and without a sign of human habitation. Then, quite suddenly at the foot of the hill you round a turn to enter Mogollon, a town the Anglos call "muggy-own."

Your eye is immediately assaulted by a big two-story yellow stucco building emblazoned with the words: J. P. HOLLAND GENERAL STORE. Small signs dangling from the railing around the porch read: GILA NATIONAL GALLERY OF ART.

A stolid stone structure stands directly across the street. It has a sign over the front door that tells you this is the MOGOLLON MUSEUM.

Both are obviously occupied and give an impression that Mogollon is more tourist trap than ghost town. But as you drive on up the narrow street you see contrary evidence. Buildings clinging to both sides of the street are in varying stages of decay, the boards the deep mellow-browns typical of ghost towns. The telltale debris of former-day mining is all about. It is quickly evident that this was a substantial community now fallen on hungry days.

It *was* substantial. It was also a late-starter among New Mexico mining camps — but one that became the state's biggest silver producer. During Mogollon's lifetime, this district produced 18,000,000 ounces of the white metal, fully a quarter of the state's entire production. The district also produced much gold.

The Apache Indians kept Mogollon from getting an earlier start. These mountains were their last stronghold. The Spanish came here first, but overlooked the minerals. They named the mountains for Don Juan I Flores Mogollon, governor and captain-general of the area, including New Mexico. He never saw them.

In the late 1860s small U.S. Cavalry units made scouting trips into the mountains. Sergeant James C. Cooney, an Irishman, led one party from Fort Bayard on an expedition to map trails and waterholes. Deep in a canyon on Mineral Creek, just north of Silver Creek, Cooney found ledges rich in gold ore. He kept it to himself until his discharge came through in 1876. Then he gathered some friends and headed for Mineral Creek.

The Apaches watched from the forest as Cooney and his friends staked claims and did a little exploratory work. After awhile they attacked and drove the party away.

But Cooney had contracted a disease from which few men ever recover — gold fever. He had seen the hint of riches gleaming in the mountain and was determined to return. He did so two years later, accompanied by William Chick and several other men. They were ready for the Indians this time, bringing two ox-drawn wagons laden with supplies. They restaked their claims and filed others, then laid out a townsite on Copper Creek, which they called Clairmont.

But the location didn't suit them and they moved a few miles south to found a village called Cooney. By early 1879, Cooney shipped a wagonload of gold ore to Silver City that assayed $200 to the ton. The Indians were quiet. Cooney and his companions began to relax a bit.

Then came April, 1880. Ranchers trapped some Apaches near the town of Alma and killed three of them. One of the victims was Torribeo, son-in-law of the great Chief Victorio.

The chief led his braves on the warpath the moment he heard the news. They swooped down on the Silver Bar Mine at Cooney like so many howling locusts, setting it afire and killing two miners. Cooney, Chick and the others escaped to the timber. The frightened miners fortified themselves at Roberts Ranch on the west side of Mineral Creek.

Victorio returned the next day, April 28.

The battle raged all day. Indians killed only one man, William Wilcox, a miner. But sharpshooting miners picked off a number of Indians by firing their guns through the cracks between the upright logs forming the ranch-house wall.

Day dawned clear on the twenty-ninth. Not an Indian was in sight. Al Potter and John Motsinger decided they would go up creek to see what had happened to the white men who had failed to reach the safety of the ranch. They got halfway there before the Apaches hit them from ambush. A rifle slug smashed into Potter's Winchester, knocking it from his hand. He quickly grabbed his six-gun from his belt and returned the fire. Under constant attack, both managed to get safely back to the ranch.

Later the same day Cooney and Chick set out for Alma on the San Francisco River to warn the settlers. They made it to Alma, then started back for their besieged friends. Their riderless horses returned to Alma two hours later. The settlers found both men slain and mutilated in a gorge now called Cooney Canyon. They buried Cooney where he lay, blasting out a crypt in a giant boulder. The rock — and Cooney — are still there, on the south bank of Mineral Creek, a few miles off U.S. 180. A marker reads:

J. C. Cooney. Killed by Victorio's Apaches, April 29, 1880. Aged 40 Years.

When Cooney's brother, Captain Michael Cooney, heard about his brother's death, he quit his job as customs inspector in New Orleans and hastened to New Mexico to take over his brother's mining interests. Captain Cooney became a guiding light in the development of the district, opening more mines on Mineral Creek and later on Silver Creek after the town of Mogollon was founded.

Three years after he arrived in the Mogol-

lons, Cooney grubstaked a prospector named Turner whom he never saw again. The next year, Cooney met Turner's uncle, who had come West to help Turner work a mineral discovery but said that Turner never showed up. Turner's skeleton was found in 1889. He had been slain by Apaches.

Captain Cooney made two unsuccessful attempts to find the rich strike that was rightfully his. Already quite wealthy, he made a third try in the fall of 1914 and early snow-storms swept the Mogollons and caught him unprepared. His body wasn't found until the following February, less than a hundred yards from the place where poor Turner's bones had been found. The bonanza was never relocated.

The town of Cooney prospered in those early years, but never became much more

Silver Creek ran down the canyon, leaving little room on either side (Mogollon)

Prizefighters striking a pose in a Mogollon saloon in boom days at the turn of the century

than a camp, its buildings built principally of logs. Many were half log and half tent. When the ore began to give out and Cooney Camp began to die, fate lent a helping hand.

The year was 1889. A grizzled prospector named John Eberle struck it rich with the Last Chance mine near Silver Creek and soon afterward built himself a cabin. It was the first building in what became Mogollon. Within weeks Harry Hermann, a lumberman, moved his mill to Silver Creek from Cooney, and the new camp was off and running. More strikes were made. More miners deserted the Cooney workings to move across the twisting three-mile trail that led to Mogollon.

There was little planning at the new camp. Silver Creek ran down the canyon, leaving little room on either side. However, cabins, huts and tents soon crowded both sides of the street running along by the creek and, slopping over, straggled up the hills on each side. Where necessary, logs and footbridges were thrown across the creek to permit entrance to the houses and buildings.

By 1892, the town in the canyon got a post office and soon afterward had a school. Two years later, fire roared through the blossoming village and almost wiped it out. The residents rebuilt with adobe and stone, a foresight that probably saved the town from total destruction in two more bad fires — one in 1904 and the other in 1915.

By 1909, 2000 people were living in this isolated canyon and Mogollon could boast seven restaurants, five stores, two hotels and fourteen saloons. An added attraction was a red-light district for each end of town. One was called Little Italy. The principal establishment in the other was Big Bertha's.

One of the notorious crimes of early-day Mogollon was the $14,000 robbery of a mine payroll by two Mexican laborers. The pair waited until the stage from Silver City deposited a strongbox containing the money with the Mogollon Mercantile Company. They waved guns at the store manager and demanded the money but he refused to give it to them. They then opened fire, killing both the manager and a clerk. Citizens formed a posse and caught both culprits, killing one in the process.

Among the more notorious saloons was one called "The Bloated Goat." Much blood reportedly was spilled in the sawdust on its rough floors.

The town had its interesting characters. One, William H. Antrim, known locally as "Uncle Billy," was Billy the Kid's stepfather. Those who knew him said he never once mentioned the outlaw's name.

Another was Ben Lilly, famous Mogollon lion hunter. Ranchers gave Ben $50 for every mountain lion he brought in and during his career he brought in 110 of the sleek animals.

Along with interesting characters, there were interesting stories, some of them departing from the truth. One of the best concerns the bearded Mogollon prospector who had a pet grizzly bear.

Now anyone knows that a grizzly bear is one of the meanest creatures to inhabit the forest. But when the prospector found a grizzly-bear cub he just couldn't leave it to die out in the wilderness. He took it home to his cabin where he fed and mothered it. Before long, the two had become bosom pals — no matter where the prospector went, the cub tagged along at his heels.

The years passed and the grizzly grew to proper adult bearhood — which meant he became enormous. He continued to be just as much of a pet as ever, trailing the prospector everywhere. At last the prospector realized he might as well make use of a good thing, particularly since he didn't have a horse, or even a mule. Thereupon he bravely climbed aboard the grizzly's back, nudged him with his heel and found he had himself a mount quite as serviceable as a horse.

The first time the old prospector rode that grizzly bear into Mogollon they say it created quite a stir — consternation, in fact. But eventually the people got used to it. Throughout the Mogollons, the bear and his rider became legendary figures.

One moonlit night the prospector was awakened by a loud noise just outside the cabin, where he always kept his pet grizzly tethered. Rushing outside, he found his pet locked in mortal combat with an even larger bear.

The battle continued to grow in ferocity, while the prospector danced around in a helpless effort to stop it. Suddenly, he found himself trapped between the two snarling animals. There was only one way out, he decided: he'd have to ride out, aboard his bear.

Promptly, he leaped on its back, grabbed hold of the fur on its neck, nudged his flanks with his bare heels and felt the bear move off downcanyon at a rapid clip.

A few miles away from the scene of the action, the prospector shouted, "Whoa!"

Wood haulers did a brisk business before oil engines were installed in mines at Mogollon

The bear kept running. The prospector shouted again, tugging hard on the soft neck fur of the Grizzly. The bear growled and moved a little faster. Suddenly he raced through a moonswept clearing in the forest and the prospector glanced down at his mount.

"My God!" he shouted. "I'm on the wrong bear."

Legend has it that the last anybody ever saw of the bear and his rider they were streaking southward across the Mexican border.

Just as incredible and perhaps more accurate were some of the stories about the miners who gouged the mountains for gold and silver. One concerns the Last Chance Mine, the discovery strike that created Mogollon.

Ten years after Eberle's discovery, the Last Chance seemed to have passed its prime but an English mining engineer, Ernest Craig, thought riches were still buried deep inside its workings. He acquired the mine in 1899 and began experimenting with various methods of treating the ore. It cost him two fortunes without success. On the third try Craig was successful. It made him wealthy and allowed him to return to England where in 1910 he was elected to the House of Commons.

There were many other mines around

Mogollon — some more productive than the Last Chance. Among them were the Little Fannie, the McKinley, Little Charlie, Pacific, Confidence, Champion, Deadwood and Crescent.

From the very beginning of the camp, transportation was always a problem. Once you have traversed that winding road so full of hairpin curves that leads here from U.S. 180 you can appreciate its magnitude. And in the early days, the only road was a much narrower shelf blasted out of the side of the mountain. There was no paving.

Over this tortuous road, ten- and twenty-mule teams hauled ore out at a cost of fifty dollars a ton. Milling cost another ten dollars a ton and usually recovered only little more

than half of the gold and silver the ore contained. In spite of these handicaps, the Mogollon district produced $4,650,000 worth of mineral, most of it silver, by 1904.

Improved methods of separating the metal from the ore gave Mogollon a boost upward in 1905. From that year to 1926 the mines were practically in continuous operation, producing $15,000,000 worth of gold and silver, two-thirds of it silver. During that period this district took out about forty per cent of the gold and about sixty per cent of the silver produced in all of New Mexico.

The top year was 1914, when the streets of Mogollon were constantly jammed with wagons and teams and miners. Then, the annual payroll was nearly a million dollars

Cinco de Mayo (May 5) celebration in Mogollon, early in 20th century

— quite a handsome sum for the day.

That was also the year a new automobile first sputtered and steamed its way into the Silver Creek Canyon country. As early as 1909 some 400 animals were used to haul supplies and mining machinery into the district and ore out. Barring trouble, stagecoaches made the trip from Silver City in fourteen hours. Ore trains took considerably longer.

The last of the big years was 1926. The veins dwindled. Mines began to close. People moved away. Within months Mogollon was practically a ghost town, abandoned to the bobcats and mountain lions that occasionally ventured into its streets.

In 1931 Mogollon again began to breathe with life as new mining operators found more ore bodies. Although of much lower grade than earlier discoveries, these kept operations going for another eleven years, producing an additional $5,000,000 worth of gold and silver.

World War II ended this. There was a brief revival after the war before Mogollon settled into a permanent slumber. Ghost town it became, but never a corpse. A few people lingered, enough to keep it from being completely abandoned. Today thirteen hardy holdouts still live in Mogollon and from the looks of things, they aren't about to give up on the town.

Miss Ethlyn Whiteside is typical. A life-long resident and until recently the official mail carrier, she is the daughter of the late W. L. (Blanco) Whiteside, pioneer lawman of half a century ago. She inherited his stamina and courage. For many years Miss Whiteside drove that twisting road to Glenwood each afternoon to pickup the Mogollon mail, also taking orders from Mogollon residents for groceries. A few winters back Miss Whiteside's pickup truck lost a wheel high on the mountain. In true postal tradition, she brought the mail through — on her back, wading through deep snow.

You'll usually find Miss Whiteside in the stone building at the west edge of town. It once housed the Mogollon Mercantile Company and now houses what Miss Whiteside proudly calls "The Silver Queen Museum." The museum is dimly lighted with kerosene lamps; there are no electric wires leading to Mogollon. They give it a faintly yellow look of age, the light flickering over relics of Mogollon's salad days.

Over there is a sawed-off shotgun which caused four deaths when this was a roaring camp. A placard explains that a saloonkeeper used it to kill three men, then was killed himself with it during a dispute with his bartender.

A miscellany of other items includes an old poker table from the Sil Gamblin gambling hall; a pool table from Todd Hilliard's saloon; the town's first telephone switchboard.

If you ask her, Miss Whiteside will point out bloodstains on the wooden floor. These are the remains of that payroll robbery of the Ernestine Mining Company in 1912 when C. A. Freeman and his bookkeeper, William S. Clark, were shot to death.

The big building across the street that was formerly Holland's General Store and is now the "Gila National Gallery of Art" is the home of an artist, Chet Kwiecinski. Up Main Street, past the gaping foundations and tumbledown buildings, you'll come upon another relic of the past — what used to be a store building. Now a freshly painted sign adorns the porch, reading: *Artcher's Ghost Town Gallery*.

Inside, artist Johnny Artcher and his wife, Nettie, have a gallery of literally hundreds of Artcher's oil paintings, plus an amazingly complete museum of relics. The Artchers "discovered" Mogollon several years ago, bought this place, cleaned out the assorted rubbish of fifty years and began fixing it up as a place to live. Artcher calls it his "own private Taos."

Among the other residents of the town are Mrs. Wray, the postmistress, who also runs a lunch counter serving delicious apple pie, and several artists like Kwiecinski and Bill Rakocy.

Artcher says that each summer more tourists are visiting the lonely little town. A few people are coming here to spend the summer in the nostalgic air of a real ghost town. The road has been paved from U.S. 180 and this has helped bring more visitors. The number is expected to keep growing.

By 1967, New Mexico 78 had already been blacktopped through Mogollon and for twenty miles east to Willow Creek, deep in the mountains. Eventually, of course, it will be paved over the mountains to link up with New Mexico 59 and form a grand scenic route through south-central New Mexico.

For the moment, however, a ghost town atmosphere still clings to Mogollon in spite of the museum and art-gallery signs. What will happen to that atmosphere as more artists and tourists "discover" it remains to be seen.

A ghost-town atmosphere still clings to Mogollon: a little church, its boards unpainted

Weeds grow tall around Chloride's falsefronts

16 | The Shangri-La of Raymond Schmidt

CHLORIDE

James Hilton created a never-never land in his novel, *Lost Horizon*, and isolated it by the Himalayan Mountains. He called it Shangri-La, a paradise where time stood still, where modern pressures didn't exist. Many seek such a place, but few find it. Raymond Schmidt has found his in a ghost town tucked away in the lonely Black Range of Southwestern New Mexico.

The town is called Chloride. Something of an island in time, isolated from modernity by miles of emptiness, Chloride lies about seventy miles due east of Mogollon. You can reach it by way of New Mexico Highways 78, 59 and 52 from Mogollon but you'll need a four-wheel drive to do it. The best starting point is U.S. Highway 85, nine miles north of Truth or Consequences at its junction with blacktop NM 52. Turn west on 52 to wander through parched country of skimpy bunchgrass, greasewood and spidery ocotillo.

The road leads through a Spanish-American hamlet called Cuchillo (Knife), hidden in a desert canyon, then climbs rapidly toward a distant, wrinkled mountain range. Soon you are in piñon country, in the foothills of the Black Range. Twenty-eight miles from U.S. 85, the highway enters a high valley where broad meadows of brown grass abound. You cross a creek that is usually dry, sheltered by cottonwoods, and ahead lies a service station dominated by a red and white Chevron sign. A smaller sign on a post indicates that this is Winston.

The paved road veers to the right. The gravel turnoff to the left leads to the buildings and trees marking the site of old Winston. Drive straight into the 1880s down the street lined by false-fronted stores, all vacant. Some are boarded up. The town has an unkempt look, thickly overgrown with high grass. An ancient gasoline pump rusts in front of an old garage. You can barely make out the faded lettering on one of the false-fronts: *Lucky Jacks Saloon.*

Leaving Winston to doze with its memories, drive on through town on the winding gravel road for another two miles to reach Raymond Schmidt's Shangri-La. Chloride sprawls around the mouth of Chloride Creek Canyon. It is a typical Western ghost town filled with crumbling adobes and unpainted frame buildings dyed brown and black and white by the elements.

Only a few houses are occupied. Raymond Schmidt lives in one: a two-story adobe planted rock-solid on a hill at the right side of the canyon. It was built in 1883 at the height of the Chloride silver boom.

Walk across the polished round stones of Chloride Creek and swing open the tired gate in the fence. It is guarded by an old-fashioned dug well, the boards bleached salt-white by the sun. A rope, a rusty pulley and a shiny tin pail hang above the well. Birds twitter happily in the limbs of the scrub oak and box elder and cottonwoods in the yard. Grama grass billows like wheat in the breeze; it is the color of honey.

Knock on the door to the Victorian house and Schmidt will answer, peering alertly at you through steel-and-plastic-rimmed glasses. A thin, almost frail-looking man who might be a retired schoolmaster, he looks somewhat younger than his seventy summers. His khaki shirt is buttoned at the neck but he wears no tie. His trousers are supported by wide green galluses.

I visited him most recently on a winter day when the sun was bright and the air almost sparkling, it was so clear. It was warm, with only a cool breeze to remind you that it was February.

He ushered us into his spotless two-room house with a smile and soon we were sitting in a comfortable old walnut rocker. A fire crackled in a small black cast-iron stove. An ornate Victorian clock ticked on the wall, chiming the quarter hour.

Only four families — about fifteen people — still inhabit this silver-boom reminder, and Schmidt is the eldest. Partly because of that and partly for other reasons, he is an institution in these parts. He is a man of many talents who amuses himself by tinkering and building things and studying the heavens through a reflecting telescope that he built himself.

His roots are sunk about as deep as possible in the history of these mountains. He was born in Lake Valley, another silver camp, and has spent most of his life in this tranquil canyon. He knows its history by heart because his family is so intimately connected with it.

Troopers of the 10th Cavalry, encamped near Chloride during the Apache campaign

From his front porch, he can look down past the well at the abandoned stores lining Chloride's main street. They are lifeless and lonely now. Schmidt can remember when they were otherwise.

He can see the stunted shape of the live-oak tree that sprouts from the middle of the street. Some folks say that it sometimes served as a gallows. The tree, still living, has grown very little in those eighty years.

We sat there that bright winter day while Schmidt talked about Chloride. It was never an important town except to those who lived there. It was never noted for its great bonan-

zas or even its rowdiness. An ordinary town, inhabited by ordinary people making their ordinary way on a hostile frontier.

It started with Harry Pye, a rough mule-skinner who freighted goods for the Army. Pye had learned how to survive in this country. He thought he knew every trick of the Apaches who used the Black Range as their private hunting preserve.

Pye spotted Chloride Canyon one day in 1879 while looking for a place to camp. He was taking a mule train up Cuchillo Creek, headed for Ojo Caliente (Hot Spring) Army post. The gulch was overgrown with brush.

It was perfect. The little creek offered water. But most important, here was cover from the watchful eyes of Indians who might pass this way, ready to lift the scalp of any likely paleface they might find.

Pye, who didn't intend that the scalp should be his, bedded down there in the canyon with his mules. When day broke he fixed himself some breakfast and walked about to shake some of the kinks of sleep from his rugged frame. Then he spotted the streaks in the rock outcrop on the side of the canyon. Excited, he took out his knife and scraped at the rock. It was silver chloride from the looks of it — and rich.

Pye was a prudent man. He knew he had a silver strike. But he was tied up with his army contract and couldn't break loose to mine the claim just now. He noted the location carefully, keeping it strictly between him and his mules. Then he chipped off a few ore samples and stuck them away in his pack.

An assay showed several ounces of silver to the ton. Pye restrained his excitement until his contract was finished. Then he assembled some friends — it was wise to travel in numbers in this unfriendly land — and returned to the canyon to stake a claim. He called it "Pye Lode." The camp was named Chloride.

The word went faster than a pig at a barbecue. By late 1880, hundreds of prospectors and miners were swarming like ants all over the Black Range, unmindful of Apaches. The following year some prospectors formed a second town, two miles from Chloride, which they called Fairview, the place now called Winston.

The Apaches waited, watching. In January, 1881, they fell upon Chloride in full war paint, uttering their bloodcurdling screams. At their head was the great Chief Nana.

A Chloride mining-camp character

The surprise was such that the Indians were able to kill two men, seriously wound a Mr. Patrick, and steal much livestock before the miners could put up a defense. Then, as suddenly as they had appeared, the savages were gone.

Chloride in the early 1880s

Incidents such as that didn't leave much peace of mind. But the memory faded in a few months. Harry Pye was like all the rest. He was so busy getting rich he forgot about the Apaches. One day they picked him off from ambush and that was the end of Harry Pye. Other similar incidents occurred but the Apaches never again made a direct attack on the camp.

From fifty residents in 1881, Chloride in two years boomed to a hundred houses, shops and a hotel. It eventually got a couple of thousand residents.

The *New Southwest and Grant County Herald* reported from Silver City in June, 1881, that Chloride "is growing up as rapidly as possible under the circumstances, considering the difficulty of having adobes made, cutting stone and etc. besides having to haul sawed lumber from fifty to one hundred miles."

But, the *Herald* added: "It already has four stores and I don't know how many saloons, assay offices, blacksmith shops and residences, mainly built of substantial material."

The same correspondent reported that there were already thirteen locations on the "Pye Lode, some of which are showing up very well in gray copper and other rich ores." Later that month, A. Rush Bowe wrote that the Ivanhoe Mine had a shaft down "sixty feet and improves in appearance every foot." Three assays ran $4652, $8050, and $68,779.50 to the ton, said Bowe.

In August, the *Herald* said Harn & Mc-Conkey were running a six-horse stage from Engle Depot on the railroad to Fairview and "lighter vehicles to Chloride City and Grafton." Chloride then had 300 population. But the paper reported some problems:

The great drawback to this camp has been the obstinacy displayed by prospectors in holding undeveloped claims, at the figures of developed property, and thus repelling capital that would have been invested in the district, owing to the immense ledges and rich assays obtained from the surface croppings. This policy has been to retard the growth of the camp, which would have been very rapid, and to cause a general stagnation of business in Chloride City.

But the *Herald* was hopeful: "The prospectors have now realized the folly of their own policy and are prepared to sell at reasonable prices."

That year of 1881 saw the Indians everywhere in the Black Range. Typical was this item from the *Herald* on August 6, 1881, published under a scare head:

LOOK OUT!
The Indians are again in the Black Range. On the 28th inst. they killed at the mouth of Cuchillo Negro Creek on the ranch of Jose M. Montoya, which they burnt, two Mexicans and one American woman. At midnight on the 29th the following dispatch was received at Fairview, Black Range:

Ojo Caliente July 29th
"Sir: It is officially reported that Lieut. Guilfoyle's command had a fight with a small band of Mescalero Apaches on the 25th inst. in the San Andreas Mountains, about 50 miles north of Membrillo Canon. Last news: Lieut. Guilfoyle was following the trail. . . . Please inform settlers and miners as far as possible.

"Very Respy. Yours,
W. W. Taylor, 1st. lt.
9th Cavalry Com'dg."

A four-team freight-wagon train, Chloride in the 1880s

A Mexican mariachi *band of boom times in Chloride*

Another report had it that on August 31 four Mexican sheepherders were killed in the San Mateo Mountains. This time a force of fifteen miners from Fairview and Chloride took the trail in search of the savages but apparently never caught up with them.

If Indians were a problem, so were outlaws. Gangs of rustlers operated in the Black Range. That same newspaper reported an incident when a "mob" of infuriated stockmen caught up with two of the thieves. "The surprised chief had only one 'pal' with him, but the two 'stood off' the attacking force so effectually that the latter withdrew after losing nine of their number . . ." reported the *Herald* with almost grudging admiration.

As a kind of aside, the paper explained that a noted desperado named "Rattlesnake Jack," who had been operating in Wyoming, had recently joined the Black Range rustlers. Earlier, it seems, Rattlesnake had frequented parts of California. There, said the *Herald,* "he rendered himself odious by his cattle-stealing propensities and murderous proclivities, and became unpleasantly notorious under the romantic alias of 'Buckskin Bob.'"

The name might have been one a dime-novel hack dreamed up. Actually, however, Rattlesnake Jack or Buckskin Bob had a real name that was completely different, reported the *Herald* with some satisfaction. It was plain Billy Dieffenderfer. Maybe that was why he took to crime in the first place.

Chloride continued to thrive, so much so that W. O. Thompson opened a weekly newspaper there, calling it *The Black Range*. This little tabloid chronicled a generally peaceful history for the town and only occasional excitement.

There was the night Harry Froehlich, Harry Reilly and William Hardin, "three gay and festive cowboys," shot up the town.

Editor Thompson was unhappy that the town justice of the peace fined the "Hoodlums" only seven dollars apiece. It provoked this bit of editorial comment: "The outrageous disturbance created by drunken hoodlums Saturday night and on Sunday last should certainly arouse our citizens to take immediate steps for the building of a 'cooler' for the safe storage of disturbers of the peace."

Among Chloride's diversions were the Big Six Saloon and what sounds like a palace of pleasure, judging from this *Black Range* item in the October 12, 1888 issue:

That assignation office on upper Wall Street is a nuisance and a disgrace to the respectable inhabitants of the west end. Such an institution should not be allowed to exist in the midst of a respectable community.

Another note appeared in another issue:

Since the episode at the Chloride Hotel Tuesday night the landlord of that hash foundry has declared himself. From now on all gentlemen boarders who make application for sleeping apartments for female "friends" must flash up their marriage credentials.

Biggest event of the year in Chloride was the Fourth of July celebration, launched at dawn with a blast loud enough to wake the dead. The one in 1888 was chronicled in *The Black Range*

"At ten o'clock a procession of mounted citizens, carrying flags, went out and met the procession of Fairview citizens who they escorted to Holme's Hall where the opening ceremonies were held," the paper said. A choir then sang *The Star Spangled Banner* and Mamie Bunker read the Declaration of Independence. This patriotic feature was followed by a rendition of *Columbia* by the choir and a "rousing and spirited oration delivered by Mr. D. H. Wenger which brought forth cheers and applause from the audience."

The baseball match between Chloride and Fairview which followed had to be cut to five innings "because of want of time." Chloride won. The game was followed by four horse races and a shooting match, which John H. Cook won.

"The lion fight," reported *The Black Range*, "which was to have taken place in the early evening was declared off on account of her majesty's indisposition." The lion was supposed to fight a dog. At 8:30 p.m., "all lovers of dancing adjourned to Holme's Hall where all enjoyed one of the most pleasant and social dances ever given in Chloride."

There were many good mines in and around the town, including such big producers as the Silver Monument, the Readjuster, the Alaska, the Atlanta, the Ben Harrison, the Buffum and a host of others. The town's salad days ended with the demonetization of silver in 1893 and the panic that followed. Mining kept going for a number of years but Chloride finally began dwindling away.

End of the bear hunt (Chloride in the 1880s)

Among the early settlers in Chloride was Raymond Schmidt's father, Henry, a most remarkable man. A native of Germany, he attended the University of Marburg for two or three years. It was there, probably, that he read books about the great American West and the savage Indians who roamed the plains. Utterly fascinated, he decided he'd come to America to see them in the flesh.

Schmidt arrived in America at the age of seventeen, pretty well prepared for life because of his good education. His first stop was Grafton, West Virginia, where an uncle who operated a store gave him a job as a clerk. But clerking was too tame for him: he wanted to see some Indians. Before long, he quit and took off for the Wild West, which he found in Yankton, South Dakota.

"There were about four hundred Indians around the train when it stopped in Yankton," his son says. "He thought he saw enough Indians after he was there a week so he went looking for a job in Leadville, Colorado."

Schmidt did assay work and surveying in that booming mining camp and in 1882 joined a survey party on an expedition into New Mexico. He wound up in Chloride. Here, he opened an assay office and like his son after him, became a kind of institution. He got interested in photography and soon proved expert at it. He recorded a priceless trove of Southwestern history on film, saving every one of the 1500 photographs he made, many on glass plates. The collection, carefully saved by Raymond Schmidt for many years, now lies in the University of New Mexico Library.

Henry Schmidt had the German gift for meticulous detail and mechanics. He liked to build things. Among his projects was probably the first X-ray machine west of the

Birds eating from Raymond Schmidt's hand

Mississippi River. An El Paso doctor located it a few years ago right here in Chloride. Apparently the only one of its kind in existence, it now reposes in a General Electric Museum.

The elder Schmidt married and moved to Lake Valley, another mining camp, but returned to Chloride after the death of his wife in 1897, bringing with him their three children. Here, Raymond and his brother and sister grew up — "practically orphans" the first years because their father had to be away so much on various mining projects.

As a young man, Raymond worked for the Forest Service, then joined Phelps Dodge at the new copper camp of Tyrone (Chapter 20) He stayed there ten years before returning to Chloride in 1928 to rejoin the Forest Service as a fire lookout.

Retired since 1945, Schmidt spends most of his daylight hours "fixing things" and sharpening saws for people. Until late 1966,

Chloride falsefronts, framed by Raymond Schmidt's dug well

Schmidt lived in a one-room cabin that adjoins the house. Then he got some free time and went to work on the larger place. An extensive two-month-long repair job made it liveable.

If you ask, he'll take you on a stroll out in the yard where the tawny grama grass grows thick and tall. Probably, he'll introduce you to a couple of "friends" — a chickadee and a nuthatch. The tiny birds eat bits of peanut from Schmidt's hand. He seems to have a way with wild things.

Farther out in the yard, the sun beams on a low wooden shed where Schmidt conceals his pride and joy — a 12½-inch reflecting telescope. The shed roof is cleverly counterbalanced so that a touch is enough to slide it out of the telescope's way. The instrument itself is a long silver-painted tube, pivoted so delicately that a child can operate it. A friend in Corning, New York, ground the mirror.

"I had ground lenses for two smaller telescopes," explains Schmidt. "And I'd have ground this one but he insisted on doing it for me."

Schmidt, however, built the rest of it from plans he found in a magazine. He shrugs away the suggestion that it took great skill to build such a delicate instrument. He displays the same skill in repairing watches and clocks.

When you ask him if he doesn't get lonely, he laughs. "No. I've been alone most of my life — I was a fire lookout for many years and doing that you get kind of used to being alone."

When he needs something he hops on a bright red Honda motorbike and zips over to Winston, or the forty-five miles into Truth or Consequences. He has his astronomy and the radio and a large collection of books for amusement.

"And quite a few people come to see me," he says.

The absence of such twentieth-century phenomena as television, movies and the telephone bother him not a whit. When you visit him here in his tranquil brown hills you can understand why.

Chloride is timeless, a refuge where at least one man has found peace.

All Winston's buildings are vacant, some boarded up

Hillsboro during the mining boom

17 | A Pair of Black Range Ghosts

Chloride and Winston are merely "openers" for the ghost hunter in the Black Range, mountains that are dotted with reminders of gold and silver rushes, Indian fights and gunplay. New Mexico 90 slices into the very heart of this historic country and will take you to Hillsboro and Kingston, a pair of nineteenth-century heirlooms. Highway 90 links U.S. 85, fifteen miles south of Truth or Consequences, and U.S. 180, sixty-five miles distant across timbered high country.

You get a sample only a few miles west of the turnoff from U.S. 85, the remains of a placer gold-mining operation. A road to the right leads to a cluster of buildings within sight of the highway. They are now part of a ranch but were once the town of Gold Dust, a place that flourished for a few years while men used hydraulic means to gouge the desert of sand and gravel. The men are gone and so is the gold but an eternal monument remains in the form of massive hills of gravel.

At a point eighteen miles from U.S. 85, the road enters the valley of Percha Creek. Almost at once you are on Hillsboro's long and winding main street. Big cottonwoods cast most of the old masonry and adobe buildings into shadow, giving the town a lazy air.

Hillsboro began because Dan Dugan and Dave Stitzel went prospecting up the Percha in April, 1877. Stitzel spotted some promising-looking "float," as ore samples are called, and showed them to his companion.

Dugan snorted. "No good! Anybody should know a formation like that doesn't carry any mineral."

Stitzel was unconvinced. He kept the rocks and later had them assayed. He got quite a horselaugh when the ore ran $160 in gold to the ton. Then the two enlisted Joe Yankie and returned to the Percha. On May 13 they located the "Opportunity" and "The Ready Pay" claims. They scraped over five tons of ore out of the mountain within a couple of weeks, hauled it to the mill on the Mimbres and cashed in more than $400.

Prospectors began drifting in to the "diggings," among them Frank Pitcher, who teamed up with Dugan. The two were exploring around "Ready Pay Gulch" one day

A Hillsboro barbershop in the 1880s

and sat down in a clump of oak bushes to rest. They picked up some loose rock, found it heavy, broke it open and saw gold. They called their claim "The Rattlesnake."

Somebody built a house in what is now Hillsboro in August, 1877. Miners threw some names in a hat to find a name for their town. The one produced was "Hillsborough," which was quickly shortened.

George Wells hit the richest strike around on a claim called the "Bonanza." The mine produced more than a million dollars. Hillsboro old-timers recalled that during the winter of 1877-78 Wells spent $90,000 in gold dust and nuggets in the stores and saloons of the town.

By 1880 Hillsboro had four saloons, four grocery stores, 300 miners and four companies of soldiers to protect them from the Apaches. The Indians were always lurking offstage, although seldom seen by the miners. They watched the goings on with keen interest, keen enough to pick off any unwary miner so his scalp might decorate the belt of a brave.

In the early 'eighties, when Victorio went on the warpath, the Hillsboro miners were kept constantly on the alert. Once the noted chief almost put in an appearance on the streets of the town. Victorio had had dealings with a half-breed named Trujillo, who kept a ranch five miles south of Hillsboro. Trujillo had twin fifteen-year-old sons who were friendly with a Hillsboro youth named Homer Tarbill. One day the twins returned to the ranch from Hillsboro with their friend and soon afterward up rode Victorio himself at the head of about ninety war-painted braves.

While the Indian chief spoke to Mrs. Trujillo the boys huddled together to watch. When Trujillo showed up, driving a herd of steers, Victorio ordered him to call his sons.

The three boys stepped forward and the Apache chieftain shook his head, pointing to the Hillsboro boy.

"He is not your son," the chief declared.

Mrs. Trujillo, hoping to save the Tarbill boy's life, insisted that he was. Victorio wasn't fooled. He boxed the woman's ears, then had his men cut some long willow switches from trees growing beside Trujillo Creek. The Indians then stripped young Tarbill of his clothes and gave him a fifty-yard head start before they started after him on foot waving those switches.

The terrified youth outdistanced his pursuers for about three miles, but then they caught up with him, switching him unmercifully right to the edge of Hillsboro. At the hill at the south edge of town the Indians gave up the chase, but young Tarbill kept going, his naked body covered with blood.

When Hillsboro became the county seat of Sierra County it got an ornate Victorian courthouse

He fell unconscious in front of Perrault and Galles' Store.

Victorio, meanwhile, took his choice of Trujillo's best cattle and his finest horses and vanished toward the South. Young Tarbill recovered and for many years served as sheriff at Dwyer, N.M. In 1885, when Geronimo went on the warpath, Tarbill was once again pursued by Apaches but escaped by riding his horse over a cliff.

With Victorio raiding all over the area, the Hillsboro miners finally fled over the mountains to the mining camp of Georgetown to amuse themselves there until the heat cooled along the Percha. Then they returned.

Hillsboro grew rapidly, gaining a population of about 2000. It also became the county seat of Sierra County and subsequently got an ornate Victorian courthouse, complete with a durable jail out in back.

When the mines played out, Hillsboro clung to life as a trading center for the many ranches that had sprung up in the area. The courthouse became the scene of several well publicized trials of rustlers and an even more noted murder trial.

As the years passed the many small ranches were absorbed into giant spreads like the vast Ladder Ranch, the headquarters of which is just northeast of town. The need for a county seat here evaporated and it was moved to Hot Springs, a town now called Truth or Consequences.

Hillsboro settled into a deep slumber, mostly deserted. In 1939, the courthouse was torn down for building material and only a few brick walls and doors and windows were left to serve as reminders of the past. Today about 150 people continue to live in Hillsboro, many of them retired. Others work on ranches.

There are people like Mrs. J. O. Hatcher,

who operates a hotel and cafe in an ancient thick-walled adobe building on the main street. She came here during World War I with her physician husband. He set up a hospital in the same building where she now operates the hotel. Mrs. Hatcher has been here long enough now to qualify as an old-timer, and is one of the few around. Only a few go back farther in Hillsboro's past.

Mrs. Lydia G. Key, a pleasant, blue-eyed housewifely woman, keeps Hillsboro traditions alive in the Black Range Museum. Mrs. Key and her husband Newburn wandered into the Percha Valley about ten years ago, towing a house trailer. They had retired after a lifetime in Florida and liked Hillsboro so well they stayed.

The museum is a good place to absorb some of Hillsboro's past. It is filled with well preserved relics of those golden days, including a fancy grand piano from the home of an early-day lawyer, and many photographs

Mrs. Lydia Key keeps Hillsboro traditions alive in the Black Range Museum

Smelter bucket, Hillsboro

Church steeple, Hillsboro

taken when Hillsboro was booming. Like practically everything else in Hillsboro, the building that houses the museum has an interesting past. Madame Sadie Orchard once operated a hotel here.

Madame Sadie came to the United States from the Limehouse district of London and wound up in Hillsboro in 1886. On a hill at the edge of town she operated a house that provided feminine companionship — for a price — to lonely miners. She also operated the hotel and a stagecoach line between Hillsboro and Lake Valley.

Sadie Orchard became famous across the frontier. She lived in Hillsboro until her death in the 1940s and spent her declining years telling anyone who would listen about her harrowing experiences driving a stagecoach, fighting off Indians and highwaymen.

The friend of many famous people, during the influenza epidemic of 1918 she and her girls distinguished themselves by their selfless devotion to the men, women and children of stricken Hillsboro.

Hillsboro has a peculiar charm that has attracted many people in recent years. Its atmosphere is unspoiled, no huckster has yet discovered it. The town retains its individuality, uncluttered by neon and billboard.

KINGSTON

From Hillsboro west, Highway 90 moves back through history along the narrow and scenic canyon of Percha Creek. This was the main route for stagecoaches between Hillsboro and Kingston and because of its many recesses it was a favorite point for ambush by both Apaches and highwaymen.

Orchard's stagecoach — Hillsboro, 1906

Left: *a house in Hillsboro in the 1880s, with the family on the porch;* right: *the same house today*

Out of the canyon, the road climbs higher and higher into the Black Range. Just seven miles from Hillsboro you come to Kingston, probably New Mexico's roaringest camp at one time. If you're not careful, you'll whip by its grave without knowing you have passed it.

Time has been far less kind to Kingston than its sister ghost down on the Percha. A ramshackle old store on the right of the road serves as a landmark. At this point Highway 90, which is paved, curves left to climb the hill and head on across the mountains to Silver City. The road to Kingston goes straight ahead to the right in front of the store.

Kingston bears little resemblance to a town at all, except for reminders like the old Percha Bank and the Victorio Hotel. Houses hide amid the scrub.

Kingston's story, which begins a little later than Hillsboro's, resulted indirectly from the gold strikes there. These discoveries sent prospectors out in all directions seeking pay dirt. Two parties of them met at the site of Kingston in the fall of 1880. One of these groups found silver on Thief Creek that November and two men with the second party, Phillips and Elliott, located the Iron King

and Empire Mines. The Iron King was the mine that later gave Kingston its name.

At that time there was no town here at all. Chief Victorio's activities the next spring drove the prospectors out and it wasn't until the following year that the strike which created a town here occurred.

The man responsible was a drunk named Jack Sheddon. Sheddon was, if anything, a Western anti-hero who had struck it rich in the rarefied air of Leadville, Colorado, then roistered away half a million dollars. When the money was gone he sobered up long enough to decide he'd better head for more productive climes. This decision brought him to Lake Valley, a boom town about twenty miles south of Hillsboro.

There, instead of the mines, Sheddon haunted the gin mills. His friends kept him going for some time. When he was in his cups Jack had a tendency to get mean and cantankerous and generally make a nuisance out of himself. Finally, he became too much for Lake Valley. The marshal loaded Jack aboard a burro with a supply of grub and a jug of whisky thoughtfully provided by Jack's friends and ran him out of town.

His destination this time was supposed to be Chloride, where Jack had heard the silver

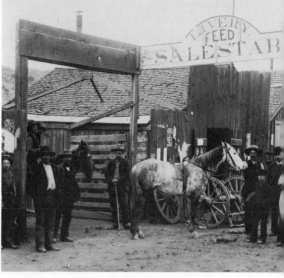

A frontiersman poses after a successful hunt near Kingston in the '80s

Livery stable in Kingston in the 1880s

pickings were good. He didn't quite make it. At about nine o'clock one August morning, Jack and his burro came upon a pleasant little park near the Middle Percha Creek about two miles from the site of Kingston.

It looked inviting. So did the jug, which was still about half full. Jack unbridled his mount there in the invigorating mountain air, sat himself down on the ground against a giant boulder and uncorked his bottle of redeye. By the time the bourbon was gone, so was Jack — dead to the world, passed out against that big boulder.

It was midafternoon before he awakened. Through a whisky haze he could see his burro grazing contentedly in the grassy little park. Struggling to his feet he suddenly noticed that the boulder against which he had been leaning had a peculiar metallic look. He picked up a rock off the ground to chip away a piece of the boulder. It felt heavy. When he broke it in two he found it was bornite, a rich silver ore.

Sheddon had himself another bonanza. He called it "The Solitaire," and it was adequate to provide him with an ample supply of whisky and games for some time to come.

With his very first drink in Hillsboro — which followed rather soon after the strike — Sheddon told the world about his good fortune. It caused an immediate exodus from Hillsboro to the new diggings.

With such a horde of prospectors on the Middle Percha it was only a matter of days before a man named A. Barnaby arrived on the scene, set up a tent and opened a store. By August 26 a townsite survey was under way, and by autumn 1800 people were in the new camp.

The late James A. McKenna, who was there, said the miners and their camp followers didn't wait for a roof to hold a dance, holding it in the open air beneath the flickering yellow light of pine knots. When it came time to name the camp, "Kingston" won out.

Trouble visited Kingston that very first winter in the form of a severe smallpox epidemic. Doctor Guthrie, something of a toper, set up a hospital in a tent, with three aging alcoholics to serve as nurses. After seven miners died, three Kingston prostitutes volunteered to nurse the sick, winning the undying admiration of every man in the camp.

In spite of smallpox and the ever present

threat of Apaches, Kingston thrived. Within a year, the population had swelled to 5000 and a year later had reached 7500. For the first year Kingston was a tent city but then it began to take on a more permanent look as substantial buildings were erected. From the very beginning, it was an exciting place where fortunes were made overnight — if not from the mountains, at the poker and faro tables in the gambling dens and saloons that lined Kingston's main street.

At the height of the boom, here amid the pine trees, at least twenty-two saloons staggered along the broad sidewalks of the main street. The men of Kingston seemed to devote most of their waking hours to the pleasures of Bacchus. The town had no church, until somebody started passing a hat in the saloons one night and quickly collected $1500 to build one.

If there was no church at first, there also was no jail and those who imbibed too heavily or committed some offense against the public morals were fastened to a snubbing post until someone had time to haul them off to Hillsboro. At last a makeshift adobe jail was built, hard against the wall of the Percha Bank. The jail somehow has outlived the town and still exists as a satellite to the bank.

At Kingston's peak, some twenty-seven mines were operating hereabouts. The great Iron King, the Grey Eagle, the U.S., the Bullion, Lady Franklin, Gypsy, Comstock, Miner's Dream, Black Colt, Savage and the famous Brush Heap were among them. Crowds were so large in the town on pay nights that it was a struggle to go ninety feet in thirty minutes.

Progress was so fast that pretty soon the town had practically everything. There were a brewery, an opera house, three newspapers, fourteen groceries, three hotels, a

Kingston residents posed on the steps of their homes, wearing their Sunday-go-to-meeting clothes

Downtown Kingston during the silver boom

A store in old Kingston

Mine camp in the Black Range, believed near Kingston, in the 1880s

G.A.R. post, Odd Fellows, Knights of Pythias and Masonic temples and, finally, a schoolhouse.

The miners who thronged the place lived at a rapid pace — sometimes dangerously. One of the most celebrated parties in frontier history occurred on the first Christmas Eve here. A saloonkeeper named Pretty Sam had just completed a fine new dancehall, fifty feet wide by 150 feet deep. Its front faced the street and the rear jutted out over the Middle Percha Creek Canyon, built on a trestle about thirty feet above the stream. Under construction for months, it was Sam's pride and joy, even boasting a polished hardwood dance floor. It was called The Casino.

Pretty Sam planned a real celebration, inviting everyone for miles around. Everything was on the house. He even hired an orchestra in El Paso and brought it to Kingston for the big night. On Christmas Eve, the place was jammed with miners and their "ladies," all spiffed up in their best bibs and tuckers.

As Jimmy McKenna told the story, the grand march was led by one Colonel Park, a former West Pointer who had fought with the Confederacy. He must have made quite a picture leading the parade, his 275 pounds jammed into his old West Point dress uniform. His partner was "Big Annie," madame of a Kingston bagnio.

There were several other "colonels" in attendance, testifying to the frontier preference for the military title. Colonel Crawford had earned his title because of his fancy clothes and fancier lies. Colonel Harris got his by sitting in a stud-poker game for forty-eight hours without getting up. Colonel Jim Finch could tell the difference by the sound between a .45 and a .45-70 Winchester, and Colonel Bob Hopper could tell the difference between Old Crow and Sam Thompson by the taste.

By midnight, the party progressed to a state of near-hysteria. Then a miner named Roach happened to awake from a drunken stupor and start hunting his lady love, who had gone to Pretty Sam's dance. As the clock tolled twelve, Roach popped in the dance-hall door, firing at the oil lamps with a Springfield rifle. In a flash, practically every man in the room had a pistol in hand and was shooting back.

Amid the screaming females and the crashing of gunfire, there followed an immediate exodus toward the rear, with Big Annie in the lead. Out the back double doors she crashed (they had been locked) to drop thirty feet to the hard rocks of Percha Canyon. Right behind her came French Joe and others. Annie survived with only minor bruises. She was too well padded to be hurt badly.

Such a boom town naturally attracted its share of up-and-coming young men. It was here that Ed Doheny first became friends with Albert Bacon Fall. Doheny went on to make millions in oil in Los Angeles and become linked with Fall (then Secretary of the Interior) in the Teapot Dome oil scandal.

Street scene in Kingston during the silver boom

George Curry was also active in Kingston. One day he was to become Governor of New Mexico. Another figure to achieve later fame was the tall, courtly Colonel Edward R. Bradley, who with his brother Jim haunted Kingston's night spots. Bradley, noted in the rough camp for his honesty, was a gambler. Later he went on to make a fortune with a casino in Florida and become a respected breeder and racer of fine horses. Bradley's horses won the Kentucky Derby four times.

Another denizen of Kingston was Sheba Hurst, whose tall tales won him a place in Mark Twain's book, *Roughing It*. Hurst is buried in Kingston's cemetery on a hill overlooking the town. Like the others buried here, Hurst lies just beneath the surface. The ground is so hard that dynamite was always used to dig the graves.

Located as it was in the heart of Apache country, Kingston had its share of Indian trouble. Once, Victorio led his braves in an attack against the town. The miners, getting ready to go out on a hunting expedition, had their rifles ready and quickly beat off the assault.

Victorio tried again, but was again repulsed, and Kingston's citizens decided to prove their bigness. They named their spanking new three-story hotel, "The Victorio" and it stuck.

Kingston was an enormous producer of silver. Up to 1904 its mines had produced more than $6,250,000 in the shiny metal. But the panic of 1893 had given Kingston its death blow, turning it into a ghost town.

Today only a few reminders of past glory still show amid the little piñon and juniper trees. A bell still hangs from its log supports on the main street. It was the gift of a miner in 1887 to the town and was used for years as a fire alarm and to summon residents when the mail arrived.

The Percha bank, a relic of boom days in Kingston

By far the most substantial structure left in town is the Percha Bank. The interior is very much as it was in the early days, even to the paneled cages that first served the bank and later the post office. The mammoth vault is richly decorated in Victorian fashion. In the back room is a tiny, narrow fireplace with a raised hearth, once used by the bank for assay purposes.

Paul Vetter, a retired Southern Pacific employe from El Paso, lives next door to the bank and keeps his eye on it. The building is owned by his son. The Vetters have bought a comfortable home here. Each August, the bank building is used for an exhibition of paintings by the Black Range Artists group.

The old Victorio Hotel is a mere shell. It has lost its top two stories and the one remaining has been stripped of even the floors. The basement is filled with a tangled mass of rubble.

If most of Kingston's structural links with the past have disappeared, so have the human ones. The man with the closest tie to the boom days is Miles Moffitt, a spare, blue-eyed bachelor whose father came here from Pennsylvania in the 'eighties.

Mr. Moffitt, born in the Pennsylvania coal-mine country, was brought here by his parents while still a child. The family didn't stay and Miles grew up back in Pennsylvania but he returned to Kingston in 1936 to make his home permanently. He now lives in a small but comfortable shingled house at the foot of a mountain.

Sitting in a rocking chair on his front porch he gestured at the mountain. "They took four million dollars off that mountain, my father said. Four million dollars —"

His voice trailed off. His eyes were far-away. Then he began to tell us about his

Miles Moffitt, the man with the closest ties to Kingston's boom days

sister, the first white child born at the now extinct mining camp of North Percha in 1886.

"They called her 'Percha'," he chuckled.

His mother tacked another name — Helen — ahead of Percha. Now living in another state, she is still called Percha.

Moffitt talked about his uncle, Johnny Moffitt, one of Kingston's gay blades during mining-camp days. He remembers that Johnny made enough in mining to buy a fine house and always wore fashionable clothes and rode a spirited horse.

His other memories of Kingston are dim, lost in the misty years like the town's brawling, lusty past. It is a past that is dead, as Moffitt and the other twenty-five or thirty people who live in the town well know.

Now they look with some encouragement to the future. New people are showing up in the old camp: people like the Vetters, who came here to retire because of the peace and quiet. There are others, also attracted by the tranquil atmosphere.

It is an ironic fate for a boisterous place like Kingston.

Lake Valley as it appeared in boom days

18 | The Solid Silver Cavern

Lake Valley is another relic of the Black Range excitement, lost amid the dusky brown foothills seventeen miles south of Hillsboro on New Mexico 27. It is remembered chiefly for an incredibly rich silver strike and for the luck — or lack of it — of George W. Lufkin.

Lufkin was a sometime soldier, sometime railroader and prospector who made his way as best he could on the frontier of the 'seventies. Born in Maine, he became a railroader early in life, then fought in the Union Army during the Civil War. Afterward, he returned to railroading and drifted west.

He was in the San Juan Mountains around Silverton, Colorado, at the time of a silver rush and saw other men get rich in a hurry. But not George Lufkin; he wandered to New Mexico and got a job as a pick-and-shovel man in the Santa Rita pit near Silver City to learn mining. When he was convinced he knew it, he moved to Hillsboro and started serious prospecting. There he found a partner, Chris Watson, who helped ward off the loneliness in the back country.

Board sidewalk and falsefront, Lake Valley today

The two were bending an elbow in a Georgetown saloon when a Chinese wandered in with a story to kindle a flame in the brain of any prospector. The Oriental had been working at Fort Selden on the Rio Grande north of Las Cruces. He quit his job to strike off across country for Silver City. He was aiming for a shortcut he had heard about which ran near a high peak close to the settlements on the Mimbres River.

He lost his way, and in trying to find it he came across a large outcrop of dark rock he thought might be iron. He broke off a chunk and stuck it in his pack. Then he found a trail and wound up in Georgetown, where he showed the rock to anyone who would look. Plenty did, and recognized it as the purest kind of horn silver.

Try as he would the Chinese couldn't find the outcrop again but his lack of success didn't stop others — like Lufkin and Watson. They studied a map, did some figuring and decided that he must have spotted the rock somewhere near McEvers' Ranch, the site of Hillsboro. They set out down the Mimbres from Georgetown, then worked their way through Gavilan Canyon and headed south to a point in the hills near a small valley containing a tiny lake. By now they had been out for weeks with nothing to show for their trouble but sore muscles.

It seemed to both men that this was their last big chance to strike it rich. Lufkin was fifty-five years old, his partner close to it. They wandered on beneath the burning sun that July of 1878, and finally came to a large dike of quartzite, just west of the small valley. They followed it through a small pass and noticed some dark outcroppings on the hillside.

The legends that come into the picture at this point are so thick it is difficult to ascer-

tain the truth. The one that calls Lufkin a cowboy says that he stopped to tighten the cinch on his saddle. Another has it that Lufkin and Watson stopped to rest in the shade of a piñon tree. Anyhow, they found some *real* outcrops of silver.

They were convinced they had a bonanza but time had run out on them. Their grubstake was exhausted. Both moved north to Hillsboro where Lufkin got a job as a cook and Watson as a miner. While they worked to get another grubstake so they could exploit their claim, the Apaches went on the warpath and the two could not return to the scene of their lucky strike. They wandered, spending some time in Clifton, Arizona, then returning to Silver City. By then the Indians had calmed down so the prospectors hurried back to their discovery, taking with them a wagon and team.

They dug about half a ton of the black ore and headed back for Silver City. Their first stop was the Red Onion Saloon, where they displayed their ore to an excited crowd of miners. John A. Miller, a well known mining man, heard the news and hastened to the Red Onion to investigate. He knew immediately that the two had struck a bonanza. He offered them $1.50 a pound for the lot, or $1500 for the wagonload.

Lufkin and Watson accepted before settling down to some serious celebrating. Miller took the ore to an assayer, who told him it ran as high as twelve dollars a pound in silver! Miller then put up the money to develop the mine and the two prospectors went to work on the claim in earnest. By the spring of 1881 they had done enough work to sell out to a syndicate headed by George Daly, a Colorado operator.

The *New Southwest* reported that the price was a hefty $225,000. Miller cleared

$100,000. The names of Lufkin and Watson appear in a list of nine others who shared in $125,000. They apparently got $25,000 for their share, plus the income they had already received from the claim. This must have been considerable: $100,000 worth of ore had been shipped from the Columbia Mine the preceding month, most of it running 500 ounces of silver to the ton.

Lufkin went East and got reacquainted with the widow of a conductor on a train he once piloted. They were married and returned to the place where Lufkin had made his strike. There he built a house and as miners drifted in, Lufkin dubbed the camp "Daly," after the man who had bought his claim. Daly soon became a roaring camp and before long people started calling it "Lake Valley." Lufkin spent his time dabbling in real estate.

Blacksmith John Leavitt walked into the picture then to try his hand at mining. The Sierra Grande Mining Company offered some leases and he took one. He chose a hole that Lufkin and Watson had started burrowing and never finished. Leavitt was willing and eager and went right to work. Two days and ten feet later, he broke into the strangest cavern the world had ever seen. It was practically solid silver!

The cave was about twenty-six feet across with a ceiling about twelve feet high. Practically every inch of walls and ceiling were covered with pure silver chloride, known as "horn silver." The dirty gray mineral is known technically as cerargyrite and is so soft it can be cut with a knife. Miners held a candle flame beneath some of the "horns" of silver hanging from the ceiling and watched in disbelief as drops of molten precious metal dripped downward.

It was the richest single silver deposit for the size of the cavern ever uncovered anywhere in the world. The Sierra Grande Company was pleasantly astounded. Blacksmith Leavitt apparently didn't realize what he had uncovered and agreed to sell out to the company for a few thousand dollars.

The company nicknamed the rich find "The Bridal Chamber," and found silver just waiting to be broken off practically anywhere they looked. Mining it was ridiculously simple. It was so near the surface that the side of the hill was knocked out and a spur track laid right into the cave. Rail cars were backed into the room and hand saws were used to cut the chunks of silver from the walls. The ore was so rich that ordinary methods of preparing the metal in concentrate form for smelting were unnecessary. The metal itself was shipped.

The biggest piece of silver taken from the Bridal Chamber was worth $80,000. By the time the room had been completely mined, 2,500,000 ounces of silver had been removed, worth $1.11 an ounce. Total production was $2,775,000.

Lufkin, Watson and Leavitt had been dealt out of the bonanza. So was George Daly, who was deprived of its rewards on the very day it was uncovered. He was in Lake Valley that day when a white woman staggered into town carrying her baby. She had been surprised at a ranch by Victorio's Apaches and terrorized for hours before escaping.

The camp was already excited by previous Indian raids and the woman's appearance was a call to arms. The men proceeded to Cotton's Saloon to fortify their courage and pretty soon a unit of the Army's Ninth Cavalry showed up. Then a scout reported that Victorio had made camp in nearby Gavilan Canyon.

A posse soon rode toward the gorge with Daly in the lead. Lieutenant Schmitt and nineteen cavalrymen rode along. The posse rode straight into an ambush in the rocky, narrow gulch. Schmitt and Daly were downed in the first volley.

The survivors took to the rocks to hold off the Indians until afternoon, when reinforcements arrived from Lake Valley. Besides Schmitt and Daly, another civilian and two soldiers were killed. Eight were wounded. One of these died later.

Daly never knew about the Bridal Chamber. Those who did said it was quite a sight. An El Paso *Lone Star* reporter wrote that the ore "hangs in beautiful, glistening, soft chloride crystals, which...when compressed yield to the pressure and assume the shape of the closed palm like dough. . . . The chlorides run about $27,000 to the ton."

Actually, all the Lake Valley mines were unusual in the quality of their silver ore. In most places, silver is associated with baser metals like lead, zinc and copper. Here, the silver chlorides were extremely high grade.

Such discoveries brought hundreds to the little desert camp. A *Las Vegas Optic* reporter gave a vivid description of the boom camp as it appeared in the winter of 1882:

. . . Water is conspicuous by its absence and the dust is terrible. The entire road was filled with loaded wagons, all on their way to this new eldorado. . . . The town is flourishing, and the town lots command a handsome figure. . . .

A shaft mine at Lake Valley during the 1880s

Hotel accommodations are scarce, but Skinny, the rustler, secured us a room for $1.50. The family washstand was a feature of this hostelry. It consisted of a cracker box and a tin basin in the back yard, a chunk of rosin soap, a filthy towel and a barrel of water with a tin dipper. A cautionary notice tacked on the barrel informed the guest that "water was very scarce." The sensitive Doc refused the primitive altar so he sought a barber shop and paid twenty-five cents for the privilege of a "decent wash" as he called it. The country is staked off by prospectors for five miles around the town in the hopes of catching on to the "other end" of the Lake Valley claims.

Such an influx carried with it certain civic problems. In the spring of 1881 a Silver City physician was shot to death in a bit of gunplay at Lake Valley. He happened to be in the neighborhood when some miners began arguing over their claims and opened up on each other with six-shooters. The good Doctor Kallenberg was laid to rest in the Lake Valley Cemetery.

By 1882 things had gotten so tough that the town imported a six-foot, two-inch gunfighter named Jim McIntire to keep order. His marshal's salary was $300 a month — an enormous sum for the day. Presumably he earned it.

A few months later the town added another lawman — the famous Jim Courtright. Within a few days he laid two ore thieves to rest with a couple of well placed shots during a running gun battle. Later on, Courtright killed three other men with his deadly guns.

Within a few months of the date of its founding, Lake Valley boasted 500 people. A year later it topped 1000 and had a weekly newspaper.

But the lodes played out and by 1888 the decline had set in and the population had dipped to 500. The panic of '93 drove the last nail into Lake Valley's coffin, but by then more than $6,105,000 in silver had been taken from the mines.

It wasn't until the population dipped to less than 100 that Lake Valley got a church. In 1896, the women of the Christian Endeavor Society bought the false-fronted rooming house that had been run by Union Army veteran Major Morgan Morgans. They covered the walls with oil cloth, hung seven coal-oil lamps from the ceiling, set up rows of chairs and opened a church. The annex, next door, was fixed up to provide quarters for any preacher who might be traveling through and could stay long enough to conduct services.

By the early years of the twentieth century Lake Valley was a ghost town with only a few residents. But while most people were leaving Lake Valley, it had a few who were just arriving in the desolate village on the edge of a desert nowhere.

In 1908 Oliver Wilson came to town with his family, fresh from a personal disaster in Kingston, at the time suffering from the same disease afflicting Lake Valley. Wilson was a Swede who had built the Victorio Hotel in Kingston and had passed up an opportunity to sell it, only to see the bank finally foreclose on it.

Among the passengers in the buggy that day when it topped the hill above Lake Valley was Wilson's daughter, Blanche, a vivacious girl of nineteen. When she looked down at the woebegone remains of the town her heart sank.

"I decided I just couldn't live here," she said.

Today, sixty years later, Blanche is one of the last holdouts in Lake Valley. Her life is a chronicle of the past half century of a ghost town.

For awhile the Wilsons ran a restaurant until they could save enough to buy a ranch.

Then, in 1916, Mr. Wilson sold a mine claim he had been developing for years. Blanche meanwhile met and married A. Lee Nowlin, who remained the Santa Fe Railway station agent in Lake Valley until the line was abandoned in 1934.

She laughs about it now. Her family didn't approve at first. "After all, he was a Texan, and Texans generally weren't held in very good repute around here in the old days," she says.

It was a good marriage, though, and the Nowlins had many happy years in the crumbling town. They ran the Continental Oil distributorship for southern New Mexico from Lake Valley and Mrs. Nowlin continued to operate it even after Mr. Nowlin died in 1937.

Mrs. Nowlin lives in a little adobe house surrounded by a picket fence that lost its paint long ago. An oldfashioned swing is suspended from the porch ceiling.

When I first visited Mrs. Nowlin it was Sunday and she greeted me on the porch wearing a delightful print dress. Her gray hair looked as if she had just come from a beauty parlor. Vivacious as a teen-ager, her blue eyes bright behind her rimless spectacles, she showed us around her spotless home and introduced us to her pets — fifteen cats in various sizes, shapes, colors and styles.

Next door to Mrs. Nowlin live Mr. and Mrs. Pete Martinez and their son. Martinez originally came here to work for Mrs. Nowlin's oil company, but has remained and now owns much property in the ghost town. The Nowlin and Martinez homes are the only two livable places in the camp.

Up on the hill, where the greasewood and mesquite grow thick and the ground is hard as concrete, the old Santa Fe Depot has been put out to pasture. Sentiment caused Mrs.

Blanche Nowlin of Lake Valley

Nowlin to buy it a few years past. Boards nailed over doors and windows help keep the prying vandals out.

Perhaps a quarter of a mile away the schoolhouse still stands in a reasonable state of preservation. Occasional church services are held there and sometimes couples come to be married. Now and then a Lake Valley resident comes home to be buried in the cemetery on the hill across New Mexico 27. Funeral services are held in the school.

Down the street from Mrs. Nowlin's place the false-front that the Ladies of the Christian Endeavor Society fixed up is on the verge of collapse. The panes are gone from the windows. The floorboards creak. The oilcloth the ladies used to cover the walls hangs in tatters and the wind sings through the loose weatherboarding.

Such things are of no concern to Mrs. Nowlin, who could, if she wished, live elsewhere. "It's so peaceful, you know," she said. "It's wonderful to wake up in the middle of the night and *hear* the silence." Her family has asked her to move to "town" in Truth or Consequences, but she steadfastly refuses.

She is comfortable and happy. She has a television set and a piano and even a telephone. Lately she has been doing some oil painting.

"This is where all my memories are," she explained. "There are seven graves over there on that hillside that I can't leave."

She served us enormous cola drinks overflowing with ice cream there on the front porch. Watching a couple of hummingbirds

Weathered window, Lake Valley

buzz about a vine, we talked about the silver rush to Lake Valley and the strange games fate plays with men who seek riches. Men like George Lufkin, who caused the boom here but missed millions by only ten feet.

He lies in a lonely desert tomb in the cemetery over there on the hill. He died penniless and was buried in a pauper's grave.

The desolate aspect of Lake Valley today

Lake Valley | 175

19 | City of the Cross

Pinos Altos is not a ghost town like Lake Valley, although it is sleepy enough to be. It dozes amid juniper and piñon trees astride the Continental Divide six miles north of Silver City on New Mexico Highway 25. About 200 persons still live here, most of them working in Silver City.

There is little about the place to tell you that it was once a hustling, rowdy gold camp of several thousand people. However, a weathered but quite modern sign on a corral fence on the south edge of town invites the visitor:

PAN GOLD HERE JUST AS
THE OLD TIMERS DID
A HUNDRED YEARS AGO

A burro keeps a bright eye out for cash customers and when one approaches, he brays unmelodiously to announce the arrival.

The sign and the burro are the last vestiges of the placer mining that created a town here. The tall ponderosa pines for which the place was named have disappeared long since, the victim of man's greed for lumber. Mine dumps slash the scrub-covered mountains, the relics of man's greed for gold.

But on a hill above town towers a cross, a symbol that man can live in peace. The story of that cross starts long before there was even a town here in the gulch of Bear Creek.

Some say it started as early as 1800, when Spanish prospectors discovered gold in the gravel in the bed of the stream. They built walls of adobe and rocks amid the pines to protect themselves against the Apaches. The Indians hadn't the faintest interest in the glittering dust that powdered the streambed. This was part of their hunting grounds. When the Spanish intruded the Indians reacted with characteristic hostility.

When they were through, a number of the Spaniards lay dead. The survivors soon departed for safer territory, leaving only some ruins of walls behind them in testimony that they had been here at all. This suited the Apaches handsomely. They had the pine-clad mountains to themselves — until history played a dirty trick on them in the form of the California Gold Rush of 1849.

By 1860 a backwash had developed from the flood of humanity that swamped the Golden Gate. Three drifters known to history as Thomas Birch, Colonel Snively and a man named Hicks were caught in that backwash. Stopping in Mesilla, New Mexico, the trio heard rumors about gold in the Bear Creek country and promptly headed that way.

They were no better and probably no worse than most of the people who created history on the American frontier. Birch, known among his friends as "Three-fingered Birch," apparently had fled from Rock Island, Illinois, with a $1500 price on his head for the murder of a Colonel Davenport.

The men made camp on Bear Creek near its junction with the Little Cherry on May 18, 1860. Legend has it that Three-Fingered Birch bent over to drink out of Bear Creek and promptly spotted gold dust sparkling in the bottom. He shouted to his companions and all three fell to panning the gravel with a vengeance. Within a day or two each man had panned a whole handful of gold but they lacked provisions for a long stay.

They returned quietly to Santa Rita, where they let Thomas J. Marston and his brother, Virgil, in on their secret. They told the two to buy supplies as unobtrusively as possible, but as anyone knows you can't muffle word about gold. By the time the three men returned to their Bear Creek diggings, other miners had shown up. The entire gulch was swarming with people within a few weeks. Seven hundred were crammed into the camp of "Birchville" by September.

Then along came somebody with some romance in his soul who decided that Birchville was much too common a name to hang on a town in such a magnificent setting. Other residents agreed. Birchville became Pinos Altos, which means "Tall Pines." The three-fingered discoverer of the place probably did not mind. He was busy trying to get some of the riches he missed in California.

Nearly every miner averaged between ten dollars and fifteen dollars a day by panning the stream. Captain James H. Tevis, an Arizona scout who arrived on Bear Creek that summer, reported he *always* cleared twenty-five dollars a day above his expenses. Sometimes, he said, he netted as much as $600!

Such easy riches attracted another form of "miner" — soft-handed fellows more skillful with a deck of cards than with a pick and shovel. A dance hall was one of the first permanent structures in camp. After all, there had to be amusement.

Six-shooters provided some of the fun. An impromptu dueling ground developed on the edge of town. The Catholic Church stands on that bloody spot today.

There was a shortage of women at first. Some camp followers — prostitutes and dance-hall girls — wandered in, but few respectable females. Thus, when Rhoda Parker, twenty-five-year-old daughter of a miner from Iowa arrived, it created a real sensation. Captain Tevis recalled:

"She seemed amused to have the miners staring at her like a lot of lunatics. She was a small woman, weighing perhaps ninety pounds, and good looking. She wore a broad-brimmed hat and tight fitting dress, with a skirt quite short. She looked to be about sixteen, but we learned that she was really twenty-five years of age."

There were some small children in camp and no teacher. It seemed natural that Miss Parker should take over this job. She was glad to do it and the miners were equally glad to cough up $2.50 apiece to pay her for her trouble.

According to Captain Tevis, Miss Parker received 300 bona fide proposals of marriage from the miners. She once showed him a whole basketful of love letters. But Miss Parker turned all her suitors down. Later, when the Indian trouble flared, she and her father left the mining camp never to return.

At least one celebrity-to-be was among the swarm of goldseekers thronging Bear Creek Gulch. Roy Bean and his brother were there. Roy later settled in a little west-Texas town called Vinegaroon and made quite a name for himself as "The Law West of the Pecos."

Pinos Altos population ballooned to 1500 by December, 1860. Tom Marston discovered the first gold vein that same month and opened what became known as the Pacific Mine. He sold it the following spring to his brother. Other hardrock strikes followed, apparently insuring some kind of permanency for the log-and-tent city along the gulch. But not all was golden.

The Apaches lurked in the shadows among the fragrant pines. They had a word for the white men who were messing up their hunting grounds. They called them "god-dammies." Just to remind the miners that they were considered interlopers, they would now and then pick off a white man from ambush and relieve him of his scalp. It was enough to give a man nightmares.

Captain Tevis never forgot his own terrifying experience when some Apaches forced him to watch while they burned two of his friends alive, then made him stand in a fire until his boots burned off.

The great Mimbres Apache Chief Mangas Colorado (Red Sleeves) decided that the only thing keeping all these men in the Pinos Altos Mountains was gold. So he rode up to the fledgling mining camp with a proposition. If they would leave, he would personally lead them to a great gold deposit Victorio had found south of the border. For an answer the miners seized him, tied him tight, gave him a sound horsewhipping and sent him back to the Mimbres country.

The Mimbres chief, smarting with pain and humiliation, took his problems over into Arizona where Cochise, greatest Apache of all, was encountering his own troubles with the "white eyes." The whites had falsely accused Cochise of murder and had seized him by treachery but he escaped, vowing eternal revenge.

The two Indians agreed to pool their braves for an attack on Pinos Altos. They would fix the "god-dammies" for once and all.

In the pre-dawn darkness of September

Pinos Altos as it appeared in the late '80s

26, 1861, the chiefs massed 400 war-painted braves on the hills around the mining camp. Stealthily they encircled the town and, when the sun peeked over the horizon, the great chiefs gave a signal and the horde of screaming savages struck Pinos Altos from all sides.

Luckily the miners and prospectors in the camp strung up and down Bear Creek kept themselves prepared for just such an event. Their guns were close at hand. Tom Marston was captain of the Arizona Scouts militia unit in the camp. He quickly organized a defense and before many minutes passed guns were barking at the Indians.

The Apaches charged again and again, only to be repulsed each time by Captain Marston's militia. The battle continued until noon when the Indians withdrew, leaving fifteen of their number dead on the field.

Casualties in Pinos Altos were considerably lighter. Two men had been killed and eight others wounded, including the heroic Captain Marston. His wounds were mortal and he died within the week.

Marston's brother, Virgil, survived the fight to continue mining. But he himself was a victim of the Apaches on May 18, 1868, while returning to Pinos Altos from Mesilla. Riding in a buggy, accompanied by two men on horseback, Marston was attacked by a band of redskins. The riders escaped and Marston fought off the savages for awhile but finally was killed.

Although the Cochise-Mangas Colorado

attack didn't achieve its immediate aim — the destruction of Pinos Altos — it had some serious implications for the community. A great many miners suddenly thought of more important things that required their presence elsewhere. The Civil War was one. To many, Union and Confederate sympathizers alike, the possibility of death on a "civilized" battlefield seemed infinitely more desirable than at the hand of the cruel Apache.

An exodus from Bear Creek followed. A few hundred stalwarts remained, however, determined not to let the redskins keep them from the riches they were convinced lay just within reach.

Cochise meanwhile had returned to Arizona to harry the settlers there. Mangas Colorado stayed in New Mexico, still seething, but biding his time. He noted with interest the arrival of a hundred militiamen under Major Waller in the Bear Creek camp. They had been sent by Governor Baylor.

The wily Apache knew that he lacked the manpower to gain victory over such a force, but trickery might succeed. Aware that the few women residents of Pinos Altos had fled after that first raid, he decided to strike at the miners in their weakest spot. Selecting the most beautiful of the young women of his tribe, he stationed them on the hillside above the town as bait.

There, in full view of the lonely Bear Creek miners, the girls paraded their charms in a kind of strip tease, sensuously combing their long black hair. It was too much for the virile young men in the camp below. Most of them started a mad rush up the hillside toward the Indian maidens.

Mangas Colorado's Mimbrenos ambushed them before they made it, hitting the whites from both sides, then cutting off their retreat down the hill. By the time it was over, the miners had suffered forty casualties.

By this time, the United States Army decided something had to be done about Mangas Colorado, who so far had shown himself to be a far more skillful general than most of the West Pointers. The Army commanders decided that if they couldn't lick him by force, they would try stealth. On orders from General Carleton, a message was sent to the chief inviting him to Fort McLane for a peace parley under safe conduct.

Mangas Colorado, who should have known better, accepted the invitation, only to be promptly imprisoned. On January 18, 1863, some soldiers shot him to death "while attempting to escape." A few days later, his wife was captured and taken to Pinos Altos, where she was murdered.

By this time, one would think that the Indians would never trust a white man under any conditions. But they did. Long enough, in fact, to sign a peace treaty that allowed them to come into Pinos Altos to barter.

Thereupon a miner hospitably invited as many Indians as would come to visit his home for a feast celebrating the new treaty. Sixty naive Apaches showed up. Once they were in the house, the host and several assorted friends opened fire on them with pistols and rifles, leaving several dead and others severely wounded.

From that day on it was unsafe for a white man to venture beyond the camp unarmed. When the Civil War ended and the men returned to town the trouble subsided, but never for very long. Once, a Navajo band drove off some oxen and were chased by a Pinos Altos posse. A hot battle in the woodlands left thirteen Navajos dead.

Finally, in 1874, the white men and the Indians agreed to stop killing each other. They agreed that a large wooden cross would be erected on a hill overlooking the town as a symbol of friendship. The Indians gave a solemn oath that so long as the cross stood, there would be no more trouble.

They kept their word. And so, for a change, did the whites.

That first wooden cross was covered with tin. It stood for thirty-three years and then crumbled away. By then, of course, all danger of Indian trouble had vanished. Pinos Altos residents erected a replacement in 1907 but this also eventually surrendered to the elements.

In 1963 George Schafer III, whose grandfather, George Schafer, settled here in the early days, started a campaign to replace the cross. Residents raised the money and installed a new one on the site of the first. It was built to last — fashioned of four-inch pipe set in concrete.

Pinos Altos really started moving about the time that first cross was erected. For a time it seemed that gold was to be found almost anywhere anybody cared to sink a pick. All sorts of strikes were uncovered. As usual, the names the miners gave to the claims were as colorful as the town itself. Naturally, there was a "Hard Scrabble" and a "Pride of the West." More original, perhaps, were "The Gopher" and "The Kept Woman."

Arrastras, primitive ore-crushing devices, were everywhere. They were the epitome of simplicity, resembling shallow cisterns of stone. A mule walked around the bowl dragging a giant granite slab that crushed the ore. It was said that at one point there were seventy-five *arrastras* in operation here.

When Grant County was split off from Dona Ana, Pinos Altos served briefly as the county seat. A courthouse was built and the first (and only) term of court set off an enormous celebration enlivened by refreshments, a brass band and two executions. Alas, Silver City politicians were already at work and

Among the relics of mining days in Pinos Altos is a rusty winch

before you could say "foul" the county seat had been moved.

An unusual aspect of the town was its flowers. Many residents strove to outdo each other in their flower gardens. Many fruit trees were planted. The overall result was to give Pinos Altos a far glossier appearance than most mining camps.

By the 'eighties and 'nineties, several thousand people were crowded into the town, which had two hotels, a drugstore, clothing stores and a Turkish bath. Then a decline set in as the gold ore began to play out.

Optimism soared in 1906, when the long sought narrow-gauge railroad reached the camp, simplifying transportation of ore to the Silver City smelters. For some time the trains accepted paying riders who would climb aboard the tops of the loaded ore cars. This practice continued until a string of returning cars came loose on the steep grade and plunged off a curve into a gulch. That ended the excursions.

If the coming of the rails was good news to Pinos Altos, the same year saw bad news as well. George Hearst, father of newspaper tycoon William Randolph Hearst, chose that

Door of the old but still graceful Mormon church, Pinos Altos

The first schoolhouse in Pinos Altos

year to sell his widespread holdings in the local mines. It was a bad omen. The end was nearly in sight.

The richest gold ore had long since been mined out, leaving much ore but of a far different variety. That which was left was complex, containing lead, zinc and other base metals. It required complicated and costly processes to separate.

People began to drift away. Stores began to close. Decay set in, but not death; now and then there were brief signs of life. In 1911 Ira Wright and James Bell struck what looked like a bonanza in the Pacific Mine, which they had leased. One load of ore weighing 18,000 pounds netted them $43,000. It was only a pocket, however. Wright and Bell did not renew their lease and the exodus from Pinos Altos resumed. Before long, the camp was practically a ghost town.

During the depression of the early 'thirties a strange new crop of goldseekers thronged the hills around Bear Creek. These were the pitiful jobless men from the breadlines, trying to scrape enough gold from the hills and the creek beds to stay alive. They dug around abandoned mines and dumps and filled the gulches with activity as they panned and operated rocker devices designed to separate gold from the gravel.

Probably they got very little except aching muscles and blistered hands. It was small comfort to them to know that the United States Bureau of Mines estimated that the Pinos Altos mines had produced more than $8,000,000 in gold, lead, silver and copper.

Today it takes a careful eye to detect boom-camp relics in the town. There are reminders of those days, of course, like that crassly commercial sign and the live jackass on the outskirts of town.

The Pinos Altos Mercantile Store and Post Office is the principal business establishment. There are only a few others: a bar, a couple of eating places and a service station. Just enough to serve a suburban bedroom community, which is what Pinos Altos is today.

Decaying rapidly is the old but still graceful adobe Mormon Church on a side street. Touches of the past can be spotted at various points. A weed-grown, hard-rubber-tired truck rusts away in the grass behind the post office. Nearby is a grindstone, somewhat the worse for wear. There are wagon wheels in endless abundance, appropriately weathered and worn.

Across the street from the store is the first schoolhouse in Pinos Altos, built of logs. It bears a metal marker but no one seems to pay much attention. On the highway overlooking what is left of the town is the quaint

In the town graveyard, Pinos Altos

little Catholic Church, the one built on the old dueling grounds. Its pale-blue door and the bell hung on a log support are its distinguishing features.

Nearby is the town graveyard, filled with old decaying headstones and many artfully carved wooden crosses. Under a juniper tree only a few feet from the road are the gravestones of Thomas J. and Virgil Marston, heroic pioneers, both victims of the Apaches.

If you are ambitious enough to hike to the top of the hill you can see the modern cross that symbolizes the peace the people of Pinos Altos eventually found in their relations with the savages of the forest.

The Pinos Altos Catholic church has a pale-blue door and a bell on a log support

Looking down on Tyrone in the days when it was called the "Million Dollar Ghost Town"

20 | The Town That Beat the Odds

Tyrone was born as a copper camp, then rebuilt as the most beautiful model mining town in the world, only to die soon after it was completed. The town that slumbered for forty-six years as "The Million Dollar Ghost Town" now is being resurrected on a far grander scale than before. Seldom does a mining town get a second chance, particularly when the second life is based on the same mineral. The odds against it are enormous, like drawing to an inside straight in a poker game.

Tyrone lies only ten miles south of Silver City (sixteen south of Pinos Altos), and a mile west of New Mexico 90. Its setting is the Burro Mountains, a lonely brown range of desert hills speckled with the twisted shapes of scrub oak and piñon and juniper.

The pale pastel hills looked just the same when man first found minerals beneath them. The Spanish probably were first but they didn't linger long and left few marks in their passing. It was the 1870s and 1880s before the Burros really came into their own. The 'seventies and 'eighties were great mining years throughout the West. Prospectors found gold and silver and other minerals in many sections. Miners who arrived on the scene of a rich strike too late quickly took off for the next hill or mountain. In those days it didn't pay to tarry; there was often too much at stake.

Some of those lonely wanderers found rich blue copper ore in the Burros. (They also found turquoise but weren't much interested because the copper seemed so much more worthwhile.) So the digging commenced and the word traveled far and wide, exaggerated each time it was repeated. The men came to the strike on foot and on horse and muleback, in wagons and buggies and carts. And just behind them followed the gamblers and the con men and the prostitutes and the dance-hall girls and in due course a camp sprouted.

Sprouted is the right word. Unplanned. It came up like a weed.

Actually, there were two camps. One was called Leopold, for obscure reasons. The other was named Tyrone by a nostalgic Irishman after a mountainous county in the far-off north of the Emerald Isle.

The two were like a thousand other Western camps, a hodgepodge of tents and unpainted shanties and false-fronts weaving in the restless wind. They were built in a hurry, to provide shelter. No one in either town took the time to worry about the niceties of civilization.

By 1904 the two towns were flourishing like weeds in a compost heap, getting uglier and dirtier every year. But forces were working to change all that. The mines had by now mostly gravitated into the ownership of the Burro Mountain Copper Company, a large concern. And about this time, an even larger firm began to eye the Burro Mountains copper.

This was the giant Phelps Dodge Company, one of the world's largest mining firms. The company was already active in New Mexico, operating coal mines at Dawson (Chapter 11). Phelps Dodge began buying stock in Burro Mountain Company until it owned all of it. This meant *everything* — mines, minerals, both little towns and, figuratively speaking, everyone in them.

By now it was 1915 and the war in Europe was creating a great demand for such things as cannon and shells and cartridges for rifles and machine guns. These required copper, something there was in abundance around Tyrone and Leopold. The price of copper soared.

Phelps Dodge decided to expand its Burro mining. The great company immediately realized that little Tyrone and Leopold were totally inadequate to take care of the population increase the expansion would bring. The answer was simple: build a new town.

At this point, the wife of Cleland Dodge, one of the principal owners of the giant company, enters the history of Tyrone. Mrs. Dodge had a burst of inspiration. She suggested to her husband that the "new" mining camp be made a model for all the world to see.

Why not prove, once and for all, that a mining town can be beautiful — more beautiful, in fact, than an ordinary city? Why not make it a pleasant place to live instead of a dirty, slatternly shantytown of company houses?

Why not? Cleland Dodge like the idea. So did his board of directors. Phelps Dodge would build a model mining town and old Tyrone and Leopold would vanish.

The company decided to go first class all the way in its endeavor by hiring the most famous architect in the world. Bertram

Tyrone's company store, framed by an arch of one of the stores across the street

Goodhue seemed to fit that description admirably. Goodhue's work first caught the firm's eye at the Panama-California International Exposition of 1915 in San Diego. Many of those grandiose buildings still exist in a San Diego park. Their style was Spanish mission, the prevailing architectural "influence" of the day.

Goodhue had also designed the United States Military Academy at West Point, the National Academy of Sciences in Washington, D.C., the University of Chicago Chapel,

St. Thomas's Church in New York and the Nebraska State Capitol at Lincoln, to name but a few of his works.

Phelps Dodge made its announcement on April 13, 1915: Goodhue had been commissioned to design a model mining camp at Tyrone. It would utilize the most modern mining techniques and would be a completely planned community, said the company.

Goodhue's master plan included a hotel, two churches, railroad station, opera house, trading post, department store, library, jail and justice court, theater, garage and service station, mining office, hospital and school. Wartime shortages prevented construction of the Catholic Church and opera house. Everything else was built.

The new Tyrone was completed in 1917 and the mining world marveled. As Mrs. Dodge had foreseen, it was unique.

A plaza, 1500 feet long by 300 feet, was the center of the town. Crisscrossed by walks and planted with grass, flowers and shrubs, it was encircled by a wide drive. The rest of the city was a picture of pale-pink stucco and red-tiled roofs and graceful arches in the tradition of Old Spain. It was bright and beautiful. Flowers bloomed everywhere.

The company store was the most imposing structure, the largest such building in New Mexico. It was three stories tall with a lofty "bell" tower, minus bell. The front was crossed by a long veranda lined with arches. The store offered groceries, clothing, dry goods, furniture and home furnishings. An undertaker was located on the premises. An elevator was available to those who didn't want to walk up the wide ornamental staircase to the mezzanine. A big warehouse behind the store was linked to it by a second-floor walkway over the railroad tracks.

Goodhue's stucco railroad station was next door, replete with splashing fountains lined with specially made Mexican tile and surrounded by the arched walkways that were a Tyrone trademark.

Another store building stood across the plaza, somewhat smaller but quite adequate. The company rented space there to outside merchants to sell in competition with every department of the company store. The same building also housed the post office. An imposing two-story structure next door housed company offices. Marble pillars flanked the ornate doorway.

A school capable of taking care of 300 pupils was erected nearby. The company built one-story apartment houses for Mexican laborers in a canyon southwest of the store, providing every modern convenience. A second apartment in another canyon housed 1500 people.

Goodhue created a Mediterranean town on the hill overlooking the plaza, with scores of neat, tiled-roof stucco houses for the miners. Designs were varied to avoid the look of a "company town." They were painted in pastel shades of pink, tan, blue and green.

The company built T. S. Parker Hospital farther out on the ridge, also in Spanish-mission style. It offered a magnificent view in all directions. The ultra-modern hospital had two operating rooms containing some of

The company store in Tyrone in 1966; a long veranda lined with arches is in front

the first ventilated operating lights in the U.S. The X-ray room was air-conditioned. The pharmacy offered an unusual filing system permitting nurses to dispense drugs from coded bins without a bottle in sight. Indirect lighting throughout the hospital was a real innovation.

Fifteen hundred people lived in the camp when Phelps Dodge started its mammoth undertaking in 1915. The population had ballooned to 4000 when the model city was completed two years later. The company bought a new Packard truck to haul forty miners to work at a time and bring back a load of children to school.

Old Leopold had disappeared. The only relic was the barred door on a mine tunnel that once had served as a jail. Old Tyrone was gone too, absorbed into the new. Miners, used to filth and disorder in mine towns, were overwhelmed. Tyrone looked like Utopia to them.

Copper production hit a peak in 1918. The world was coming up roses in the Burro Mountains. The mines were designed to turn a profit on fifteen-cent a pound copper; in 1918 it was selling at twenty-eight and one-half cents.

Then the war ended and copper prices plummeted. Soon afterward the rich veins of copper began to pinch out. By 1921 the mines were producing ore containing only two-per-cent copper. With the price drop, other mines producing richer copper were being forced to close.

In 1921 Cleland Dodge paid a personal visit to the beautiful little city he had created there in the tawny hills. A great crowd of miners met him in the sun-splashed plaza and offered him a proposition.

If he would keep the camp open, they would accept a twenty-five-per-cent cut in wages. Sadly Dodge shook his head. It just

Burro Mountain Copper Company office-building entrance, Tyrone

wasn't financially feasible. Tyrone must die.

As he decreed, death came within two weeks. The company was helpful, running a special train to El Paso filled with Mexican workers. At El Paso the Mexican government provided free transportation to agricultural areas in Chihuahua. Other miners drifted away to other mine camps, as miners have done time out of mind.

Some, who got jobs in Silver City, continued to live in the pretty little stucco houses on the hill. A crew of watchmen was kept on duty by the company to protect buildings from vandals. Windows were boarded up on all the grand buildings around the plaza. The lovely green lawn in the square died from lack of water. The dusty green of Russian thistle (tumbleweed) and chamiso took over.

Plaster began to fall off the buildings of

Tyrone. Roofs began to leak. Vandals broke off the colored tiles in the depot and carried them away. The company fenced off the buildings to keep visitors from being hurt by falling debris. And there were plenty of visitors.

Ghost town it had become, and a magnetic one. For unique as it had been in life it was more so in death. Tyrone's new reputation was as the most unusual ghost town in the West, an offbeat tourist attraction that drew thousands annually.

It presented a sad picture, this once great town abandoned to the sagebrush and the cactus and the wild things that inhabit these mountains. It was an intriguing place of sunlight and shadows, a place that made you think of Granada or Valladolid or Madrid, or some ancient city of the Middle East or Asia.

And always there remained the residents on the hills, who were permitted to rent those little houses at reasonable rates. They came and went, hardly aware of the sad decaying beauty there in the plaza.

As in the case of every ghost town, there were tantalizing rumors that Tyrone would bloom again. Nobody paid any attention to them. It was just small talk.

Phelps Dodge, however, hadn't given up on its unique creation. In the 1950s, the company conducted a large core-drilling project to determine the extent and the grade of the ore still underground. When the job was completed in 1958 the drillers packed up their tools and moved away. The latest rumors quickly died.

Meanwhile a mystery apparently unconnected to Tyrone was intriguing farmers

Elaborate façade of Phelps Dodge company store, Tyrone. Right, *Arched walkways were typical features of the Tyrone buildings designed by Bertram Goodhue*

along the Gila River. Ben Ormond, Sr., a resident of the area, and his son spent nearly ten years buying land and water rights along the river in the name of the Western Pacific Land Company.

The mystery was solved in 1966 in New York City. Robert G. Page, Phelps Dodge Corporation president, announced that the firm would spend $100,000,000 developing a completely new copper operation at Tyrone. Water for the gigantic operation would come from water rights on the Gila, acquired by the company's "wholly-owned subsidiary, Western Pacific Land Company."

The new mine would be completely different from the old shaft-and-tunnel mines. It would be a mammoth openpit copper mine similar to the one run by Kennecott at Santa Rita. To get at the ore it would be necessary to strip off some 50,000,000 tons of overburden, a project expected to take eighteen months. The pit itself would cover about 100 acres. The company owned mineral rights to 10,000 surrounding acres.

Immediately after the announcement crews began moving heavy machinery into old Tyrone to build a power plant, machine shops, buildings, wells, a pumping plant and pipelines. The Santa Fe Railway began re-laying tracks along the abandoned roadbed of old.

So big was the project that Phelps Dodge expected it would take three or four years to get the mine in full production. It will boost total United States copper production by three and one-half per cent, no insignificant amount. The mine will increase Phelps Dodge's own copper production by twenty per cent. Already the firm was producing 275,000 tons of the metal a year. Tyrone suddenly came alive again. Trucks and bulldozers began to thunder in the streets. The company reopened its ornate old office building. The move was only temporary. The principal copper deposits lie deep beneath the center of the old plaza. When the giant earth-moving machines moved into the million-dollar ghost town the first thing they did was to destroy the old department store and the grandiose depot. Eventually, said Phelps Dodge, even those fifty or so houses on the hill would have to go also.

However, a contract was let quickly and construction started on a completely new city, which will be a "model" community, according to the company. This new 120-acre townsite was laid out in the foothills between the mine and Silver City. It has winding, paved drives. Millions are being spent to erect more than 200 two- and three-bedroom houses for mine employees.

All are of Spanish style and all will be ultra-modern, just like those houses built so long ago over the fabulous plaza there in the Burros.

There was a familiar ring to the words of the *El Paso Herald-Post* story describing the new townsite:

The residences, of Spanish architecture, promise to make the new Tyrone the outstanding example of mining town architecture in the Southwest.

It sounded just like 1915 all over again.

Columbus the day after Villa's raid

21 | The Mark of Pancho Villa

Pancho Villa changed the future for Columbus, a little town on the plains thirty-two miles south of Deming on New Mexico 11. The Mexican bandit led his forces in an attack on the then prosperous little community one dark March night in 1916. It was the first invasion of United States soil by foreign troops since the War of 1812. Columbus has never been the same since.

That single overwhelming event changed the place forever. Until then, the prospects were bright. True, it had gotten a late start as New Mexico towns go. Colonel A. O. Bailey, a Civil War veteran who had moved West for the health of his son Frank, laid out the town in 1891. He chose a townsite three miles north of the Mexican border town of Las Palomas, which was to have been the northern terminus of a Mexican railroad that never came to be.

Judge B. Y. McKeyes of Deming apparently chose the name Columbus, after first suggesting "Columbia," after the Columbian Exposition. But the Post Office Department rejected that one and Columbus was the second choice.

Colonel Bailey had only fair success at promoting his town until 1903, when Columbus became a stop on the new El Paso & Southwestern Railroad, connecting El Paso

Pancho Villa in 1914, about two years before he led his dorados in the Columbus raid

within a short time became one of the leading citizens of Columbus. Ravel opened a general store that was an almost overnight success, then later built a three-story hotel called "The Commercial" on Taft Avenue. He soon became interested in other business ventures in the town.

By the spring of 1916, Columbus seemed to be doing quite well. Better, in fact, than its promoters had expected. The population had already topped 700 and more people were moving in. The town had a bank, two other hotels and a weekly newspaper, *The Columbus Courier.*

That spring there was little in the way of local excitement to stir things up in the town. Some townsfolk were concerned about the possibility of United States involvement in the war in Europe, but not many: the thunder of guns seemed very far away from the arid plains of southwestern New Mexico.

A few rumors were adrift that Francisco "Pancho" Villa, Mexican bandit and revolutionary, might raid *some* border town. Hardly anyone in Columbus paid any attention to the reports. After all, just across the tracks were stationed nearly 500 members of the Army's 13th Cavalry. Anyway, latest reports were that Villa would raid Ciudad Juarez, across the border from El Paso.

What the good residents of Columbus didn't know was that Villa had picked out his target as early as February 16. The swarthy, mustachioed guerrilla leader was then hiding out in the rugged mountains of Chihuahua, licking his wounds. Fighting a war against the Carranza government of Mexico, Villa had come to grips with his enemy the previous November at Agua Prieta. On the verge of victory he saw it snatched suddenly from him because of two abrupt actions by the United States.

and Douglas, Arizona. When the United States designated the fledgling town as an official port of entry, Columbus was on its way. Settlers began moving into the town, which was the trading center and rail connection for a vast ranching area in the plains of southern New Mexico.

Promoters helped things along by soliciting both businesses and residents for the town. One man thus lured was a Jewish immigrant from El Paso named Sam Ravel, who

The Wilson government had recognized the Carranza government, then let Carranza reinforce his beleagured forces by shipping 3000 troops and artillery on trains across United States territory from Eagle Pass, Texas to Douglas, Arizona.

The result had been a shattering defeat for Villa. The bandit leader retreated into the mountains with only a tattered remnant of his army. He was bitter and furious at the United States for what he considered a betrayal but his first concern was arms and men.

At Hacienda San Geronimo, Chihuahua, 120 miles south of the border, Villa pondered his problem and thought of Sam Ravel, from whom he had bought supplies three years before. Villa, apparently believing he still had several hundred dollars' credit with the Columbus merchant, sent General Candelario Cervantes to Columbus to buy some guns from Ravel. When the Mexican showed up in Columbus that February, Ravel not only wouldn't sell him guns, he threatened to throw him out of the store.

When Villa heard the news he flew into a rage. Eleven days later, he moved out of his headquarters at the head of his *dorados*. He knew exactly where he was going.

On March 1 his *Villistas* raided the Edward John Wright ranch at Pearson, Chihuahua, taking Wright, his wife and baby and another American prisoner.

On March 7, Villa reached the Boca Grande River only thirty miles southwest of Columbus. He led a rag-tag army of 500 mounted Mexicans, many of whom had joined him along the way. They were spoiling for trouble. When they spotted a group of cowboys from the Palomas Land and Cattle Company on spring roundup, they attacked. They killed three of the cowboys in the first volley, then took others prisoner.

Juan Favela, superintendent of the outfit, managed to escape and he rode at a gallop toward the border. He found a lieutenant and three troops of the 13th Cavalry and poured out his story. They told him to take his report to Colonel Herbert J. Slocum, commanding officer at Columbus.

Favela climbed back aboard his horse and went on to Columbus. He found the colonel and related the story to him. Colonel Slocum seemed uninterested.

"You just run your business, Juan," said the colonel. "And I'll take care of running the Army."

Favela said Colonel Slocum also warned him not to say anything about the incident around Columbus because it would "upset the town."

It was now becoming pretty obvious that the wily bandit was up to something. General John J. Pershing at Fort Bliss was studying intelligence reports that Villa planned an attack north of the border — possibly El Paso — with an army of 15,000 men.

On March 8, the same day Villa's band killed the three cowpokes at Boca Grande, the *El Paso Times* carried this front-page story:

Information received in El Paso last night from the 13th Cavalry, stationed at Columbus, New Mexico, was to the effect that Villa had been sighted 15 miles west of Palomas Monday night, and was camped there all day Tuesday. What his plans are at this time is not known.

The article also reported that Villa was allegedly planning on attacking Palomas, the Mexican town only three miles south of Columbus.

Pershing knew that Villa was in that vicinity. Army Intelligence had told him on March 7 that the bandit was camped south of Columbus.

Meanwhile, Villa, camped in Boca Grande, was alarmed that the Americans might have been alerted by those who escaped his clutches at the cattle camp. It was March 8. Villa fretted, then sent Lieutenant Colonel Cipriano Vargas and another officer into Columbus to scout. They returned at noon, convinced that there were only about thirty U.S. troopers on the post.

At four p.m. Villa mounted Taurino, his favorite roan, and led his "army" toward Columbus. It was a colorful but ragged group. Tall Mexican *sombreros* were everywhere. Many of the bearded riders wore double bandoleers of cartridges. They wore tattered clothing and some of them had no weapons.

Villa reached the border about one a.m. on March 9 and cut the fence at a point about two and a half miles west of the Palomas gate. The raiders moved quietly to a point within a few hundred yards of Columbus. Villa assembled his men and gave them their battle orders. He said he would remain with the reserve.

"*Vayanse adelante, muchachos!*" Villa commanded and his troops formed a skirmish line facing east.

It was deathly still in the desert that moonless morning. Darkness enveloped the sleeping town. Only a few people were awake in Columbus and in the military post south of the tracks.

One of them was Lieutenant John P. Lucas, a veteran of Phillippines action. He had been in El Paso with the regimental polo team and had returned on the midnight train, known locally as the "drummers'" or "drunkards'" special.

Lucas arrived at his quarters and routinely checked his single-action revolver. His roommate, Lieutenant O. C. Benson had removed the shells. For some reason, it suddenly seemed important to Lucas that the pistol be reloaded. He moved some boxes to get to his trunk and find shells. Then he fell into bed and almost immediately went to sleep.

He was awakened soon afterward by the whinny of a horse just outside his adobe quarters. He sat up, listening. More horses passed his window. Lieutenant Lucas's pulse raced. He reached swiftly for the .45 he had so painstakingly reloaded and slipped to the window, peering into the blackness.

Then he spotted the *sombreros* and heard men speaking in Spanish, their voices low. They were using military terms. The horsemen were moving directly toward his quarters.

Lieutenant Lucas was alarmed. He stepped backward to the center of his room, thumbing back the hammer of his six-gun. He pointed it at the door, waiting.

Across the Deming road, Private Fred Griffin of Troop K paced back and forth before regimental headquarters. He heard a noise and whirled, swinging his rifle into firing position. Peering into the darkness he saw shadows moving toward Lieutenant Lucas' quarters. The men were mounted. . . .

"Who goes there?" he challenged.

"*Viva Mexico!*" came the shout.

The entire group of horsemen spun about and charged the young private. Griffin triggered his 1903 Springfield as the guerrillas opened fire on him. A 7-mm. Mauser bullet slammed Griffin back against the headquarters wall and he slumped, continuing to fire and operate the bolt on the rifle until it was empty. Two other bullets thudded into his lifeless, crumpled body. Three Mexicans lay dead in front of him. The battle of Columbus had begun.

Some of Pershing's expeditionary force on review before starting in pursuit of Villa's raiders

Rifles began cracking from all over the west and north sides of town, almost like firecrackers on the Fourth of July. The hoofs of horses thundered on the dirt streets. Mexican shouts came from all sides:

"*Viva Villa! Viva Mexico! Muerte a los gringos!*"

A bullet slammed into the clock on the wall at the depot, stopping the hands at exactly eleven minutes past four.

Surprise completely on their side, the *Villistas* quickly enveloped the town and the army camp. A group headed for Sam Ravel's store on Broadway, where Sam's sons, Arthur and Louis, were asleep in the back room.

They were awakened by shouts in Mexican and loud pounding on the front door. Arthur, fourteen, went to open it. His elder brother, Louis, crouched under some hides, out of sight. The door burst inward the

moment it was unlocked and a couple of bearded Mexicans grabbed Arthur, demanding the whereabouts of Sam Ravel.

He had gone to El Paso to see a doctor, gasped Arthur. The Mexicans didn't believe him. They tore the store apart searching for Sam, then started carrying off everything they could lay their hands on. They asked Arthur to give them the safe's combination but he told them he didn't know it.

The *Villistas* now took Arthur to Taft Avenue and the Commercial Hotel, figuring Sam might be there. Two of them held the youth in an iron grasp. The guerrillas already had the hotel surrounded. Ten or fifteen of them rushed inside and dragged out three men and a woman. One of the men was John Walton Walker. He was torn from the arms of his bride of twenty-eight days and shot to death on the stairs. The Mexicans shot the

During Pershing's punitive expedition Army biplanes were stationed at Columbus and flew reconnaissance flights over Mexican territory

other three men dead, then aimed their guns at the woman.

She shouted, *"Viva Mexico!"* and the *Villistas* lowered their guns and let her go free.

The raiders hauled Steve Birchfield from an upstairs room, searched him and took his cash. They threatened to shoot him because he had so little money.

"No, *muchachos*," said Birchfield. "That's all the cash I have on me, but I do have my checkbook. I'll just write out what you want."

The Mexicans examined the checkbook skeptically, until one of them, Eligio Hernandez, vouched for Birchfield. The Mexican had once been helped by the American. Birchfield cheerfully wrote checks payable to each of the Mexicans and they spared his life.

The *Villistas* put the hotel to the torch after they sacked it. The dry wood caught like kindling and within minutes orange flames roared skyward. The fire illuminated the entire central section of town with a garish, flickering light.

The two Mexicans holding Arthur Ravel started back to the store. Just before they reached it gunshots dropped both raiders. Arthur, still in his underwear, started running and didn't stop until he had covered three miles.

Those first shots back at the camp had aroused the garrison. Private Griffin's challenge had undoubtedly saved Lieutenant Lucas's life. We left Lucas in his quarters, gun in hand, facing the doorway. He heard Griffin's voice and saw the raiders turn on the sentry.

When the gunfire subsided and the Mexicans moved on, Lieutenant Lucas ran across the road to Private Griffin. Lucas was barefooted and only partly dressed. He saw that Griffin was dead, then hurried to the barracks, shouting:

"Turn out the men and follow me!"

Lucas commanded the machine guns of the 13th. From the barracks he ran toward the guard tent where the guns were locked up. There he found Private J. D. Yarbrough, his right arm shattered by a dum-dum bullet, firing on a band of raiders with his pistol held in his left hand.

Lucas and some of the soldiers who were now joining him put the Mexicans to flight, then had to batter the locked door to the guard tent down to get at the Benet-Mercier machine guns. The lieutenant ordered one gun taken to the front of the depot where it could control the point where the road crossed the tracks. Only a few rounds were fired before the gun jammed. Within minutes, the soldiers had three other machine guns in place, chattering into the night.

Lieutenant James P. Castleman, officer of the day, was having an extremely quiet tour of duty. So much so that he had greeted the "drunkards' special" when it arrived, then checked the camp and returned to his quarters.

It was about 4:15 a.m. when he heard the shots fired by and at Private Griffin. Drawing his .45, the lieutenant raced out of the O.D. quarters to find himself facing a sombreroed Mexican with a rifle pointed directly at him. An instant later the *Villista's* rifle belched fire and smoke, but the bullet somehow missed. The Mexican dropped an instant later, hit by Castleman's bullet.

Rifle fire was rattling from all over the camp. With bullets whistling all around him, Castleman ran for the guard tent, then the stables and finally to his own unit, Troop F. Mustering his own troop and others whose commanders were trapped in Columbus, Castleman led an advance on regimental headquarters, where Private Griffin had fallen. The *Villistas* retreated and Castleman and his men began a sweep into Columbus, across the tracks, starting a slow movement around the business district. The troopers paused and fired steadily until enemy fire fell off, then moved forward again.

At one point, near the tracks, the Mexicans

Some of Pershing's wagons moving across the Chihuahua desert in pursuit of Villa after the raid

made a stand but were quickly driven back with heavy casualties. Before long, Castleman's troops had formed a line facing west at the eastern edge of the business district.

By this time, the Commercial Hotel had burst into flames, brightly illuminating the street and the raiders. Other buildings now were aflame and the Mexicans presented good targets to Castleman's troops on the east and Lucas's machine gunners on the south.

There were still a few raiders in the army camp. A band of them charged the adobe building housing the army kitchen, where cooks were preparing breakfast. Startled, the cooks fought with anything that came to hand, from butcher knives to boiling water. They killed one raider with an ax. When the cooks grabbed the shotguns they used to hunt small game and began firing them at the Mexicans, the raiders quickly withdrew.

In Columbus A. B. Frost and his family were awakened by the first sounds of gunfire. Hastily dressing, Frost put his wife and three-month-old baby in the family car and backed it out of the garage. As he wheeled down the street, he was struck by a bullet, but managed to continue. After he got on the road for Deming another shot hit him and he collapsed. Mrs. Frost then got him into the back seat and drove the family to safety in Deming.

Mrs. G. E. Parks, telephone switchboard operator and wife of the editor of *The Columbus Courier*, played one of the heroic roles of the wild night. Mr. Parks was in the country that night and Mrs. Parks and her baby were at the little telephone exchange building just west of the Hoover Hotel. When the firing started, she clutched her baby to her breast and quickly rang Deming.

Bullets tore through the paper-thin walls of the little building, shattering the window-glass. Cut by flying shards, Mrs. Parks stayed at her post, first reaching Captain A. W. Brock of Deming. Brock immediately gathered forces to go to the relief of embattled Columbus. Mrs. Parks stayed at her switchboard until the last shot had been fired.

Sometime during the battle Villa released Mrs. Maude Hawk Wright, one of the captives he had taken almost ten days before at a ranch deep in Mexico. The woman had been torn from her husband and her baby, put on a mule and forced to make the hard journey northward with the *Villistas*. Throughout the grueling trip she slept in the sand and subsisted on some half-raw mule meat. The bandit leader admired her courage and turned her loose south of Columbus. She found out later that her husband had been murdered but that her baby was safe.

It was about 5:30 a.m. when Colonel Slocum arrived on the scene and took command from Lieutenant Castleman. The American troops steadily pressed the battle, forcing the Mexicans to retreat, even over the protests of their chieftain.

By 7:30 a.m., in the full light of day, the last of the *bandidos* were moving southward in an orderly retreat. They carried with them an enormous amount of booty, including 300 rifles, eighty good cavalry horses and thirty mules.

Major Frank Tompkins, whose unit was isolated during much of the Columbus battle, led a band of troopers in pursuit of the fleeing Mexicans. They caught up with them south of the border and although greatly outnumbered, attacked fiercely. Major Tompkins and Captain George Williams were wounded.

The Mexicans eventually withdrew, to

The Columbus depot still stands, donated to the town by the railroad as a parting gesture

continue their retreat. The United States troopers returned to Columbus; their ammunition was running low.

The chase cost Villa much of his booty, including many of the horses. He also lost about 100 men, downed by the sharpshooting American cavalrymen during the pursuit.

Back in Columbus, Colonel Slocum and his aides surveyed the smoldering wreckage. The Mexicans had burned an entire block. Dead and wounded men littered the streets. As the officers walked through the dust and smoke, someone pointed out a *Villista* officer, lying wounded and bloody — but still alive — in the dirt.

"Let him bake in the sun," snapped one officer, striding on.

Later, one of the soldiers in the body-gathering detail hit the Mexican in the head with a rifle butt and threw him alive on a pile of bodies consigned to a makeshift crematory.

Ninety *Villistas* lay dead on the streets of Columbus and in the army camp. Twenty-three were wounded. The American toll — military and civilian — was eighteen dead, including a woman, Mrs. Milton James, wife of the railroad pumper. Eight others were wounded. Soldiers gathered dead *Villistas* and horses, piled them in stacks, doused them with oil and burned them.

Within a week, General Pershing moved through Columbus and into Mexico with 10,000 troops in pursuit of Villa. The force stayed south of the border for nearly a year, fighting several battles with the Mexicans, but never catching Villa. Curtiss Army biplanes were stationed at Columbus for a time and flew reconnaissance flights over Mexican territory. It was the first such use of airplanes by the United States Army.

Why did Villa attack Columbus? Historians still debate the question.

Bill McGaw, publisher of *The Southwesterner*, says he has evidence the United States government paid Villa $80,000 to make the raid. He contends the reason was to create a border incident to warrant calling out the National Guard to make the United States ready to enter World War I.

Another theory is that Villa vented his spleen on Columbus because Sam Ravel refused to sell him guns. Villa's enmity for Ravel is well established. Sam was obviously a prime target that bloody morning. Also, the Mexican desperately needed guns, horses and supplies and was anxious to repay the United States for Agua Prieta. Columbus was convenient and relatively isolated.

Whatever his reasons, the raid was costly for Villa. But history shows that it proved even more costly to the little town on the plains.

Columbus was a different place when the smoke died and the dust settled. The heart went out of the town. Prosperity waned. The population began to drift away.

Today only a few hundred persons stick it out. Concrete foundations poke disconsolately up amid the bunch grass and the tumbleweeds. Even the railroad is gone, abandoned in 1963 by the Southern Pacific, successor to the El Paso & Southwestern.

The depot still stands, donated to the town by the railroad as a parting gesture. The stalwart residents of Columbus have set up a unique city library in the depot. It is operated by Patricia Truscott, who organized it. The library is open twenty-four hours a day, seven days a week. Anyone who wants a book signs for a key at the Columbus telephone office, unlocks the library and returns the key after making a selection.

Because of this, the two-story depot gleams fresh and bright with paint beside the railroad bed which residents use as a road to drive to El Paso. The sign on the tower stands out boldly: COLUMBUS

The memory of that bullet-punctured night in 1916 still remains etched in the minds of some residents. Deputy Sheriff Jack Thomas, a grizzled eighty, shakes his head.

"We came out of our homes shootin'," he declares.

Strangely, time seems to have dulled the bitterness one would expect to remain as a result of the pillage.

The New Mexico Legislature created a state park on the site of the Army camp. Nobody in Columbus raised so much as a peep when the politicians in Santa Fe named it "Pancho Villa State Park."

Columbus residents held a big barbecue in the park in 1963. The guest of honor was Pancho Villa's widow, who came all the way from Chihuahua city for the event.

The heat makes the town seem to cringe, clutching the earth closely as if for protection — Shakespeare

22 | Improbable Shakespeare

If a haunted town exists anywhere, it has to be Shakespeare, a ghost village with a history quite as improbable as its name.

Shakespeare clings to precarious life in the desert two and a half miles south of Lordsburg. To reach it, turn south off U.S. 70-80 onto Main Street, then bear right when the road forks and you're practically there.

Little is left of the town — six or seven adobe buildings overwhelmed by a vast expanse of brown landscape and blue sky. It is like a mote afloat on an ocean of dry land. The rolling hills around it bristle with mesquite, prickly pear, greasewood and yucca,

In summer the sun sears everything with the kind of heat that pours from an open oven. It makes the town seem to cringe and clutch the earth closely as if for protection. You look a little longingly toward the Burro Mountains, a distant purple pile misted in the haze on the northern horizon. That heat was something the first settlers had to contend with a hundred years ago. But they managed.

It all started because of a water hole, first used by wandering Apaches and later discovered by pioneers making the arduous trek to California in covered wagons. They began

A crumbling wagon, Shakespeare

calling it Mexican Springs, a name that stuck for awhile.

In 1858 John Butterfield linked St. Louis and San Francisco with his Overland Mail stagecoach route. It was an impossible road of desert and mountain and hardship. The main route passed north of Mexican Springs, but a road through here was used as an alternate. It brought permanent residents. The Concord coaches were stopped by the Civil War but they returned again a few years after Appomattox, this time operated by National Mail and Transportation Company.

"Uncle" Johnny Evensen arrived amid the greasewood at Mexican Springs to open a stage station in 1867. It too was an alternate stop but Indian ambuscades on the main route caused Mexican Springs to be used frequently. Uncle Johnny, then fifty-three, was destined to live at this woebegone desert watering place for the rest of his life.

"Mexican Springs" seemed somewhat undignified to Uncle Johnny and his bosses. General U. S. Grant was a popular hero at the time, so they renamed the place "Grant." Its population was two: Evensen and some nameless hostler.

There were occasional visitors to sample Uncle Johnny's beans and bacon and sourdough biscuits and antelope steak. One of them was W. D. Brown, a dropout from a government survey party. He stopped with Uncle Johnny for a time while prospecting in the nearby Pyramid Mountains.

Brown found ore that looked promising but he was prudent enough to realize it might be more profitable to let somebody else do the work of gouging it from the mountain. He headed for San Francisco to show the samples to William C. Ralston, leading spirit and organizer of the Bank of California.

This was a time of frenzied mining-stock speculation and promotion and Ralston, already a millionaire, was one of the greatest promoters of all. When an assay report on Brown's ore showed a fantastic 12,000 ounces of silver to the ton, Ralston was off and running. His destination was lonely Grant, out there in the burning New Mexico desert.

It was quite an event for Uncle Johnny and his hostler when the great Ralston showed up to sup at their humble table — not to speak of the men he brought with him. It was late February, 1870, and before many days passed they had staked claims all over the Pyramids. Ralston was a master organizer who left little to chance. He laid out the Virginia Mining District covering six by twenty miles. Then he platted a town right around Uncle Johnny's stage station. It contained three parallel streets and cross streets and was divided into lots and blocks.

Obviously "Grant" was an inappropriate name now. The town became "Ralston City."

The desert wind must have carried the word of the Pyramids silver strike, because only a few days after Ralston showed up other prospectors ambled in. One was John Bullard of Pinos Altos. He took one look at the ore, scratched his head and climbed back aboard his burro. If this stuff was really silver, he knew where there was plenty of it near Pinos Altos. He went and sure enough it was, and that was the beginning of Silver City.

But Bullard went by himself. Soon tents and adobe shacks began blossoming like cactus flowers after a rain all around Uncle Johnny.

Ralston returned to the coast to organize the New Mexico Mining Company, capitalized at 6,000,000 pounds sterling. He started selling stock all over the United States and Europe.

Back in Ralston City, trouble flared. Prospectors found that Ralston's men had already staked out all the choice claims. Objecting, they ran square into some Texas hardcase gunmen Ralston had imported to protect his interests. Luckily nobody got killed.

Ralston's competitors took their troubles to court and tangled the whole shebang in a morass of legal red tape. By then, however, Ralston and his associates didn't particularly care. They had found that the great bonanza lay in small pockets and most of the ore was low grade. Ralston moved out quietly so as not to disturb the stock selling.

It didn't take the several hundred residents of Ralston City long to realize what was going on. They disappeared almost as rapidly as they had shown up. Ralston City became a ghost town, except for Uncle Johnny and his hostler. Johnny stayed on, climbing the small hill near the spring every day to watch for the stage so he'd have time to put his beans and biscuits on.

While he kept a weather eye on the wagon ruts, a couple of seedy-looking Forty-niners showed up in the mahogany halls of the Bank of California in San Francisco. Their names were Philip Arnold and John Slack. They acted most secretive about some bags of precious stones they wanted to leave at the bank for safekeeping.

It took a little prodding to elicit the information that Arnold and Slack had discovered — of all things! — a diamond field. Ralston was one of the first to hear. After all, it was *his* bank. He snapped at the diamonds like a roadrunner going for a rattlesnake.

He sent sample stones to Tiffany's and they were pronounced genuine. The whole lot of uncut stones was appraised at $120,000. Ralston then hired Henry Janin, a noted mining expert, to examine Arnold and Slack's diamond field.

Like many another secret, this one was soon spread upon the front page of practically every newspaper in the land. Promoters and confidence men enjoyed a boom selling suckers on the story that they knew the location of the diamond field.

Arnold, Slack and Ralston and company kept their mouths shut tight about the actual location. Reports circulated far and wide about the locale, and all were different. It was in Colorado, or Wyoming, or Utah, or Arizona, or New Mexico Territory.

Meanwhile Janin returned. The field was genuine, he declared. He found diamonds in cracks in the rocks, in ant hills, and in pack-rat holes. It seemed there were diamonds practically everywhere one looked. The field, he told Ralston, was of unbelievable richness. Ralston paid him $2500 in cash and a thousand shares of stock in the $10,000,000 San Francisco and New York Mining and Commercial Company that he organized.

Ralston then paid Arnold and Slack the tidy sum of $600,000 for their diamond field. They promptly vanished from public view, never to be heard from again.

The printing presses got busy once more

Avon Avenue, Shakespeare, from the porch of the old general store

and the stock certificates came rolling off in frantic haste. The *San Francisco Chronicle* reported on August 1, 1872, that the first shares, at forty dollars per share, were gone in twenty-four hours.

By now practically everybody in the West was trying to figure out where the diamond field was. When the *Chronicle* reported on July 31 that the field was within 1000 miles of San Francisco, "at a point not far from the boundary line of New Mexico," somebody quickly spotted lonely little Ralston City and the Pyramid Mountain mines. It was well known as a Ralston promotion.

The National Line's creaking coaches suddenly began dropping off droves of passengers at Uncle Johnny's stage station. The trickle became a flood. By the end of the summer Ralston was booming as never before. Buildings were refurbished and others built until the main street was lined with businesses, including seven saloons, a couple of stores, barber shop, assay office, Chinese laundry, restaurants, boarding houses and so on. Buildings and tents sprouted on the other two streets, along with a full blown red-light district.

The seven saloons were an absolute necessity. It was enough to make a man thirsty just to look at all the crowds and the confusion. Wagons and horses and people jammed the streets, churning up clouds of choking, powdery dust. Every place in town bulged. By day, men prowled the desert and the Pyramids looking for gems. By night they jammed the gin mills to drink and carouse and perpetrate mayhem.

The only law was that enforced by Ralston's Texas gunmen, who still hung around. Murder became commonplace, a not unexpected fact considering the fact that people like the notorious Curley Bill Brocius and his gang were swaggering along the streets.

Within weeks more than 3000 people were jammed into the desert village. Nobody was finding any diamonds, a fact which seemed to bother no one in particular.

As Ralston City boomed along a spoilsport suddenly turned up in San Francisco. Clarence King, government geologist and member of the Fortieth Parallel Commission, decided to investigate the diamond strike. Ralston told King the location of the field. King took a German friend along and the two explored the great discovery. They dug around and found some diamonds and were suitably impressed — especially so when the German found one gem bearing lapidary marks. Quite a field indeed, to contain *cut* diamonds!

The two wired Ralston that the great diamond field had been "salted." It was a phony.

General D. D. Colton, company manager, took some aides and hastened to the scene, then made a grim announcement to the San Francisco papers on November 26, 1872. The company, he said, was the victim of a colossal fraud. Police started looking for Arnold and Slack, who were nowhere to be found.

It took awhile for the news to reach burgeoning Ralston City. The result was something like a delayed-action fuse. One might have thought a dam was about to break and wipe out the town, so rapid was the exodus.

Within a couple of days hardly anybody was left but faithful Uncle Johnny. The stagecoach service dwindled to twice a week. Uncle Johnny opened a saloon in conjunction with the stage stop to help make ends meet. A couple of other saloons remained open, as did the store. Ralston became a haunt for outlaws.

Most of those who had flooded Ralston City were convinced that the diamonds lay on the slopes of Lee's Peak in the Pyramid Mountains. They weren't even close: just

Shakespeare during the boom of 1879

before the bubble burst, the *San Francisco Chronicle* disclosed that the diamond field was seventy miles south of Green River Station, in Summit County, Colorado.

The diamond fiasco ended Ralston's association with his namesake town. His pyramid of wealth crumbled a few years later and he first went bankrupt, then for a swim in San Francisco Bay, from which he never returned. He left behind him some mementoes in New Mexico.

Some of those hired Texas guns, now footloose, still hung around the Ralston City area. They began rustling cattle from Mexican ranchers south of the border. Their activities provoked some bloody incidents with the Mexicans and a number of men on both sides were killed.

By this time, Ralston City and the Pyramids had a reputation for fraud known throughout the West. People stayed far away. But Colonel William Boyle and his brother, General John Boyle of St. Louis, kept an eye on the mining district. They thought there were good mineral possibilities

in the area. Both were natives of England, a fact they would never forget.

They waited patiently until the old court cases had been forgotten and the mining claims had lapsed. Then they moved in, filing claims on the Jerry Boyle and the Bonnie Jean and other mines once owned by Ralston. Forming a company to develop the property, they were faced with the big problem of Ralston City's reputation. Who would buy stock in a mining operation here?

So they changed the name to something pleasing to a British ear. Ralston City became "Shakespeare." Main Street became "Avon Avenue," and the principal hotel "The Stratford." The hotel was nothing fancy. Unbleached muslin tacked onto two-by-four framing separated the rooms. But Mrs. Ross Woods soon earned the Stratford's dining table an enviable reputation.

Shakespeare became a United States post office on October 27, 1879. The first postmaster, appropriately, was Uncle Johnny Evensen.

Other people moved in and staked claims.

Soon wagonloads of silver ore were being hauled out of the Pyramid mines and Shakespeare basked in prosperity once more.

Mrs. Emma Muir arrived in Shakespeare in 1882, when several hundred people lived there. The houses were of thick-walled adobe with small windows that could be sealed by heavy wooden shutters.

"These were reinforced by rocks piled behind them when Indians threatened, which was most of the time, so the rocks were kept neatly piled nearby," she wrote.

The town never had any plumbing and water had to be carried from the spring.

"Shakespeare had no church, no club, no school, no fraternal organization," wrote Mrs. Muir. "Even during my growth from childhood into womanhood, after the railroad had pushed through New Mexico, it had no bank; and men either carried their money in leather belts or buried it in tin cans. Nearly all the money was gold."

If, as Mrs. Muir wrote, Shakespeare had no "fraternal organization" it had some saloons. The Roxy Jay was the best. It contained a fancy mahogany bar imported at great cost from St. Louis.

The Roxy Jay was lighted brightly by a score of kerosene lamps. It offered gaming as well as dance-hall girls. There was a certain moral tone to the place: the girls were taken back to Lordsburg each night and never (well, hardly ever) spent the night in Shakespeare.

Shakespeare's men strove diligently to keep that moral tone. Consider the case of "Arkansas Black," who moved to Shakespeare during the boom of '79 and opened the Silver Dollar Saloon. Affable if not handsome, Black was charming and soon became popular with both male and female residents — particularly the latter.

One of his conquests was married. She began to entertain Black almost daily, whenever her husband was at work in the mines or out of town. Such an affair couldn't be kept secret. The other married women soon indignantly told their husbands about it.

The husbands got together and decided they would have to do something. They sought out Arkansas after dark and told him they wouldn't tolerate such goings on in Shakespeare. He'd better leave town, they said.

Ore wagons and mule teams in the Shakespeare boom

The Stratford Hotel — left, *during the boom of '79;* right, *today*

Black went for his six-gun but he was restrained. The men conferred again, deciding that if Arkansas wouldn't leave they'd just have to hang him.

A corral stood just down Avon Avenue from the general store. The gate had a bar across the top. The vigilantes led Arkansas to the gate, looped a rope around his neck and quickly hoisted him high.

"You gonna leave town, Arkansas?" they asked, and let him down until his feet touched the ground.

"Hell, no!" sputtered Arkansas.

They hauled him up again, to hang for a little longer. The next time they lowered him he refused again, with much profanity. The third time, they let him swing until he practically gave up the ghost. Just before life fled, they dropped him to the dirt.

"How about it, Arkansas?"

Black was unconscious so they revived him with a bucket of water. Arkansas was furious: he told them that if they'd give him back his pistol, he'd shoot it out with the bunch of them right then and there.

Roxy Jay, the saloonkeeper, arrived on the scene at this point and made a suggestion that would have done credit to Solomon. After all, reasoned Roxy, everybody liked good old Arkansas. It was the woman who was the bad one. Why not make her leave town?

The proposal was agreeable to Arkansas and the vigilantes. The latter paid a call on the woman, who left town the following morning with her husband in tow.

Perhaps because of that near-disaster at the corral gate the proprietor later removed the crossbar, leaving any prospective necktie parties without a scaffold. But American

ingenuity triumphed when the need arose.

A party of seventy vigilantes took Russian Bill and Sandy King from Shakespeare's makeshift calaboose on September 8, 1881, and hanged them. The mob used the big wooden beam that spans the dining room of the Grant House, Shakespeare's second hotel.

They left the two swinging overnight. The next morning, the stagecoach pulled in and a passenger looked in the door and saw the grisly sight.

"Wh-what did you hang them for?" asked the frightened tenderfoot.

Uncle Johnny pondered that question for a moment, then shook his head.

"Well, Russian Bill here stole a horse, and Sandy King was just a damned nuisance."

The bodies were cut down and removed and the tables pushed back into place and the Grant House served breakfast as usual to the stage passengers.

Months afterward, the Shakespeare postmaster got an inquiry from a Russian noblewoman through the American consul. She had not heard from her son, William Tattenbaum, for some time. Could the postmaster explain his whereabouts? He could, and did.

"Dear Madam," he wrote; "I am sorry to report your son has died of throat trouble."

Thus died Russian Bill, one of the strange characters who roamed the West. A well educated man, he spent about three years around Shakespeare and was fond of quoting Keats and Shelley to anyone who would listen. He was something of a frontier dandy, sporting fringed buckskins in Wild Bill fashion. His hair was blond and curly.

Sandy King was a different type. At the moment of his death he was out on bond on a murder charge in Silver City. When he arrived in Shakespeare he bought a bright silk handkerchief. The store clerk asked for money and Sandy whipped out his six-shooter and shot off the end of the clerk's finger. The vigilantes were unable to find him guilty of attempted murder so they found him guilty of "being a damned nuisance" and had done with it.

Curly Bill Brocius was another notorious gunfighter who haunted Shakespeare's dusty streets. He headed the gang of which Sandy King was a member. A six-footer with a fondness for flaming red neckties, Curly Bill loved to shoot coins from the quivering hand of anyone who would hold them.

He ran up against Wyatt Earp one day over toward the Arizona line and took a load of buckshot in the abdomen. He was brought back to Shakespeare and died in the general store. He may be buried in the basement.

The noted and mysterious John Ringo also frequented Shakespeare. He too was well educated. Gunmen like Ringo and the others found Shakespeare to their liking while it prospered. But a mining decline set in during the latter part of the 'eighties. Shakespeare died after the panic of 1893.

Meanwhile the upstart town of Lordsburg, just two and a half miles distant, blossomed with the coming of the railroad. When the town first began Lordsburg residents had to get their mail at Shakespeare.

Shakespeare experienced a brief revival in 1907, when some of the old claims were reopened. The Stratford Hotel opened its doors for a time but the new breath of prosperity proved only a gasp. The final indignity came when the railroad laid a spur track up the middle of Avon Avenue to reach the "85 Mine." The tracks are still there.

The busted town got a reputation as a hangout for bootleggers during the 1920s. Repeal and the depression drove the few remaining inhabitants out.

The current residents of Shakespeare arrived in 1935. Frank and Rita Hill had been wiped out by the depression on their cattle ranch near Separ. They bought Shakespeare with the little money they had and made it the headquarters for a modest ranching operation. The spread now totals seventeen sections, nearly 11,000 acres, counting the range the Hills lease — not very much in a country as hard and dry as this.

Others might have come to the old ghost town and treated it as nothing more than some eroding adobe buildings better off out of the way. But the Hills were enchanted by the history here. They have tried their best, with meager means, to preserve what is left of a colorful chapter of the Southwest's past.

Lanky, weatherbeaten Frank Hill has the look of a rancher who has been battling drouth and the land most of his life. Rita is a vivacious, graying woman who looks the perfect part of a ranch wife. She has written a fine little booklet about the town. Their beautiful, black-haired daughter, Janaloo, shares their life in the ghost town.

Mrs. Hill and Janaloo supplement the ranch income by running a dancing school in Lordsburg while Frank tends the ranch. The Hills have about seventy cattle — a most unusual herd. The Hills know everyone by name.

"We had to sell Marilyn Monroe last week," Mrs. Hill chuckles. "But her daughters, Audrey and Doris will take her place."

All three Hills keep alive a dream that Shakespeare may someday be restored. It is a bright-burning dream, quite as brilliant as the diamonds once believed "salted" out there in the Pyramids.

They have used painstaking care to collect relics of boom days and are trying hard to preserve the remaining buildings. Much

Frank and Rita Hill, with daughter Janaloo; Avon Avenue, Shakespeare, in background

remains to be done. The front wall of the Stratford Hotel verges on collapse and only a stout cable keeps it from tumbling in a desert gale.

Frank and Janaloo, a few years back, rode horseback all the way to San Diego in a bid to publicize the town. They produced a little play along the way. But the trip was a financial failure and didn't produce the publicity the Hills had hoped for.

To get money to prop the buildings up they charge the few visitors who come by seventy-five cents for guided tours at ten a.m. on weekdays and ten a.m. and two p.m. on Sundays. They are expertly guided journeys backward in time, with much to see.

The Grant House still stands. Bullet holes pit its saloon walls: a favorite frontier sport was shooting at flies. Windows in the Grant House dining room still contain glass and screening. The heavy wooden beam from

The Grant House — Shakespeare today

which Sandy King and Russian Bill swung that tragic night seems strong enough to endure for yet another eighty years.

Farther down Avon Avenue you can walk into the Stratford Hotel and reflect about what Shakespeare's finest inn has finally come to. Bean Belly Smith shot a man to death in the dining room one lost morning long ago in a gunfight over an egg.

The Hills live in the old general store, which serves as both house and a museum full of relics. The Hills have fixed things up comfortably in spite of the fact that electricity has never reached Shakespeare. The spacious store room is their living room. It is supposed to be haunted. They say that sometimes when you walk across one creaky corner you can smell sulphur. Just a whiff, really, as if someone had just struck a country match — or a demon had opened the doorway to hell.

The Hills say they have smelled it, but are unconcerned.

"Some say it's the ghost of the man buried in the basement," chuckles Mrs. Hill.

And, looking around you at improbable Shakespeare, you are inclined to wonder. It is easy to believe in spirits in Shakespeare. They seem to hover at your shoulder, just beyond sight, to disappear with the wind that rustles the branches of the mesquite and greasewood.

If memories are ghosts there must be many here. Like Sandy King and Uncle Johnny and Russian Bill and Bean Belly Smith and Curly Bill Brocius. Most of them lie in the cemetery down the road toward Lordsburg.

Together they make up a specter of a rough and sordid but always colorful era that is lost to us forever.

May it rest in the peace it never knew.

Sources

The Leading Facts of New Mexican History, by Ralph Emerson Twitchell. Torch Press, Cedar Rapids, Iowa, 1912.

The Lapidary Journal, November, 1962.

History of New Mexico, by Frank D. Reeve. Lewis Historical Publishing Company, Inc. New York, 1961.

The Bonanza Trail, by Muriel Sibell Wolle. Indiana University Press, Bloomington, 1958.

New Mexico, a Guide to the Colorful State (American Guide Series) New Mexico Writers' Project. Hastings House, New York, 1940.

The Story of Madrid, by Joe Huber. Privately printed. Albuquerque, 1963.

New Mexico, a Pageant of Three Peoples, by Erna Fergusson. Alfred A. Knopf. New York, 1964.

Abert's New Mexico Report, 1846-47. Horn and Wallace, Albuquerque, 1964.

New Tracks in North America, by William A. Bell (1867-68). Horn and Wallace, Albuquerque, 1965.

Violence in Lincoln County 1869-1881, by William A. Keleher, University of New Mexico Press, Albuquerque, 1957.

The Fabulous Frontier (12 New Mexico

Items), by William A. Keleher. The Rydal Press, Santa Fe, 1942.

A Fitting Death for Billy the Kid, by Ramon F. Adams. University of Oklahoma Press, Norman, 1960.

The Western Hero in History and Legend, by Kent Ladd Steckmesser. University of Oklahoma Press, Norman, 1965.

The Authentic Life of Billy the Kid (1882), by Pat F. Garrett. University of Oklahoma Press, Norman, 1954.

Fort Union and the Winning of the Southwest, by Chris Emmett. University of Oklahoma Press, Norman, 1965.

Forts of the West, by Robert W. Frazer. University of Oklahoma Press, Norman, 1965.

A Treasury of Western Folklore, Edited by B. A. Botkin, Crown Publishers, Inc., New York, 1951.

Arrott's Brief History of Fort Union, by James W. Arrott. Rodgers Library, Highlands University, Las Vegas, N.M., 1962.

Illustrated New Mexico 1885, by W. G. Ritch (Fifth Edition) Bureau of Immigration, Santa Fe, 1885.

Vicente Silva and His 40 Bandits, by Manuel C. de Baca, translated by Lane Kauffmann. Edward McLean, Libros Escogidos, Washington, D.C., 1947.

Vicente Silva and his Forty Thieves (The Vice Criminals of the 80's and 90's), by Tom McGrath, privately printed, 1960.

Old Mining Camps of New Mexico 1854-1904, selections from the writings of Fayette A. Jones. Stagecoach Press, Santa Fe, 1964.

Boom and Bust on Baldy Mountain 1864-1964, by Lawrence R. Murphy (thesis, University of Arizona), November, 1964.

The Maxwell Land Grant, by Jim Berry Pearson. University of Oklahoma Press, Norman, 1961.

Maxwell Land Grant — A New Mexico Item, by William A. Keleher. Argosy-Antiquarian Ltd., New York, 1964.

Satan's Paradise, by Agnes Morley Cleaveland. Houghton Mifflin Company, Boston, 1952.

Directory of Mines of New Mexico, by Lucien A. File. State Bureau of Mines and Mineral Resources, New Mexico Institute of Mining and Technology. Socorro, N.M., 1965.

Black Range Tales, by James A. McKenna (1936), Rio Grande Press, Chicago, 1965.

Cabezon — A New Mexico Ghost Town, by Jack D. Rittenhouse. Stagecoach Press, Santa Fe, 1965.

The Columbus, New Mexico Story, by F. Stanley. Privately printed, Pep, Texas, 1966.

Pancho Villa at Columbus, the Raid of 1916, by Haldeen Braddy. Texas Western College Press, Monograph No. 9, 1965.

Then and Now Here and Around Shakespeare, by Rita Hill. Privately printed, Lordsburg, 1963.

I have consulted the files of many newspapers to obtain material for *Haunted Highways*.

The principal newspaper sources have been the *Albuquerque Morning Journal;* The *New Southwest and Grant County Herald*, published at Silver City; *The Black Range*, published at Chloride; the Santa Fe *New Mexican;* the *Las Vegas Optic*, and others.

I used the files of the *San Francisco Chronicle* extensively in research on the great diamond fraud.

Index

(Page numbers in italics refer to illustrations.)